M000290512

UNWANTED HERO

THE FLYING CAREER OF SQUADRON LEADER
DONALD BARNARD DFC, 1937-1955

COLIN PATEMAN &
OLIVER CLUTTON-BROCK

FONTHILL

To the memory of a brave man who did his duty as he saw it,
and to all those who helped and supported him along the way.

Fonthill Media Limited
Fonthill Media LLC
www.fonthillmedia.com
office@fonthillmedia.com

First published 2012

British Library Cataloguing in Publication Data:
A catalogue record for this book is available from the British Library

ISBN 978-1-78155-079-3 (print)
ISBN 978-1-78155-162-2 (e-book)

Typeset in 9.5pt on 13pt Sabon.
Printed and bound in England

Connect with us
 facebook.com/fonthillmedia twitter.com/fonthillmedia

CONTENTS

Foreword   7

Acknowledgements   9

Preface   11

1. Early Days   15

2. Diary – Part 1: Shot Down; In Northern France   51

3. Diary – Part 2: To Marseille, and the South of France   71

4. Diary – Part 3: Departure for the Pyrenees, Spain, and the UK   97

5. The Fillerin Family – The PAT/PAO Line – The Crew   120

6. RAF, 1943-46   144

7. Civilian Flying, 1946-55   175

   Appendices   191

   I.   The Message Attached to the Pigeon at Renty

   II.   Convoy MKF7, Gibraltar–Gourock, 20-25 January 1943

   III. East Dakota Losses, June-October 1945

   IV.   Aircraft Types (and Engines) Flown by Donald Barnard

   V.   The Medals of Squadron Leader Donald Barnard DFC

Endnotes   214

Bibliography   223

Every day you may make progress. Every step may be fruitful. Yet there will stretch out before you an ever-lengthening, ever-ascending, ever-improving path. You know you will never get to the end of the journey. But this, so far from discouraging, only adds to the joy and glory of the climb.

Sir Winston Churchill

FOREWORD

Air Commodore G. R. Pitchfork MBE, BA, FRAeS

In the language of modern society and instant headlines, laced with the overuse of superlatives and exaggerated accolades, the word fortitude is rarely used, yet it captures the qualities of many people in this book, not least the main character, the Unwanted Hero, Donald Barnard.

In a number of respects he was typical of those I describe as 'the Many', whose exploits and courageous service rarely receive recognition. Yet, by any standards, his wartime career was remarkable but would have gone untold had the authors not brought him to public attention.

In any one of four very different elements, his service is worthy of recording. He survived almost two tours as a bomber pilot operating over Germany, and the authors remind us of the tragic losses suffered by Bomber Command. It is ironic that their sacrifice has only just been recognised, with the commemoration of the Bomber Command Memorial in London, in the year this book is being published. Donald Barnard was shot down and evaded capture, he went on to test over 1,000 Spitfires and by the end of the war he was flying dangerous missions over the inhospitable jungles of Burma. All required courage and fortitude, but none more so than during the events that followed his being shot down and his return to freedom.

In reading of his successful evasion in detail, we are alerted to the courage, endurance, and resolve of others – those who helped him. I am sure the authors would be the first to agree with me that I should highlight the unbelievable courage of the 'helpers', those ordinary but gallant people in enemy-occupied territories who saw it as their duty to help Allied airmen, knowing that they could, if discovered, pay the ultimate price for their actions, as so many did. The courageous deeds of all the remarkable aircrew who evaded capture and their equally remarkable helpers should live for ever and be an inspiration to future generations. Thanks to books such as this one, they will be remembered.

Few people survived the Second World War after such a sustained period of operational flying over such a long period of time. That Donald Barnard did so is testimony not only to his skill and courage but also to his resourcefulness and fortitude.

Graham Pitchfork
Gloucestershire

'Our First Reply': On 4 September 1939, fourteen Wellington aircraft from Nos 9 and 149 Squadrons attacked the entrance to the Kiel Canal at Brunsbüttel, the first bombing raid of the war. Two of the aircraft of No. 9 Squadron, L4268 and L4275, were lost with all crew members, the first aircraft to be shot down on the western front.

ACKNOWLEDGEMENTS

Our special thanks go to Ralph Forster, the sole surviving member of Donald Barnard's crew; his daughter and son-in-law, Alethea and Russell Wheeler; Geoff and John Buckell, sons of Albert Buckell; Patricia Glensor; and Richard Oliver, Donald's nephew. The family members of Donald and his crew have contributed greatly by sharing a wealth of personal information and photographic images with the authors.

We are also most grateful to Air Commodore Graham Pitchfork for kindly agreeing to write the Foreword to this book, and to the following, who generously assisted us in the compilation of Donald's story: Rosemary Agnew; William Barons (RAF retired); Bruce Bollinger (USA); David C. Boughton; Ted 'The Lad' Cachart; Bill Chorley; John Clinch; Philippe Connart (Belgium); Sebastian Cox, Head of Air Historical Branch (RAF); Ron Cuskelly (Australia); Agnes Fillerin (France); Philippe Goldstein (France); Jimmy and Isabella Jackson, and Ken Jackson (re 2 CAACU and personal photographs); Keith Janes; Joss Leclercq (France); Diana Morgan; Edouard Reniere (Belgium); Rog Stanton; Robin A. Walker.

The authors also wish to acknowledge the extraordinary photographs of Monsieur Lenglet, who processed the German Luftwaffe officers' camera film in 1942.

And, finally, our thanks to Squadron Leader Chris Golds AFC, RAF (retired) for allowing his painting 'Our First Reply' to be reproduced on the cover of *Unwanted Hero*. The Wellington depicted in the painting represents the identical type of aircraft flown by Donald Barnard on No. 99 Squadron in 1939.

Wanted Poster with Geneviève Fillerin, Sergeant Forster, Pilot officer Glensor, Squadron Leader Barnard, Monique Fillerin and Madam Fillerin, October 1942.

PREFACE

Several stories have been told of RAF evaders and the daily determined battles they fought to seek freedom from enemy-occupied territory.

This book has been co-written with Oliver Clutton-Brock to ensure that one such story is told. Having researched evaders and RAF personnel for many years, I was fortunate to acquire documentation and memorabilia of the late Squadron Leader Donald Barnard DFC at an auction in 2004. One of the items secured was a large-format diary written in pencil by Donald of his escape from enemy-occupied France, a story that is both personal and unique in content. It details the courageous efforts of the clandestine escape line that aided his escape. There can never be too many stories told that pay tribute to the selfless individuals who worked for these escape lines, especially the Fillerin family, who first looked after Donald. Norbert Fillerin, his wife, and three children placed themselves at risk, as did thousands of others, of paying the ultimate sacrifice. By the time that Donald had made contact with them in September 1942, thirteen other soldiers and airmen had already been sheltered at their home.

A unique item saved from Donald's 1942 evasion was an original 'Wanted' poster, produced and published by the Germans during the search for the crew from Donald's crashed aircraft. This poster had been procured by one of the Fillerin family, who put it up in their garden shed. With resolute defiance of the Germans, they then photographed themselves, Donald, and two of his crew in front of the poster while the frantic search for the British airmen continued. Donald took the poster with him on his long journey to freedom and, although aged, it remains intact to this day.

Oliver was invaluable in providing his expertise and knowledge, having recently (2009) published his book *RAF Evaders*, in which Squadron Leader Donald Barnard's evasion is mentioned, and to whom, therefore, some of Donald's story was well known.

What was not generally known was the fact that Donald, who had been awarded the Distinguished Flying Cross in 1942, was to be dismissed from the RAF after a general court martial in 1946. The reader will, I hope, be inspired by the facts and circumstances surrounding that court hearing process.

Colin Pateman
Sussex
2012

Recherches
des AVIATEURS ANGLAIS

En leur adressant l'appel ci-après le *SOUS-PRÉFET de St-OMER* invite ses Administrés à lui donner la plus large publicité. Il leur rappelle en outre que des instructions antérieures rendent toute complicité passible de *LA PEINE DE MORT*. Il compte sur leur sagesse et sur leur concours.

Le Sous-Préfet,
L. SEGUY.

Le 17 Septembre 1942, vers 1 heure du matin, un bombardier Anglais a été contraint d'atterrir au hameau de Neuville, commune d'ALQUINES.

Des cinq hommes de l'équipage, on a été pris et les quatre autres sont en fuite. C'est pourquoi je vous prie d'adresser un appel urgent à la Population pour l'inviter à collaborer à la recherche des fugitifs. L'assurance est donnée, que toute personne qui adressera à la Kommandantur des renseignements susceptibles de procurer l'arrestation de ces aviateurs, **pourra désigner pour chaque fugitif arrêté, un PRISONNIER de GUERRE Français qui sera rapidement libéré.** La discrétion la plus absolue est assurée.

Par contre la Kommandantur attire l'attention sur les sanctions graves qu'encourent ceux qui favorisent l'évasion. Les noms des fugitifs sont les suivants :

1. SQUADRON LEADER Barnard.
2. PILOT-Officer R. E. Gleuser.
3. Fl. SERGANT BUCKELL.
4. SERGANT FORSTER.

Signé HAUPTMANN und Kreiskommandant :
GOTTWALD.

Wanted poster identifying Barnard's crew.

When Colin asked me if I would be interested in helping him put together the story of Squadron Leader Donald Barnard I had no hesitation in agreeing. As Colin says, I was already familiar with some of the story of his evasion and of two of his crew, but here was the chance to get the fuller picture.

Alas, Donald died in 1997. Despite the fact that he appears to have written few letters throughout his life and, apart from the account of his 1942 evasion, seems to have made no written record of his exciting and interesting flying career, we have, undeterred, put together as much of his history as we can. And so, with the addition of some personal memories, I believe that the story that we have been able to uncover is well worth the telling.

Oliver Clutton-Brock
Wiltshire
February 2012

IX Squadron Mk1 Wellington bombers, of the type flown by Donald Barnard on operations from August 1940 to January 1941. Note the squadron crest below the cockpit window.

CHAPTER 1

EARLY DAYS

Childhood in St Lucia, British West Indies

Set in the Caribbean Sea, between 12 and 16 degrees North and between 60 and 62 degrees West, are the three former British colonies of St Lucia, Grenada, and St Vincent and the Grenadines, that together make up the Windward Islands, themselves part of the group of islands called the Lesser Antilles.[1] Apart from Trinidad, Tobago, and Barbados, they are the furthest east and furthest south of the Caribbean Islands.

The largest of the Windwards, and considered to be the most picturesque of the group, is St Lucia.[2] The island is mountainous – its highest point, Mount Gimie, is 3,145 feet above sea level – and is largely covered with forests and tropical vegetation. Its principal exports sixty years ago and more were sugar, limes (and their oil), coconuts, copra, cocoa, charcoal, bananas and other fruit, bay rum, syrup, and molasses.

Capital of the island, in the north, is Port Castries (population 24,118 in 1943). At the opposite end of the island to Castries lies the town of Choiseul. It was here that the Barnard family lived, vastly rich plantation owners, and where Donald Beausire Barnard was born in 1918. His middle name, unmistakably French, was taken from the surname of his great-grandfather, a French nobleman from Alsace. Given the turbulent history of St Lucia this is not altogether surprising, for the island was fought over many times by soldiers and sailors of Britain and France. Though Spanish explorers were the first foreigners to land on the island, at the end of the fifteenth century, it was the French who were the first to colonise it, which they did in the seventeenth century, naming it after Saint Lucy of Syracuse. Keen to get their hands on the riches of the Caribbean, the British seized control of the island between 1663 and 1667, and over the years they were at war with the French no fewer than fourteen times until, in 1814, the British took control of St Lucia once and for all.

The French, however, were the first to create sugar cane plantations, and there was a ready supply of labour in the local population, the Caribs. But, maltreated and overworked by their white masters, and with their bodies unable to fight European diseases such as smallpox and measles, they died all too easily. To replace the indigenous Caribs, therefore, the whites brought over, in the most inhumane and shameful conditions, thousands of African slaves to work in appalling circumstances on the plantations. The result of this forced influx was

The Barnard family home in St Lucia. (*Richard Oliver*)

that by the middle of the nineteenth century those of African origin outnumbered
the Caribs.[3] Though the whites, predominantly the British, continued to wield
power on the island, the influence of the French never completely disappeared,
and today, despite English being the official language, an Antillean Creole based
on the French language is spoken by four-fifths of the population. It was with
this heritage, therefore, that the Barnards flourished on St Lucia. Despite owing
allegiance to the British monarchy, the Barnards, as mixed race, self-made
entrepreneurs, were first and foremost British West Indians, and Donald, though
he was later schooled in England and was to spend much of his later life there,
never considered himself to be English or British.

The Barnard family was long-established in the British West Indies by the time
of Donald's arrival. Research by Donald's nephew Richard Oliver shows that they
were already settled in the Caribbean in the eighteenth century, and that Donald's
great-grandfather Samuel, born in Antigua, is believed to have been a free coloured
born about 1797. He migrated to St Lucia as a teacher around the middle of
nineteenth century with his son, also Samuel, who was born in Antigua on about
6 June 1832. On 16 December 1862, the younger Samuel married Isabella Parker
in St Lucia, and had seven children (six boys, one girl). She was the granddaughter
of Joseph-Gabriel de Beausire and a coloured woman, and, it is said, of Admiral
Sir Hyde Parker (1739-1807) and Elizabeth, a coloured woman from Martinique,
who was reputed to be exceptionally beautiful.

Florence Barnard 1881-1954.
(*Richard Oliver*)

George Barnard 1869-1952.
(*Richard Oliver*)

Donald with his mother and two sisters, *c.* 1930. (*Richard Oliver*)

Their fourth child, George Ernest Beausire Barnard, was born on about 12 October 1869 at Choiseul, St Lucia, and on 7 June 1905, when living at Park Estate, St Lucia, he married Florence Winifred Hendy, in St Andrew's Church, Fulham, London.[4] Details of the ceremony were published on 24 June 1905 in 'The Weddings of the Week' column of *The Gentlewoman*:

> The officiating clergyman was the Revd C. S. Staples. The service was fully choral and the church tastefully decorated with flowers and palms. The bride, who was given away by her uncle (Mr. James), wore a robe of soft white satin with chiffon tucks, and a court train with chiffon and orange blossom. She wore a net veil over a coronet of orange blossom, and carried a shower bouquet of exotics, which, with a diamond and sapphire ring, was the gift of the bridegroom …
>
> … The bridegroom was supported by his brother, Mr. H. W. Barnard, as best man. After the ceremony a reception was held at 22, Gloucester Walk, Campden Hill, W., by the bride's aunt, Mrs. Arthur Stopford, and later in the day the bride and bridegroom left for Devonshire for their honeymoon.

Donald Barnard with two of his
sisters St Lucia, *c.* 1930.
(*Richard Oliver*)

George and Florence also had seven children, three girls and four boys, Donald
Beausire Barnard being their youngest. He was born on 21 October 1918 at the
end of the Great War into the privileged, ruling classes of St Lucia.

When Donald was born, his father was already approaching fifty years of age
and his mother was in her late thirties. Donald grew up as a bit of a 'savage', as
apparently did other siblings, and, with little incentive for him to seek proper and
formal education, the young boy eschewed the classroom for a wilder and more
interesting outdoor life.

This is not to say that his parents were negligent towards his education.
Whatever this might have been in St Lucia, he was sent to England in 1929, where
he attended Pinewood Preparatory School in Farnborough, Hampshire, though
given his background in the West Indies it was not easy for him to fit into the
education system. Little enough is known of Donald's time at Pinewood, but in
1933 he went not far away to Cranleigh School in Surrey. A prestigious public
school, though with a relatively short history, Cranleigh had opened in 1865 as
'the Surrey County School for parents of the middle class or moderate incomes'.
By the time that Donald arrived, the school accommodated some 300 pupils
boarding in six houses.[5]

Acting as Donald's guardian *in loco parentis* during his time at Pinewood
was one of the school's masters, Mr C. A. Ranger, but at Cranleigh this role was
assumed by his eldest sister, Naomi Isabel (known as 'Nibs'), who was a good
twelve years older than him. Having come over to England, Nibs had married

George Davern in the spring of 1934 at Steyning in Sussex, though during Donald's time at Cranleigh she is noted as living at Chard, near Yeovil, in Somerset.

At Cranleigh, though not academically brilliant in any way, Donald rose in time to become House Prefect of East House, and played rugby for the school in the 1936 and 1937 seasons, gaining his 1st XV colours. He also played 2nd XI cricket, and boxed for the school from 1934 to 1937, becoming captain in his last year. Cranleigh School also had a long-standing association with the Officers' Training Corps (OTC). Set up prior to the First World War, the OTC became established in universities and public schools across the country, its aim being to prepare schoolboys for the basic skills and discipline required in military service. Cadets, as students in the OTC were known, attended Corps camps and wore the dress of military life. Donald experienced all the skills of shooting, drill, and military bearing during his Cranleigh School OTC service between 1934 and 1937. In his last year he passed the OTC exam Certificate A, Part 1. Had he decided to join the Officer Cadet Reserve on leaving school he would have had to have been 'between the ages of 18 and 31, must have ceased to attend a Public or Secondary School, and must hold Certificate A or B of the Officers' Training Corps'.[6]

Donald applies to join the RAF, September 1937

Having completed his formal education, Donald left Cranleigh in the summer of 1937 with no notable distinction other than a slight stammer and that he had been 'a bit of a nuisance'. So, barely three months short of his nineteenth birthday, Donald was now cast alone into the adult world and, rather than return to his home on St Lucia, his immediate refuge lay at his brother Hugh's house at 8, Talbot Road, Bayswater, London W2. Whether or not he was persuaded by the Royal Air Force's publicity drive that was under way at this time, he decided to apply to the RAF to become a pilot on a short service commission in the General Duties Branch, for which one had to be at least 17½ years of age.[7] Short service commissions were 'mostly for four years' service in the first instance, followed by six years in the Reserve'.[8]

As Donald was over the required minimum age, the RAF required him to attend No. 2 Central Medical Board for his medical examination on 9 September 1937. Pronounced 'Fit as Pilot' and having successfully passed the entrance examination, he was now a probationary member of the RAF. Noted on his RAF records, and which undoubtedly would have helped his chances of acceptance by the RAF, was the fact that he had passed the OTC exam Certificate A, Part 1.

In 1935 the British government had heard that Hitler was ordering the expansion of the German Air Force to equal that of the French, which boasted some 1,500 machines. The RAF were far behind in numbers, and so it was agreed by the House of Commons that, by March 1937, 'the first line of the Royal Air Force was now to be built up to 123 squadrons, or 1,512 aircraft.'[9] In 1936, estimates were revised,

Donald Barnard in RAF service
wearing the rank of Squadron
Leader.

and the basic target, for completion by March 1939, was 1,736 frontline aircraft in 124 home-based squadrons, plus a further ten squadrons for overseas. To man the many new squadrons the authorities created the RAF Volunteer Reserve (RAFVR), with the intention of recruiting 800 men per year for pilot training. When the scheme began in April 1937, eager young men flocked to the colours in such numbers that some 5,000 of them had enlisted by September 1939.[10]

The RAF were now in a hurry and, with members of the RAF and RAFVR all in the same boat, Donald, who was RAF not VR, began his flying training on 25 October 1937 at No. 1 Elementary & Reserve Flying Training School (E&RFTS), which was lodged with the Civil Flying School at Hatfield Aerodrome in Hertfordshire.[11] This was a private airfield of some 150 acres that had been bought by the pioneering aircraft designer Geoffrey de Havilland in 1930. Work began on facilities in 1933, and in 1934 more extensive work was undertaken, with a large factory and administration buildings being constructed, together with a flying-school building and the necessary flying control. In the same year the de Havilland Aeronautical Technical School (founded at Stag Lane in 1928) moved to the new airfield.

Located to the west of the town of Hatfield itself, it was not an altogether ideal site for flying, for on the east side there was a 75-foot high aircraft factory chimney, and to the west radio masts towered up to 200 feet or so. Nevertheless, it was here, at No.1 E&RFTS, that qualified RAF instructors gave initial flying training to would-be RAF pilots. On 25 October 1937, Donald recorded his very

first entry in his flying logbook: a 25-minute air experience flight with a Flying
Officer Ross in a de Havilland DH.82A Tiger Moth.

Flying logbooks were issued to all aircrew according to their trade – pilot,
observer, etc. – and it was their duty to complete them according to the appropriate
headings therein. As an official document, a pilot's logbook required its keeper to
provide evidence of all flying hours undertaken, and was submitted for checking
and endorsement by supervisory ranks either at the end of each month or on a
posting to a new squadron or establishment on a training or operational base.
Here the pilot would be required to produce his logbook for inspection.

Donald recorded his second flight with Flying Officer Ross in the Tiger Moth on
26 October, but this time he took control of the aircraft, getting a feel of its controls
and general handling. On 8 November, the logbook has the remark 'satisfactory'
against taking-off and landing into wind, but on 24 November Donald was able
to write proudly in his logbook, 'First Solo Good'. This was achieved after sixteen
hours of instruction on the Tiger Moth over a period of just seventeen days. Rapid
though this may seem, with the huge demand for trained pilots that was to come
with the RAF's expansion during the Second World War, it was not uncommon for
a pilot to go solo after eight or ten hours of instruction.

That flying was inherently dangerous was brought home very forcibly to
Donald when, as he noted in his logbook on 17 December, one of the instructors,
T. Q. Smith, was killed in a flying accident. Having completed the course, Donald
was assessed by the Chief Flying Instructor at Hatfield as a student pilot of
'Average' ability,[12] and his logbook was annotated with a total flying time of 57
hours and 10 minutes.

It was not until 25 January 1938 that Donald achieved the lowly rank of
Acting Pilot Officer on probation. On this date the Air Ministry announced in
The London Gazette that he and one hundred and four others 'are granted short
service commissions as Acting Pilot Officers on probation with effect from 9th
Jan. 1938' in the General Duties Branch of the RAF. His commission was to be
effective for the four years from 25 October 1937 to 25 October 1941. There was
no mention in *The London Gazette* of each officer's personal and unique RAF
service number, as it was not then the custom to do so, though it would be during
the Second World War. Donald's, however, was 40352.

On 23 January 1938, Acting Pilot Officer Barnard began further training at
the relatively new airfield of RAF Brize Norton, some 5 miles south-west of the
Oxfordshire town of Witney. Though building had begun in 1935, it was not until
13 August 1937 that the airfield's first occupant, No. 2 Flying Training School (FTS),
was able to move in. In due course, 2 FTS would become part of No. 23 (Training)
Group, whose headquarters were in Grantham, Lincolnshire. Another of the units
within this widely dispersed Group was the School of Air Navigation at Manston
in Kent, to which Donald would be sent in due course for further training.

At Brize Norton, Donald was introduced to the Hawker Hart biplane, at that
time a fast two-seater aircraft in service across the RAF. He made steady progress in

flying training, and in May 1938 graduated onto the advanced training squadron at 2 FTS. He now flew such aircraft as the twin-engined Airspeed Oxford, which would later earn a reputation as a 'flying classroom' for navigators and wireless operators, and the Hawker Audax, the usual complement of which on navigation exercises was pilot, observer, and rear gunner.

A frequent signature in Donald's logbook while he was at 2 FTS was that of the Chief Flying Instructor (CFI) who signed off Donald on 24 June 1938 with the impressive red-ink stamp: 'Qualified for award of Flying Badge under King's Regulations'. The CFI, Squadron Leader Thomas Howell French DFC, further endorsed the award of the pilot's 'wings'.[13] Pilot Officer Barnard, though now qualified to wear the RAF 'wings' on his uniform, underwent further training for several more months, at the end of which he was assessed by the CFI as 'Average', but with no areas of fault.

It was the RAF's policy at this time for pilots to be versed in the intricacies of aerial navigation, and so the next challenge that Donald was to face came when he presented himself at the School of Air Navigation, RAF Manston, Kent, to attend No. 43 Short Navigation Course. On 4 November 1938, Squadron Leader R. J. Cooper, CFI at Manston, signed off his logbook, which now showed that he had flown over fifty hours on navigation.

Despite the urgency to train as many pilots as necessary to keep pace with the increase in the German Air Force, RAF prewar pilot training was not hurried, and only after he had been under training for over a year was Pilot Officer Donald Barnard, now a qualified pilot, considered ready to join an operational RAF squadron.

His first posting was to No. 215 (Bomber) Squadron at RAF Honington in Suffolk. The squadron had been formed at Coudekerque in France from No. 15 RNAS Squadron during the last year of the First World War, but was disbanded in October 1919 after an existence of barely eighteen months. As part of the prewar expansion of the RAF, however, it was re-formed from 'A' Flight, 58 Squadron, at RAF Worthy Down in October 1935, and was equipped with the lumbering, two-engined Vickers Virginia Mk X.

Commanding Officer of 215 Squadron when Donald joined, on 5 November 1938, was Wing Commander Sylvester Lindsay Quine MC, who had seen active service in the First World War with the 3rd Cheshire Regiment and Royal Flying Corps.[14] Relinquishing his commission in the Cheshires with effect from 24 October 1919, he was appointed to the RAF with an impressively early service number of 08062. He continued to serve in the RAF after the First World War, and was promoted wing commander in May 1937. By November 1938, he had under his command two squadron leaders, three flying officers, and thirteen pilot officers, the most junior of whom were Donald and Pilot Officer Norman Leonard Lewis.[15]

On 215 Squadron, Donald was introduced to the Handley Page Harrow, a large, two-engined aircraft with a fixed undercarriage, which, as one distinguished author put it, was 'frankly a stop-gap; designed as a transport, it was pressed into service as a bomber in 1937 purely to meet the exigencies of expansion. In its original rôle it continued to do good service until 1944, but all the Bomber Command squadrons converted to Wellingtons in 1939.'[16] Donald flew solo on the Harrow within a few days, but continued to learn his trade by flying with other squadron pilots ranging in rank from sergeant to wing commander.

Only a few weeks into his time on 215 Squadron such was the lack of serviceable aircraft that it was proving impossible to maintain training requirements; on 9 February 1939, Wing Commander Quine accordingly annotated Pilot Officer Barnard's logbook with the entry: 'On attachment to No. 75 (B) Sqd. Progress to date limited by shortage of aircraft.'

Possibly on leave for the rest of the month, Donald joined 75 Squadron on 1 March 1939, which, conveniently, was also based at Honington and was also flying the Harrow. The commanding officer this time was the famous 1920s High Speed Flight and 1929 Schneider Trophy pilot Wing Commander David D'Arcy Alexander Greig DFC, AFC.[17]

Donald's time was spent on night flying sorties, including practising flare dropping and navigation, along with camera and bombing exercises. At the end of May 1939, Donald had accumulated a grand total of just over 300 hours' flying. His flying progress was marked by the addition of another red-ink entry stamped into his logbook on 9 June 1939: 'Qualified 1st Pilot Night on Harrow aircraft with effect from 9.6.39'. This was a most significant endorsement for Pilot Officer Barnard, as he was now permitted to fly the stately aircraft as first pilot in both day and night situations.

Donald's time on 75 Squadron was to be short, for he was posted on 19 June 1939 to 99 (Madras Presidency) Squadron at RAF Mildenhall, also in Suffolk. Here he converted onto the twin-engined Vickers Wellington bomber, popularly known as the 'Wimpy' after the Popeye cartoon character J. Wellington Wimpy. The squadron was the first to be fully equipped with this modern bomber, which was able to fly close to 245 mph and to carry a larger bomb load over a greater distance than other types, both of which were important developments. Though the fitting of a single Browning machine-gun in the nose was also considered to be a significant improvement, the ammunition feed systems to it and to the twin rear guns were not very effective.

By now, June 1939, there was no hiding the fact that war with Germany was imminent, and conversation in the squadron mess when Donald joined would certainly have been full of the impending crisis.[18] There was no hiding the fact, too, that aircrew at this advanced stage of training would almost certainly be involved in the inevitable conflict, and they did not have long to wait for, at eleven o'clock on Sunday, 3 September 1939, two days after German forces attacked Poland, war was declared on Germany, with Donald still under training.

On 4 September, however, he was back with 215 Squadron, which had become a Reserve Squadron two days earlier. Further training exercises in the Wimpy were undertaken, and he qualified as '1st Pilot daylight' on that aircraft on 10 October 1939.

Donald Barnard taking off in Harrow K6947 on 11 April 1939. This aircraft was destroyed when it crashed into high ground at Kincardineshire in 1943.

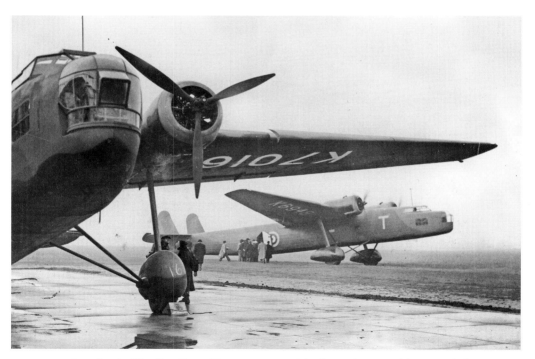

215 Squadron's Handley Page Harrow K6948 'T', flown by Donald Barnard from November 1938 to June 1939.

Six days after he had qualified, a detachment from 215 Squadron went to RAF Jurby on the Isle of Man. Donald, flying in Wellington L4390, took just over an hour and a half to complete the journey. On 27 October, he flew with Squadron Leader J. B. S. Monypenny[19] to RAF Aston Down, Gloucestershire, in Wellington L4385, though it is not known what their business was there.

Donald rejoined his squadron, which was now at RAF Bassingbourn in Cambridgeshire, but only for a few days before he was again detached, on 7 November 1939, to 148 Squadron at RAF Harwell,[20] which was then in Berkshire, 148 having been a 'Group pool' squadron since early in the previous year. Donald's time at Harwell ended in January 1940 when, once again, he returned to 215 Squadron at Bassingbourn where, as a measure of his status on the squadron, he was employed in the instruction of 'under training' aircrews.

With the significant reorganisation that had been taking place within the RAF as a result of the need for more pilots, pressure was mounting to introduce a faster training programme. One of the ways in which this was to be manifested was the creation of Operational Training Units (OTUs), where airmen could finish off their training before being sent to a frontline operational squadron. In consequence, Donald found himself posted, with effect from 4 April 1940, to No. 11 OTU, not surprisingly at RAF Bassingbourn, which he joined on 6 April.

Though his logbook records many flying sorties with crews under training, this was a frustrating time for him. Here he was fully trained and raring to go, but all he could do was read about RAF bomber operations against the enemy.

Donald goes to war

Donald's patience was soon to be rewarded, however, when, having been promoted flying officer on 6 August 1940 (seniority 25 July), he made another request to be assigned to operational duties. This time, on 14 August 1940, it was granted with a posting to No. IX (B) Squadron at Honington.[21] Its commander, Wing Commander Ernest Alton Healy (16053), was yet another of those experienced, long-serving RAF officers who were to provide the backbone of the frontline squadrons in the early months of the war.[22] He had been promoted wing commander on 12 March 1940, and appointed to command IX Squadron on 24 July.

IX Squadron, then serving in No. 3 (Bomber) Group, was operating the Wellington bomber, an aircraft so frequently flown by Donald that his confidence in it must have been sky high. As second pilot to a Pilot Officer Hoey he joined an experienced crew, and late in the evening of 16 August climbed into Wellington T2505 for his first operational sortie of the war, one for which he had waited a very long time. Their target was Gelsenkirchen in the Ruhr region of Germany. T2505 took off at 2240 hours on the night of 16 August and returned safely at 0404 hours the next morning, though Donald was suffering slightly from a fragment of an anti-aircraft shell that had struck his head.

Above & right: 99 Squadron at RAF Mildenhall, August 1939, in front of an Mk 1 Wellington Bomber. Pilot Officer Barnard is standing in the middle row, furthest left.

An artist's impression
of Barnard's sixteenth
bombing raid on
Gelsenkirchen on
10 November 1940.

Despite his first completed operation being 'in the bag', there was still a long way to go before his first tour of duty could be finished. The powers that be had decided at a conference at RAF Hospital Rauceby that a tour of operations would be limited to 200 hours, which in effect meant having to fly between twenty-five and thirty operations.[23]

A newly appointed flight commander to IX Squadron, Squadron Leader S. G. Pritchard, was looking for a second pilot, and he selected Donald. Their first flight together was on the night of 17/18 August, when Bomber Command made what they hoped would be a concerted effort by just over 100 Blenheims, Hampdens and Wellingtons to bomb five airfields in Germany and The Netherlands. One of the participating Wellingtons, R3296, with Squadron Leader Pritchard and Donald aboard, took off at 2040 hours on its way to bomb Diepholz aerodrome. Unable to locate the target through 10/10ths cloud, however, they returned safely at 0510 hours.

Even after a year of war, bombing at night was still extremely problematic for Bomber Command crews, who not only had to navigate their way to a point in the sky several hundred miles away but who then had to place their bombs on the practically invisible target several thousand feet below. Bomber Command operational crews were no doubt heartened by the truth-bending but morale-boosting message from Air Marshal Sir Richard Pierse:

> Signal addressed to the Air Officers Commanding Nos 2, 3, 4, and 5 Groups from the Air Officer Commanding-in-Chief, Bomber Command, on the 18th August 1940.
>
> Heartiest congratulations to all Groups, Stations and Squadrons on the outstanding success of their recent operations.

With the Luftwaffe attempting to obliterate the RAF before the German Army could attempt its invasion of Britain, it was Honington's turn to suffer three serious aerial attacks. The first, on 17 August 1940, resulted 'in a number of seriously ill, dangerously ill and fatal casualties'.[24] The second, at 1615 hours on 19 August, was by a single bomber which dropped high explosive and incendiary bombs. Slight material damage was inflicted, but eight service personnel were killed and a further sixteen were seriously injured. Most of the casualties had been caught in the open as they crossed the parade square on their way to the mess hall. A third raid, on 28 October, delivered by a solitary Dornier Do17 at 1825 hours, resulted in heavy damage to the north-west wing barrack block. Two Wellingtons received significant damage, several bomb craters were formed across the aerodrome, one hangar roof was badly holed, and again further casualties were caused to the airfield contingent. The Luftwaffe were to attack RAF Honington no fewer than sixteen times during the Second World War.

Despite the enemy's raids on Honington, Donald again flew with the Pritchard crew, on the evening of 19 August to Hanover, where they bombed a goods train from only 1,000 feet, returning safely to their now badly damaged base. Donald flew as second pilot, again with the Pritchard crew, on operations on 24/25 August to Knapsack, on 26/27 August to Frankfurt, on 1/2 September to Bitterfeld aluminium works, and on 7/8 September to Strasburg.

This last sortie was not the usual bombing operation, for Bomber Command airmen were being called upon to attempt to set fire to trees. British Intelligence had learnt of the build-up of enemy ammunition dumps in certain forested areas, and so the task of setting them alight to destroy them was given to Bomber Command using small incendiary bombs. These incendiary devices, however, even if dropped in the right place, were of somewhat limited value:

> The smallest incendiary devices developed and deployed operationally were those codenamed 'Razzle' and 'Decker'. They were probably the least successful [of all of the incendiary devices developed]. Both depended upon phosphorus pellets drying out and igniting spontaneously. 'Razzle', a sandwich of celluloid strips and pellets, 3 inches by 1 inch, was rushed into production during the summer of 1940 in time to attack the German harvest. Burning time was increased in 'Decker' by introducing

latex rubber into the sandwich and increasing the surface area to 4 inches by 4 inches. Bomber Command aircraft dropped a considerable number during the summer and autumn, but despite reasonably dry conditions the Germans found them to be no more than a minor nuisance – except for those who foolishly put them in their trouser pockets as souvenirs ...[25]

At the beginning of 1940, British Intelligence had reasoned that a German invasion was likely early in July of that year – the clues were the withdrawal of German shipping from Norway, U-boats being brought back from patrol, and so on – but when it did not materialise no further alert was issued until early September. RAF Photographic Reconnaissance aircraft had been on constant watch for any signs of a build-up of invasion shipping but had seen nothing of any real interest until, on 1 September, a significant increase in the number of barges gathering at Ostend was noticed. Over the next three days a further 100 barges appeared at Flushing, with additional concentrations at Calais and Dunkirk. Yet more were seen at Ostend on 5 September, and a report was also received by British Intelligence that all German Army leave was to be stopped with effect from 8 September. Such was the anticipation of an imminent invasion that at precisely 8.07 p.m. on 7 September the codeword CROMWELL was issued by the British government to all home defence forces, bringing them to 'immediate action'.

As with other squadrons in Bomber Command at this time, IX Squadron was on permanent standby and played its part in trying to prevent the expected invasion somewhere along the south or south-east coast: 'The invasion barges provided good targets as they were quite visible in the moonlight of September, particularly since they lay along the coast. Led by their C.O., Wg. Cdr. E. A. Healy, the Squadron must have destroyed many.'[26]

With the invasion problem out of the way, temporarily or otherwise, Flying Officer Donald Barnard was to fly only once more with Squadron Leader Pritchard, an air test, on 14 September 1940. From this date onwards Donald was to command his own bomber as first pilot. As fate would have it, Squadron Leader Pritchard and his crew failed to return from an operation eight weeks later, shot down by flak near Bremen on 14/15 November. Fortunately, all six of the crew baled out over Holland to become prisoners of war.

Squadron Leader Pritchard's desk was soon occupied by a new 'A' flight commander, Squadron Leader K. M. M. Wasse, who first applied his signature to Donald's flying logbook on 30 November 1940. Kenneth Michael Macleod Wasse (37058), another RAF 'veteran', had been granted a short service commission with effect from October 1934. Steady promotion followed until he became a squadron leader on 20 September 1940, the qualifying rank under RAF rules for filling the post of a flight commander on a Bomber Command squadron.

In March 1941, Merlin-engined Wellingtons were delivered to the squadrons in 3 Group, including IX Squadron; these Wimpys were now capable of carrying the massive 4,000 lb HC bomb, the famous high capacity 'cookie' or 'blockbuster'. On the raid on Emden on the night of 31 March/1 April 1941, considered to be the first raid using what later became known as the Pathfinder technique, Squadron Leader Wasse's crew in R1513 and another from the squadron dropped incendiary flares to light up the target for Wellington W5439 (Pilot Officer Franks) of 149 Squadron, whose crew dropped the first ever 'cookie' blast bomb in anger.

For the rest of the war the 4,000 lb 'cookie' would be an important weapon in Bomber Command's arsenal. It was a modernised version of a high explosive blast bomb, the 1,650 lb SN, that had been used to some effect during the latter stages of the First World War. Plans had been made during the last years of peace before the Second World War for a bomb weighing up to 4,000 lb, but without an aircraft capable of lifting such a load to Germany it was not until the Luftwaffe began dropping its parachute G mines on England in 1940 that these plans were accelerated. In the autumn of that year a firm commitment was given to proceed with its production and, as mentioned, it was ready for use at the end of March 1941.

At first the only readily available high explosive was Amatol, which had been developed during the First World War, but it was progressively replaced by newer explosives such as Cyclonite (a mixture of RDX and TNT), Torpex, Amatex, and Minol. Minol was a mixture of 40 per cent TNT, 40 per cent ammonium nitrate, and 20 per cent powdered aluminium (which increased the blast effect). Various developments led to differing proportions of these basic components. As the Amatol/TNT mixture proved to be a relatively insensitive type of explosive, it allowed armourers some level of safety during transit and storage. The fuse, or initiator, designed to set off the 'cookie' was made from a far more sensitive explosive. This was fitted only at the time of loading the bombs into the aircraft's bomb bay.

Later in the war the standard load for a 'heavy' bomber would be a 4,000 lb HC bomb and a number of 4 lb incendiary bombs, the large bomb to blast the target apart and the incendiaries to then set what was left on fire. A shocking example of this technique was to be given on the night of 11/12 September 1944 when over two hundred 'cookies' and 286,000 4 lb incendiaries were dropped on Darmstadt. Even the Nazis saw this as an extreme example of 'terror bombing'. They had good reason to think so, for the city was ripped apart. Some 12,300 of its inhabitants were killed and 70,000 made homeless.

Incendiary bombs were designed to ignite after impact and to be capable of generating a great heat in the immediate area. The 4 lb bombs contained thermite pellets within a magnesium alloy body; after the pellets had reached a high enough temperature, the magnesium case ignited and continued to burn for seven to ten minutes thereafter. These small incendiary bombs were carried in Small Bomb Containers (SBCs), which Donald frequently referred to in his logbook, using the term 'Cans'. One standard container carried a total of 90 x 4 lb bombs. Ironically, the conception of the 4 lb incendiary in 1934 had derived from a demonstration of

Flying Officer Barnard (far left) with two fellow squadron pilots enjoying a game of mixed croquet.

such devices in December 1933, one of which was a German electron-cased bomb, electron being a mixture of mainly magnesium and zinc. At the start of the war in 1939 the RAF possessed a stock of 5 million of the 4 lb incendiary, with factories geared up to produce as many as 60,000 per week as and when required. By the time that Donald was dropping these fire-raisers the original Mk 1 bomb had become the Mk III and then the Mk IV, the changes to the original design being necessitated by a shortage of magnesium.[27] The Wellington was able to carry 810 4 lb incendiary bombs in containers, a total load of 3,240 lb.

Though Wasse left the squadron shortly after the Emden raid at the end of March, he returned as its commanding officer with effect from 20 June 1941, having in the meantime been promoted wing commander and awarded the DFC (gazetted on 6 June 1941). He survived the war and continued to serve in the RAF as a squadron leader for a few years thereafter.

Now, in September 1940, a first pilot in his own right, it was Flying Officer Barnard's turn to fly with a second pilot. Pilot Officer Guy Paul Wentworth Austin (77130), from Cape Province, South Africa, was the man chosen, and so they commenced operations together under their new flight commander. September was to prove another busy month for Donald, with operations to Calais on the 15th, Hamm on the 17th, and then back to Calais on the 21st to finish off the invasion barges.

Berlin was the target on the 23rd, the first time that Bomber Command had attempted to concentrate a significant strength of bombers over one city on a single raid. A total of eighteen different targets – railway yards, power stations, gasworks and factories – were to be bombed by over 100 aircraft during a three-hour period. Donald recorded dropping eight 250 lb bombs over the target in a flight that took over seven hours to complete. Because of the significance of the target, the Air Officer Commanding-in-Chief of Bomber Command, Air Marshal Sir Richard Pierse, arrived at RAF Honington on the following day in order to meet personnel of IX Squadron, and no doubt to discover at first hand how the raid had gone.

September came to an end for Donald with operations to Boulogne on the 25th and Frankfurt on the 28th. Pilot Officer Austin proved to have been a good choice as second pilot, the South African officer becoming a popular member of the crew. He flew on seven successful operations alongside Donald, but the partnership was to end at the close of September due to a minor medical problem with the index finger of Donald's left hand which, requiring an operation, removed him from operational flying duties during October.

Pilot Officer Austin continued flying on operations with IX Squadron, but on 15 October 1940, flying with Squadron Leader J. O. Hinks and his crew on an operation to Magdeburg in Germany, their Wellington, T2464, was lost. There were no survivors, and all are buried in the Berlin 1939-45 War Cemetery. Donald simply recorded Austin's death in his logbook as 'Killed in Action'.

Donald was admitted to the Littleport Annexe of RAF General Hospital, Ely, Cambridgeshire, for treatment to his finger on 25 October. Though the hospital had been opened, with limited facilities, only in August, it was at least considered to be 'perhaps the most modern and well built of all the RAF hospitals'. Construction had begun in early 1938 after it had been appreciated by the RAF authorities that war with Germany would bring many new airfields to the flat Fen region with consequent casualties. On the outbreak of war temporary accommodation was needed while the hospital was finished, and the place selected to bridge the gap was a convalescent home at Littleport, a village 5 miles north of Ely, which had in times of peace been used by members of the Transport & General Workers' Union: 'It consisted of a series of standard-type wooden huts estimated to accommodate at capacity 250 equipped beds and the necessary ancillary services such as laboratory and X-ray departments.'[28] Here, Donald's left index finger was attended to surgically, and sick leave was granted up to a maximum of fourteen days.

He returned to his unit ready for operational flying within ten days, but missed the excitement of another Luftwaffe raid on Honington airfield. This time the enemy bomber was shot down, crashing in front of a hangar, the incident finally leading to the decision that flying personnel should be billeted overnight not far from the aerodrome in Ampton Hall, a large stately home, built in 1892 to replace the old hall that had been destroyed by fire seven years earlier.

In order that he could be passed fit for flying duty, Donald was instructed on 5 November to take one of IX Squadron's aircraft on an air test with Flying Officer J. N. Loring, Station Medical Officer, sitting alongside him.[29] Donald was passed fit and returned to the operational strength of the squadron. The rest of November saw a further flurry of operations for the squadron, with Donald flying his Wellington on raids to Bremerhaven on the 5th, Essen on the 7th, and Gelsenkirchen on the 10th. Two days later they went back to Gelsenkirchen, followed by Hamburg on the 16th, and then the same target on the 24th.

The final raid for November was to Cologne, on the 27th, where they dropped 3,000 lb of bombs. The RAF were now beginning to install night cameras in their bombers, and IX Squadron was to do so for the first time with one aircraft nominated to use the camera. That aircraft was to be last over the target and would deploy a powerful photoflash bomb after its bomb load had also been dropped. The aircraft chosen to carry the camera was Donald's Wellington, T2473, and he recorded taking photographs at 10,000 feet. When they were developed after the raid they revealed the bombing to have been well off the intended target, a disappointing result, with fires, flak and lights showing up as streaks across the photographs.

The damning evidence that few if any of the bombers at this time ever got close to their intended target was provided by the Butt Report, completed on 18 August 1941 by Mr D. M. Butt of the War Cabinet Secretariat. Having examined about 630 photographs taken on night operations in June and July 1941, he reached the following conclusions:

1. Of those aircraft recorded as attacking their target, only one in three got within five miles.
2. Over the French ports, the proportion was two in three; over Germany as a whole, the proportion was one in four; over the Ruhr it was only one in ten.
3. In the full moon, the proportion was two in five; in the new moon it was only one in fifteen.
4. In the absence of haze, the proportion is over one half, whereas over thick haze it is only one in fifteen.
5. An increase in the intensity of A.A. fire reduces the number of aircraft getting within five
   miles of their target in the ratio three to two.
6. All these figures relate only to aircraft recorded as attacking the target; the proportion of the total sorties which reached within five miles is less by one third.[30]

Donald was to take T2473, again with the camera, on a raid to Düsseldorf on 7 December. His logbook records 'photo taken at 10,000 ft minus 35 centigrade – on return got frostbite'. When the photographs were examined, they revealed that this time the bomb load had been dropped very close to the target. One photograph showed several lights that had been tracked across the target area.

Five aircraft failed to return from the Düsseldorf raid on 7/8 December. One of them, Wellington Mk 1c R3220, WS-L, flown by Flight Lieutenant D. G. Stanley,

Düsseldorf, 7 December 1940, the day of Barnard's 22nd bombing raid at 10,000 feet and -35 °C.

was from Donald's squadron. As the indications were that R3220 might have ditched in the North Sea, Donald and his crew took off next morning in order to fly a square search pattern over the sea, but after three hours they failed to find any evidence of the missing aircraft. Sadly, however long they, or anyone else, had searched the North Sea for the missing crew, they would never have found them, for their Wellington had crashed at Stene on the southern outskirts of Ostend, Belgium.[31]

On a non-operational flight during that first week of December, Donald went to Tern Hill in Shropshire to collect Wellington R1244. It was a short, two-hour trip with a second pilot whom he records as Sergeant Parkes. Donald later noted alongside Parkes' name: 'Interned France but escaped'. It was a little over a month later, on a raid on Turin in northern Italy on the night of 11/12 January 1941, that Sergeant S. M. P. Parkes and crew, flying in R1244, lost an engine on the way to the target. The crew loyally refused their skipper's invitation to abandon the stricken aircraft, and all survived the subsequent and brilliantly executed wheels-up landing in a field in Vichy France. After many trials and tribulations all six of

Parkes' crew returned to England via what was proving to be the usual route to Spain and Gibraltar. Three of the crew, however, having returned to operational flying, were not so lucky a second time and were killed in action.[32]

Donald was back in action again on 16 December with Mannheim the target. This was at the time the largest raid on Germany, with 134 aircraft sent to attack one target, and was undertaken following the heavy attacks by the Luftwaffe on Coventry and Southampton. It was the first time that bomber crews were not given a specific industrial or military target at which to aim their bombs, and was the start of what the RAF euphemistically called 'area bombing' and what the Germans more appropriately called 'terror bombing'. In the event, the majority of the RAF's bombs fell in the residential part of the city, with consequent death and destruction. Wellington T2473, with Donald at the controls, came back to find bad weather over England – it had been forecast – but landed safely.

A repeat attack on Gelsenkirchen on the 19th ensued, followed by a daring operation to bomb Venice two nights later on 21 December. Donald wrote in his logbook: '1,500 miles at 68 gallons per hour!', and at 10 hours and 40 minutes in duration this was by far the longest operation that he had flown. On the Venice trip the crew of T2473 were to experience what was at that time one of the major problems confronting all bomber crews, namely the inability to 'see' through thick cloud. Having navigated their way to the approximate target area, the crew found it covered with deep cloud, and so, relying heavily on the skill of the navigator, dropped their bombs at the estimated time of arrival. It was an unsatisfactory way to end the outward trip, but it was the best that could be done in the circumstances. Pathfinder aircraft with sophisticated flares and radio aids to assist the main force of bombers were still a long way off, though, as mentioned, IX Squadron with Michael Wasse, were to set the ball rolling.

The year 1940 closed with Donald having flown a total of twenty-two Bomber Command operations, and with a total of 967 hours and 25 minutes' flying time recorded in his logbook. He was now approaching the end of his tour, when he would be rested from operations, but on 3 January 1941, IX Squadron were back on operations with a visit to Bremen, followed by yet another trip to Gelsenkirchen on the 9th. Donald was informed that he would be regarded as having completed his tour of duty with the squadron following one final sortie to Italy. On 11 January, the crew took off at 1733 hours to bomb the Royal Arsenal at Turin, another very long trip, and bombs were accurately dropped on target, the railway yard and the arsenal itself. The Wellington touched down at 0205 hours with, no doubt, a great sense of relief being felt by Donald and the rest of the crew – Pilot Officer Waldron, Sergeant Peters, Sergeant Barrow, Sergeant Rogers and Sergeant Jackson. It was on this operation that the Parkes crew had come down in Vichy France (see above).

On 14 February 1941, Flying Officer Barnard presented his flying logbook to the Officer Commanding 'A' Flight, Squadron Leader Wasse, who endorsed the total time recorded as just over 1,000 hours. The new commanding officer of IX Squadron, since 16 January 1941, Wing Commander R. G. C. Arnold, also congratulated him on the achievement of having completed a tour of operations, but clearly did not regard it sufficiently highly to warrant the award of a 'gong'.[33]

Tour expired – posted to Operational Training Units

It was Bomber Command's policy for operational aircrew on completion of a 'tour' to be rested from operations, and this usually meant a posting to one of the burgeoning Operational Training Units which, for aircrew under training, was the last step before joining a frontline squadron. Donald's next logbook entry, therefore, was to read: 'Posted to No. 20 O.T.U. Lossiemouth'. Though being posted to an OTU was indeed seen as a rest from operations, sadly, in too many cases, it brought just as much danger as if one were still on an operational squadron. Official records give the grim statistic that over 8,000 lives – instructors and 'under training' crew alike – were killed in training accidents.[34] But with ever increasing losses in the air war over occupied Europe the pressure to train student aircrew was immense and so, for just over a year, from February 1941 to March 1942, Donald was kept hard at it, flying many training sorties to get the pupils on 'the top line'.

After a short spell at Lossiemouth he was posted, with effect from 9 May 1941, to No. 22 OTU at Wellesbourne Mountford in Warwickshire. His long spell at OTU ended on 27 March 1942, by which time he had added over 300 further flying hours to his total. There was some compensation for all his efforts, when, on 25 July 1941, he was promoted to the rank of flight lieutenant.

It was the exception rather than the norm for operational aircrew to survive two tours of duty. This must have been in Donald's mind as he embarked upon his second tour in Bomber Command when, on 27 March 1942, he arrived at RAF Binbrook in Lincolnshire. On the following day he reported to Binbrook's 'satellite' airfield at nearby RAF Waltham (Grimsby), home to 142 (Bomber) Squadron commanded by Wing Commander A. B. Olney (37116).[35]

For the next few operations Donald flew from either Binbrook or Waltham. Binbrook had been the home of 12 Squadron since September 1940, though during July and August of that year they had shared the aerodrome with 142 Squadron. On leaving Binbrook in November 1941, 142 moved 5 miles up the road to Waltham, formerly the civil airport for the town of Grimsby, which lies a couple of miles to the north. As the new airfield had been completed only that November, 142 Squadron were the first to use it, and it was the newness of Waltham that was the reason for 142 continuing to share facilities at Binbrook. Though the large, four-engined Short Stirling and Handley Page Halifax bombers had been in service with Bomber Command since the previous year, and the mighty Avro Lancaster was about to be unleashed upon the Third Reich, 142 Squadron continued to fly the twin-engined Wellington on night bombing operations.

On April Fools' Day 1942, Donald flew with second pilot Sergeant A. Harker on a 3-hour round trip from Binbrook. The wireless operator for this trip was

Sergeant Ralph Forster wearing a sidcot
suit & early 'B' Type flying helmet.
(*Ralph Forster*)

Sergeant Ralph Forster, whom we shall meet again. Donald was given a few
days of local flying to gain the benefit of landmark recognition, but on 5 April,
in Wellington Z1338, he flew as second pilot to the squadron commander, Wing
Commander Olney, on his (Donald's) first bombing raid, to Cologne, on a trip
lasting 10 minutes short of 7 hours. Without doubt his skills were being checked,
for on the following night, on a raid to Essen, Donald again flew as second pilot,
but this time with Flight Lieutenant E. F. K. Campling DFC.

Campling was an experienced pilot, who had had a close shave in the previous
year when, very short of fuel, he had just managed to cross the North Sea on
the way back from a raid. In October 1941, 142 Squadron had re-equipped with
the Mk IV Wellingtons, which had American-built Pratt & Whitney Twin Wasp
engines, much thirstier than the Merlin, consuming some 145 gallons per hour
compared to the 85 of the Merlin. This led to fuel problems on the first operation
that 142 flew with the Mk IV, when apparently only a quarter of the squadron's
Wimpys managed to get back to base without having to land elsewhere first.
One of them, Z1210 (Sergeant T. E. Parker, RCAF), disappeared somewhere in
the North Sea, but Campling just scraped in to the North Coates airfield on the
Lincolnshire coast. It was a very close call, for he ran out of fuel before he was
able to get his wheels down.[36]

It was the luck of the draw that Donald Barnard would survive the war but
that Campling, who would also prove to be an outstanding bomber pilot, would

not. Having survived all that the German defences could throw at him from the ground, sea and air, Campling was to lose his life at the age of 23 on nothing more dangerous than an air test over England. On 8 April 1944, in Lancaster R5672, he took off from RAF Hemswell with eight passengers on board. At some point during the test, and for some unknown reason, the aircraft was seen to dive into the ground, with no survivors.[37]

After these two flights under observation in April 1942, Donald began another long sequence of operational sorties, with his crew members undergoing several changes, though all were content in the knowledge that their skipper was an experienced captain. One of those who flew with him on various occasions was navigator Pilot Officer E. J. R. Yates, RNZAF (NZ.403787), who was to lose his life on 27 July 1942 when fourteen of the squadron's Wellingtons were detailed to attack Hamburg on the night of 26/27 July. Three failed to return. The crew of one of those that did return, Wellington Z1289 (Flight Sergeant N. J. Warfield), were forced to jettison their bombs off the island of Sylt when attacked by an Me110. As a result of the attack, Warfield was wounded in the hand and Pilot Officer Yates was killed. For whatever reason, the wireless operator, Sergeant William Lusk Harper, baled out and was never seen again.[38]

Also damaged in the attack was the rear turret manned by Sergeant John Howarth. With total loss of the hydraulics that powered it, Howarth had to operate his turret manually, but nevertheless managed to shoot down their attacker. Leaving the unserviceable turret he then went forward to see to Warfield, but the pilot was in such a poor state with his injured hand that it was Howarth who flew the damaged aircraft back to England. It should be remembered that the only able-bodied airmen still aboard were himself and wireless operator/air gunner Sergeant Walter Gilroy. After the long journey home, and nearing base, Warfield recovered sufficiently to take the controls from Howarth and to make a safe landing.

Sergeant Howarth was awarded an immediate DFM for his gallantry, gazetted on 14 August 1942. Commissioned (50972) in March 1943, he was killed in action on the night of the infamous Nuremberg raid, 30/31 March 1944, when Lancaster ND361, 460 (RAAF) Squadron, was shot down, probably by Oberleutnant Richard Delakowitz, 7./NJG4, for his third victory.

Walter Gilroy, as luck would have it, was to survive the war. Tour-expired on 142 Squadron in September 1942, he was promoted warrant officer, and in that rank was awarded the DFC on 17 November 1944 whilst serving on 7 Squadron, though his commission (183879) had been gazetted a month earlier, on 17 October.

Others to fly in Donald's crew were 650464 Sergeant A. E. Elphick, wireless operator/air gunner, who completed his tour of duty in June 1942; Sergeant F. H. Lang, RCAF, air gunner, who, having survived his first tour of duty and transferred to the RCAF, was killed in action on 427 Squadron on 12/13 June 1944 (Arras) as a flying officer (J.17144) on his second tour of ops; Pilot Officer J. S. Gronow

(46209), another wireless operator/air gunner, who completed his tour on 142 Squadron in early August 1942; R.59119 Sergeant T. E. Parker, RCAF, pilot, who was also killed in action, on 21/22 October 1941 (Bremen) with the loss of Wellington Z1210; 754105 Flight Sergeant A. Harker, pilot, who served on operations on Donald's squadron for only twelve days before his Wellington, Z1396, failed to return from Kassel on 27/28 August 1942;[39] 759288 Sergeant A. E. Buckell; 1053891 Sergeant R. Forster; R.65502 Flight Sergeant E. B. Key, RCAF, air gunner, who managed to complete his full tour of duty in early August 1942; and Flying Officer R. B. Ingalls, RCAF (J.4771).

All too frequently, operational aircrew on a squadron would find themselves as what were termed unofficially 'spare bods', often as a result of having been taken off operations due to ill health or injury when, during their absence, their regular crews went off on ops with a replacement and failed to return. It is possible that Donald was not allocated a regular crew, as his first operations appear to have been made with various 'spare bods'. Squadron Leader A. B. Olney (later promoted wing commander) is recorded as completing several operations during January and February 1942 with a number of the men listed above. This would suggest that Pilot Officer Ingalls, Pilot Officer Gronow, Sergeant Key, Sergeant Forster and Sergeant Harker were indeed part of his regular crew. The reason for Squadron Leader Olney's removal from operations is not known, but his crew were distributed throughout the squadron.

Canadian Flying Officer Ross Baxter Ingalls, RCAF, who was a comparatively old 27, was to be awarded the DFC on 11 August 1942, the citation for which read:

> As air observer Flying Officer Ingalls has participated in numerous operational sorties over enemy occupied territory. His coolness in the face of the heaviest defences has contributed materially to the successes obtained. Whatever the circumstances, he shows the greatest determination to locate and bomb his objective. He always endeavours to impart his knowledge to those of less experience.

Ingalls was to have a distinguished wartime RAF career, later earning the DSO on 14 August 1944 whilst serving on 582 Squadron, one of the elite Pathfinder squadrons. The citation for this award read:

> Since being awarded the Distinguished Flying Cross this officer has completed very many sorties, involving attacks on a wide range of important and well-defended targets. His navigational ability has been of a high order throughout and he has played a good part in the successes obtained. He has at all times displayed a high degree of courage and determination and his example has impressed all.

Ingalls left the Barnard crew having flown on ten operations with them (seventeen times altogether). It is possible that he became 'tour-expired' along with others of the crew who had flown with him during that period, and that he may have completed his tour of duty on 142 Squadron at the end of October 1942.

Hamburg was to be the next target, attacked on the night of 9/10 April. The following night, the Barnard crew were sent to Essen but, unfortunately, the intercom system failed while they were over Holland, forcing the operation to be abandoned. This was a wise decision, for any bomber being flown without the ability to communicate between the various crew positions was even more vulnerable to prowling enemy night fighters. Essen was once again the target on 12 April, and this time no issues prevented the completion of the operation.

Such was the pace of operations for Donald and his crew that they had only one night's rest before the next operation, to Dortmund. This proved to be an eventful sortie. Taking off from Waltham (Grimsby) at 2217 hours with a load of incendiaries the target was attacked from 12,000 feet, but the Wellington was caught in a cone of searchlights at 11,000 feet. Once locked into the multiple beams, the dangers of being hit by shells from anti-aircraft guns increased dramatically, and great skill and effort were required from the pilot to shake off the searchlights. Donald's answer to the crisis was to put the aircraft into a steep dive, but it was only when they were just 2,000 feet from the ground that they managed to escape the beams. By the time that they were nearing the English coast the Wimpy was low on fuel, requiring them to land at Manston in Kent at 0500 hours. After some rest and a check over the aircraft, Donald and crew flew on to Binbrook.

Towards the end of April 1942, Donald was required to attend No. 1503 (Beam Approach Training) Flight at RAF Mildenhall in Suffolk for a seven-day course. Known in the RAF as BAT training ('blind as a bat'), the trainee pilots were instructed in the skill of flying blind. Once in the air in their Wellingtons or Oxfords the instructors shielded the aircraft's instruments from the pilot, and the flying exercises were then completed by the trainee responding and acting upon the interpretation of signals being transmitted to the aircraft from ground beacons. It was by being able to 'read' these signals – dots on one side of a solid beam pointing down the centre of the runway in use, dashes on the other – that a pilot was able to 'find' his to way to an airfield and to make a direct approach for landing safely in adverse weather conditions, such as fog.

During the course Donald received instruction from Pilot Officer Parish and Pilot Officer Swain, recording himself as 'second pilot' in his logbook. The exercises were all flown by him with the familiar Wellington Mk 1c aircraft. It appears that Donald took the opportunity to experience a new aircraft type, the Stirling bomber, on 24 April when he flew a 25-minute air test in N3682 with Squadron Leader Speare as first pilot. This particular Stirling was in service with 149 Squadron, also based at RAF Mildenhall. The Stirling was a massive four-engined bomber standing on high landing gear. Compared to Donald's familiar Wellington, this was an opportunity not to be missed.

Donald returned to 142 Squadron in time to fly one more operation in April: an attack on Cologne on the 27th. This operation again saw his aircraft caught in the beams of several searchlights over the target area, but this time he was not so lucky. Heavy flak hit the Wellington, causing some damage. Fuel supplies once again became low, forcing him to land at RAF Marham in Norfolk. The aircraft, Z1416 'N', required some work over the following day, but was made ready to return to Grimsby late on 28 April. The next operation was another trip to Mannheim, on 19 May. It was another small but vital detail that prevented Donald and his crew from completing the sortie, namely an insufficient oxygen supply. So, once the bombs were dropped on an aerodrome in Holland, they returned to Binbrook.

All Bomber Command crews returning from an operation had to undergo a debriefing from their Squadron Intelligence Officer (IO), whose duty it was to elicit as much information as he possibly could about the sortie from the often tired and frightened airmen. Donald and crew were no exception on this night, as the IO tried to establish which aerodrome had been subjected to the bombing. Though classed as a secondary target, the operation was added to the tour of duty.

On 29 May 1942, Bomber Command paid a visit to the Gnome et Rhône works at Gennevilliers in Paris, with 142 Squadron putting up four Wellingtons on the raid out of a total of seventy-seven of all types. All four of 142 Squadron's aircraft took off shortly after midnight, but so poor was the visibility over France that they spent 40 minutes trying to locate the target. Donald reduced the height of his aircraft to 4,000 feet, but was forced to leave the area due to the weather. The bomb load was jettisoned over the sea on the return trip and the aircraft was then diverted to Abingdon aerodrome in Berkshire due to the poor weather conditions over their home station. At 0534 hours the engines of Donald's Wellington were switched off. Later that day the crew flew back to Grimsby, where they were briefed for another raid for that same night.

Not surprisingly, this raid proved to be a failure, with reconnaissance photographs showing little or no damage to the factory. A local report further stated that 38 houses were destroyed and 49 damaged, with 34 civilians killed and 167 injured.[40] The Gnome et Rhône company was famous for its aero engines, especially those used during the First World War, but with the fall of France in June 1940 it was ordered to produce the BMW801 engine for the Germans. It was only with the greatest difficulty that the company, despite having another factory at Limoges, was able to produce only 8,500 engines, against the Germans' estimate of 25,000, by 9/10 May 1944 when a raid by 56 Lancasters (5 lost) and 8 Mosquitos of 5 Group paid it and another factory a visit. The factory at Limoges had received the attention of twelve Lancasters of 617 Squadron (none lost), led by Wing Commander Leonard Cheshire, on 8/9 February 1944. There were few, if any, local casualties on the ground, unlike the raid on the Paris factory when a report suggested that 24 Parisians were killed and 107 injured. It was not just the RAF crews who suffered.

After the failed Gennevilliers attack in May 1942 it was all hands to the pump when Bomber Command's commander-in-chief, Air Marshal Sir Arthur Harris, was determined to put on a show that would make any doubters of his force's usefulness think again. He came up with a plan to put as many aircraft as possible – at least 1,000 – over the target in as short a space of time as possible so that the enemy's defences would be saturated. The unfortunate city to be finally chosen as the target was Cologne (Köln) after weather conditions prevented an attack on the first choice of Hamburg. Prime Minister Winston Churchill, who was prepared to accept losses of 100 aircraft (a staggering loss rate of 10 per cent), had agreed by 20 May to the concept of this huge number of aircraft simultaneously attacking one target. After a colossal effort by all involved in Bomber Command, and other Commands, on the evening of 30 May 1,047 assorted aircraft, 602 of them Wellingtons, set off to bomb Cologne. This was to be the first of the 1,000-bomber attacks.

One of the many Wellingtons was Z1416 'N', flown as usual by Donald and his crew of Sergeant Scores (second pilot), Flying Officer R. B. Ingalls, RCAF, Sergeant A. E. Buckell, Sergeant R. Forster, and Flight Sergeant E. B. Key. Taking off at 2256 hours, they arrived safely over the target, dropping their bomb load on the south-western area of the city from a height of 12,000 feet. Donald later reported that the entire target area was on fire. Damage to the city was immense, with over 3,300 buildings destroyed and thousands more damaged to one degree or another, resulting in over 45,000 citizens being made homeless. Bomber Command losses were roughly half of Churchill's acceptable total, but fears among the crews of possible 'friendly' aircraft collisions over the target area proved to be unfounded as the multitude of bombers entered the target area according to their planned timings and headings. Donald wrote in his logbook: '1st 1000 plan attack 44 lost'. German night-fighter pilots claimed to have shot down thirty of the raiders. One of the claimants was Oberfeldwebel Heinz Strüning who, though he did not in fact account for any British aircraft on this night, was to meet Donald and crew a few months later.

The second 1,000-plan attack took place two nights later, 1/2 June 1942, with the target this time being the industrial areas of Essen. Bomber Command failed to get the full complement of aircraft on this second attempt, falling short by nearly fifty, but Donald and crew – as above but without Sergeant Scores – were aboard one of the 956 assorted aircraft to take off. Despite a forecast of reasonable weather over Germany and the target, and despite the dropping of many flares over the Essen area, crews were hampered by poor visibility on the ground, whether caused by a natural haze, low cloud, or by smoke. Inevitably, scattered bombing occurred, with much damage being caused to the towns of Duisburg, Mülheim, and Oberhausen. The concept of large-scale bombing raids was acknowledged to be a success, with Donald having taken part in both of these important developments in the history of the RAF.

He made an intriguing entry in his logbook on 4 June 1942. After an engine had been changed in Wellington Z1416 he air tested it in the company of a Vickers employee, Mr Chaplin. Donald later endorsed his logbook entry for that day, showing Mr Chaplin as having become a prisoner of war. The circumstances in which this might have happened can only be guessed at, for it was extremely unlikely that the authorities would have allowed a civilian to have been put into such a position that there was the possibility of his either being killed or captured. There were, however, rare and unauthorised instances of ground personnel going off on a bombing operation, and getting away with it.

During the first week of June, Donald was advised of a secondment to Thruxton, five miles from Andover in Hampshire, an airfield that had been taken over by Army Co-operation Command in 1941. On 8 June 1942, Donald and crew were ordered to take a Wellington there in order to undertake parachute-dropping exercises. The full complement of men carried in his aircraft was Sergeant Hooper as second pilot, Flight Sergeant Buckell, Flight Sergeant Key, Sergeant Stubbins, Corporal Thorn, Leading Aircraftman Pritchard, and Leading Aircraftman Mackie. They flew over in Donald's personal Wellington Z1416 'N', and were immediately deployed on training exercises, the first of which involved the dropping of dummy parachutists in daylight. These were followed by similar ones at night, and they progressed to carrying eight fully equipped men, who were dropped on live exercises on various dates.

Earlier in the year, on 27/28 February 1942, British Combined Forces had carried out the daring Operation Biting, the parachute raid by men of the newly formed British 1st Airborne Division to capture parts of a German Würzburg radar set located on a cliff-top immediately north of the French village of Bruneval, and some 12 miles north of Le Havre. As the British Combined Operations team were also planning Operation Jubilee, a landing in force at Dieppe (which happened on 19 August 1942), one wonders whether or not this parachuting activity at Thruxton was anything to do with Jubilee.

On 9 July, the Barnard crew completed their secondment and returned to 142 Squadron at Grimsby to continue their operational duties over occupied Europe. They went to Duisburg in Z1416 on 14 July with a load of two 1,000 lb and three 500 lb bombs on what would prove to be a five-hour operation. A problem developed, however, when one of the 1,000 lb bombs hung up in the bomb bay after the rest of the load had been dropped over the target from a height of 9,000 feet, but a safe landing was made at base.

As a result of Donald's impressive performance in having completed thirty-nine operations, Wing Commander Donald Geoffrey Simmons (36077), the commanding officer of 142 Squadron, recommended him for the award of a non-immediate Distinguished Flying Cross:

Particulars of Meritorious Service. 12 Sorties (65.25 hours) flown on operations on this his second tour. This Officer has completed thirty nine operational sorties over Germany and enemy held territory. On all occasions he has pressed home his attacks with a determination and courage that have shown a complete disregard for his own safety.

His skilful airmanship and superb captaincy have on many occasions resulted in the target being located and bombed despite the heaviest defences. He has made many journeys to the most heavily defended areas of the Ruhr, and on more than one occasion it has only been his exceptional skill as a pilot that has enabled his aircraft to penetrate the searchlights and guns surrounding the target area.

Recommended for an award of the Distinguished Flying Cross.

Group Captain C. D. C. Boyce (26007), commanding RAF Binbrook, endorsed the recommendation on 24 July, adding the following remarks:

This Officer is a sound captain with a long record of good honest operational work without anything outstanding. He tempers dash with discretion, thereby keeping the complete confidence of his crew. He is a skilful and experienced pilot who takes an unusual amount of pains in pre flight tactical planning of each operation with his crew in order to ensure its success.

Recommended for the award of the Distinguished Flying Cross.

The Air Officer Commanding No. 1 Group, Air Vice-Marshal R. D. Oxland CBE, agreed with the recommendation on 30 July 1942.

Returning to his second tour of duty, Donald and his crew flew on 26 July on the raid to Hamburg carrying nine containers of incendiaries. They were by now much more of a settled crew around Donald, but added to the old names of Key, Forster, and Buckell a new name appeared, that of Pilot Officer Raymond Glensor, RNZAF, who was to experience a nerve-racking first trip with the Barnard crew. They were approximately 70 miles west of the target when the Wellington came under heavy anti-aircraft fire. Donald dived the aircraft to ground level, but not before it had suffered two direct hits. After 6 hours 40 minutes in the air, Wellington Z1416 landed at Grimsby, and on the following day Donald flew the damaged bomber to Binbrook for repairs.

On the last day of July 1942 another operation, involving a massive 630 Bomber Command aircraft, was launched against Düsseldorf. Donald's Wellington again carried a load of nine 'cans' of incendiary bombs. Though the raid took only seven hours to complete in the darkness, Donald recorded in his logbook that two hours of that were spent on instruments.

During August 1942, Donald and his crew flew a number of operations, the first of which was to Duisburg on the 6th with a load of one 250 lb, two 500 lb, and two 1,000 lb bombs. A further three operations followed between the 11th and 27th to Mainz, Düsseldorf, and Kassel, where they dropped incendiaries, leaving Donald now only two operations away from reaching the required total of twenty to complete his second tour of duty.

His regular crew now comprised Pilot Officer R. E. Glensor, RNZAF, Flight Sergeant A. E. Buckell, Sergeant R. Forster, and Sergeant H. James.

Raymond Glensor RNZAF.
(*Patricia Glensor*)

On 9 September, Donald took a new Wellington, DF550, on a local sortie with the CO of 142 Squadron sitting at his side. The duty shown in his logbook was 'Local for W/Cdr', Wing Commander D. G. Simmons, a prewar pilot, who was to command 142 Squadron for eight months during 1942. During that period he examined and signed Donald Barnard's logbook on several occasions and was, of course, responsible for the recommendation for the pending DFC for Acting Squadron Leader Barnard. Wing Commander Simmons departed 142 Squadron in November that year.[41]

Regarding the attack on Bremen on 13 September, Donald noted in his logbook that his Wellington, Z1416, was the first on 142 Squadron to carry a 4,000 lb bomb.[42] This was another operation that was not to be without its problems for Donald and crew, for not long after leaving the English coastline the generator burnt out as a result of a malfunction in one of the two engines. In consequence, all power to the lights, radio and identification transmitter was lost, and the propeller, slowly turning, caused so much drag and slowed down the aircraft's progress to such an extent that they had no choice but to jettison the large bomb.

Bomber Command aircraft frequently experienced bomb load malfunctions. Occasionally one or more bombs would hang up within the release mechanism causing, understandably, serious concern for the crew. Donald made reference to a similar problem on 14 July 1942 when a 1,000 lb bomb hung up over Duisburg. Any landing was likely to jolt the aircraft, thereby inducing the release of the

Wellington Bomber being loaded with an early 4,000 lb bomb. Barnard undertook the first 142 Squadron raid with such a bomb load on 13 September 1942.

Wellington Bomber receiving its bomb load for operations that night.

Wellington Queen being bombed up for operations. Note the wartime censorship of aircraft details.

bomb onto the concrete runway with potentially catastrophic consequences. In such circumstances the captain would first seek to jettison the problem load into a designated area in the English Channel.

This time the crew managed to jettison the bomb, and Donald noted in his logbook: 'Bomb dropped in minefield terrific explosion'. From the explosion created by the 4,000 lb 'cookie' it is clear that Donald was of the opinion that it must have landed in a minefield by pure chance.

Another opportunity to carry a 4,000 lb HC bomb took place on 16 September with a return to the difficult target of Essen. Albert Buckell noted that, to accommodate the bomb, a section of the fuselage floor had to be cut away. What was not fully appreciated at the time was the effect that this would have on the Wellington's aerodynamics once the bomb had been dropped. Though Donald makes no mention of it, the downward suction caused by the air rushing through the hole in the floor prevented the bomber from maintaining, or gaining, height. Unaware of this problem, Donald and crew (navigator Pilot Officer Raymond Edwin Glensor, RNZAF (NZ.403442), wireless operator 759288 Sergeant Albert E. Buckell, front gunner 1053891 Sergeant Ralph Forster, and rear gunner 1381761 Sergeant H. M. James) climbed aboard their new Wellington, DF550 'N'.

With everything checked to his satisfaction and, having been given the green light from the duty officer in his caravan down the runway, Donald opened the throttles for take-off at 2044 hours to join 368 aircraft from Bomber Command all bent on doing their bit to flatten Essen.

Donald recorded what followed in red ink in his flying logbook, the lack of punctuation only serving to heighten the drama:

> Took off at 20.50hrs starboard blower failed to work at 11,000 ft arrived over target at 13,000 ft bomb dropped in target area. Heavily engaged by predicted flak S/C [set course] base 9,000 ft 160 mph attacked by Me110 starboard engine and cowling believed badly hit. Both oil pressure zero u/c lights and petrol gauge failed to function a/s u/s oil pumped by reserve tank pipeline severed. Heavily engaged by flak and searchlights over St Omer evasive action down to 4,000 ft starboard engine revved to 3,000 although put in coarse pitch and throttled back. Attempted to feather engine seized up and stopped aircraft became practically impossible to control, crew ordered to abandon at 3,000 ft w/op left at 1,500 ft (Last crew member to escape) I attempted to leave but aircraft stall turned and went into power glide, climbed back into seat levelled out at 600 ft over a hill, touched down at approx 150 mph no a/s [air speed] or flaps. Ran 250 yards on belly a/c and self undamaged. Unable to destroy aircraft, time of landing 2359 hours.

The navigator, Raymond Glensor, had been keeping a track of their position over France with headings prior to the attack and passed these to the wireless operator, Albert Buckell. In the desperate situation after the attack, and with an increasingly inevitable crash, Albert was able to send two radio messages that enabled a fix to be made of their position. The fix also provided the crew with a good indication of their location over occupied France, somewhere near Armentières. The final SOS fix plotted DF550 somewhere between Béthune and Alquines in the Pas-de-Calais area of north-eastern France.

Of the 369 aircraft that had set out that night against Essen, DF550 and 38 others failed to return, a colossal and unsustainable loss rate of 10.6 per cent, with 142 Squadron losing three of the seven Wellington bombers that had been despatched. Two of the three, Z1380 and Z1480, crashed in Germany with no survivors.

As Donald was to record, Wellington DF550, QT-N, was attacked by a German night fighter during the return leg from Essen at close to midnight and came down in Northern France near the village of Alquines. But who was the Luftwaffe night-fighter pilot who attacked Wellington DF550 on that night in September 1942? Many postwar accounts exist with various claims by many night-fighter pilots, and it is not uncommon to detect errors in them. Without correlation of time and location being in close proximity, only the available evidence remains to indicate the most probable connection.

Dr Theo Boiten, author of *Nachtjagd War Diaries*, suggests that the Luftwaffe night-fighter pilot most probably responsible for the attack on DF550 was Oberfeldwebel Heinz Strüning of 7./NJG2. Strüning, an ace night-fighter pilot whose skills had been developed during many hours of operational flying, had on too many occasions been able to call out over his radio the night-fighter pilot's victory cry of 'Pauke, Pauke'.[43] Records indicate that his twenty-third victory was gained at 2334 hours on 16 September 1942 but, unfortunately, no location is confirmed.

With an ultimate total of fifty-six victories claimed during the Second World War, Strüning was awarded the Knight's Cross and Oak Leaves, but his luck ran out on 24 December 1944 when he was killed by the crew of a Mosquito of 157 Squadron RAF. Squadron Leader R. D. Doleman (pilot) and Flight Lieutenant D. C. Bunch DFC (navigator) were providing night-fighter support to ninety-seven Lancasters of Bomber Command on their way to bomb Cologne/Nippes railway yards. Hauptmann Strüning, Staffelkapitän of 9./NJG1 as he had now become, attempting to add to his total of victories latched on to one of the Lancasters in the bomber stream. But just as he had spotted his target, so Doleman and Bunch saw theirs and thus Strüning's fifty-sixth victory was to be his last. Forced to bale out of his blazing Messerschmitt Bf110 G-4 G9+CT, Strüning struck the tail and fell to his death somewhere in the Duisburg area.

Bunch, who had already been awarded the DFC in July 1943 (on 219 Squadron), was to receive the DSO on 9 March 1945, the citation for which reads:

> Flight Lieutenant Bunch has completed a very large number of sorties and continues to render most valuable service. He is a highly skilled member of aircraft crew and has assisted in the destruction of 7 enemy aircraft. He has at all times displayed a high standard of determination and devotion to duty.[44]

His skipper, Robert Doleman, was awarded the DFC a week before his navigator's DSO, but equalled the latter's medals with his own DSO in September 1945.

By the time of these awards, Donald Barnard was many miles away, on the other side of the globe almost. But that's another story.

CHAPTER 2

DIARY – PART 1: SHOT DOWN;
IN NORTHERN FRANCE

Sometime after his return to England, probably later in 1943, Donald wrote an account of the near-fatal mission to Essen on 16/17 September 1942, describing the landing of his Wellington bomber in northern France, his evasion through France, and his return to the United Kingdom via Spain and Gibraltar. Reproduced below is his story as he wrote it, except for names which have been inserted where, for example, he put 'Flight Sergeant B my wireless operator' or 'my navigator P/O G'. Place names, too, have been corrected where necessary, as has some of his punctuation. The authors' explanatory notes, comments and additions are in square brackets.

The Diary, which we have divided into three chapters to make it more manageable, covers a period of four months during which Donald, Ray Glensor (navigator), and Ralph Forster (front gunner) were escorted through France and over the Pyrenees to neutral Spain with the help of the PAT escape organisation, eventually reaching Gibraltar.[1] Donald and Ray Glensor landed in Scotland on 26 January 1943, but Ralph Forster, after three months in Spanish prisons, was flown back to RAF Hendon on the night of 19/20 April 1943.

* * *

September 16th 1942 to January 27th 1943

133 days

Sometime during the morning of September 16th 1942, the loud speaker system on the camp announced that the two Flight Commanders were required in the operation room. B Flight Commander being absent, his 2nd in command went along with me and we were informed by intelligence that the Squadron was on that night and that so many aircraft were required. Soon after the wing commander came in and all three of us got down to the job of deciding who was to go and who was to stand down. The target was to be ESSEN, which is where the heart of Germany's steel works is centred, and which is naturally very heavily defended.

Sergeant Forster in front of the 'wanted' poster naming Barnard's crew.

The wing commander asked me whether I would like to go and frankly, much against my will, I said yes. I had my reasons for that decision owing to the fact that I had tried twice recently to carry out an operation. The first time I had failed to even get into the air and the second time I had to return owing to engine trouble. Two more operations I had been due to partake in had been cancelled owing to bad weather. This time I decided nothing was going to stop me.

My aircraft was a new one and had never completed a raid. She had in fact given me considerable trouble ever since I had had her, which was not very long. However, the wing commander referred to her as the Flagship, but as far as I was concerned, she never deserved such a title. She was certainly different from the other aircraft on the squadron, having much more powerful engines and capable of carrying one blockbuster.

The wing commander decided I was to take off last as I was carrying such a large bomb, because should I crash during take off while the other aircraft were still on the ground, the chance of them flying that night would be rather small.

That evening however I persuaded him to let me take off first, while it was still light. I collected my crew and drove out to the aircraft which was lined up with the others on one of the runways not being used that night. The engines were started and tested. Just before taxi-ing out for the take off, Flight Sergeant Buckell my wireless operator called out that the wireless generator had burnt itself out. As this piece of news was told over the radio telephone, everybody in the aircraft heard it and the swearing and cursing that followed this announcement was frightful. I immediately called up flying control and asked for the wireless repair van as well as telling the W/Cdr my predicament. The answer was that if I could get it fixed in 20 minutes I could go.

In a few minutes, the van and the Engineer Officer appeared. My navigator P/O Glensor and I climbed out and spoke to the E.O. The amount of trouble that this aircraft had given was steadily mounting. P/O Glensor told the E.O. that if we brought N for NUTS back that night, we should bring her back in pieces. There's many a true word spoken in jest. There and then, we decided to re-christen her N for "No Bloody Good".

Eventually everything was ready, but I had no idea how many of the 20 crews there were left, if any. At 10 to 9 on the night of September 16th we took off and at 9 o'clock were passing over the aerodrome heading due East.

Nothing was said until the Dutch coast was reached, and one or two searchlights were reported. At 11,000 feet I engaged the superchargers, but the starboard one failed to function. However, before reaching the target I managed to reach 13,000 feet. The Ruhr was as busy as ever.

A short while before reaching the target, we were subjected to such a heavy concentration of predicted flak, the black bursts being so close. There was no alternative but to dive. I yelled to Glensor who was doing the bombing, to get rid of our load and by the time this was done we were down to 6000 feet. The flak was still following us, then suddenly the aircraft lifted. Our load had gone but where it fell I've no idea and frankly at that time I couldn't care less.

We climbed up to 9000 feet and flew on a southerly course, as ordered, so as to leave Cologne on our starboard side. Everything was much quieter and no flak or searchlights indicated that the city was near. Very annoying because to fly over that heavily defended area without knowing it would be extremely dangerous, especially if you were the only aircraft overhead. Suddenly in front and a little to our starboard, several searchlights came on, wavered slightly then stopped, forming a cone and in the cone a silvery object twisted and turned. They played with the aircraft they'd caught for a while, then it looked as if every gun had opened up – poor devil, he didn't stand a chance. After a few shots he caught fire and fell slowly to earth with burning pieces falling off him. All the while he fell, the guns mercilessly pumped shells into him. He eventually hit the ground, exploded in a shower of sparks. As though to make certain, the German gunners continued to fire at the burning aircraft. If that unfortunate bomber had not flown over Cologne, thereby identifying the city for us, I am quite certain we would have incurred a similar reception and perhaps come to a similar end.

South of Cologne, we turned onto a Westerly course for home flying at 9000 feet, the airspeed reaching 160 mph. Everything was going smoothly and in less than two hours we expected to be over England. Unfortunately our troubles were only just beginning.

About 11 o'clock I asked the front gunner where the light flak which I could see through the bomb aimer's window was coming from. Before he could answer, the rear gunner called out that we had been attacked by a fighter. I dived steeply, so steeply that both engines faltered, due to the petrol being pulled away from the carburettors. I levelled out at 7000 feet, turning as I did so. The rear gunner apparently had not seen the fighter till it had completed its attack. He said he thought it was a Me110. I asked if anybody was hurt, but all were O.K.

When the flap was over, I checked the instruments in the cockpit, particularly the engine ones, to see if they were registering any damage which the engines may have suffered. I noticed with a shock that both oil pressure gauges were reading zero. At the same time a smell of burning was coming from the starboard side of the aircraft. Told the navigator to go and pump oil to the starboard engine from the reserve tank which should have held 15 gallons, as I had visions of one or both engines packing up through lack of oil. While he was doing this the pressure on the starboard engine rose slowly to 60 lbs, normal being 80 lbs. I then told him to pump the port engine, but he called out soon afterwards that the pump handle was so slack and easy to move that the tank must be empty. By this time the pressure on the starboard engine had again dropped to nothing. It became obvious that there was serious damage to the oil system somewhere.

I made a further inspection of the cockpit and found that the air speed indicator was also reading nothing, that the undercarriage lights were out, though the wheels were up, and that the indicators showing the amount of petrol left had stuck.

We flew on expecting both engines to seize up. About 11.45, searchlights were reported about 50 yds astern, so I started to weave, then flak was reported between the searchlights and the aircraft. The bursts got uncomfortably close, so more violent evasive action was taken. Both searchlights and flak were now very close and very persistent. The aircraft was dived and we eventually escaped from them, but not before losing several thousand feet of precious height. The navigator informed me that the source of the disturbance was St. Omer.

Immediately after this, the starboard engine began to behave in a queer manner, the revs increased at an alarming rate and eventually showed 3000 plus. I throttled right back but it made no difference so I

Rear gunner Sergeant Howard
James. (*Joss Leclercq*)

pressed the feathering button and asked the navigator to look out of the
window to see whether the propeller had feathered but apparently not
only had the engine seized up, but the complete lack of oil had prevented
the propeller feathering. The aircraft then became difficult to control
and was losing height slowly so I used more power from the remaining
engine to attempt to keep height, with the result that the aircraft tried to
fly in circles. Partially succeeded in this despite both the navigator's and
my attempts to keep it straight, he by hanging on to the rudder pedals
with his hands. It then became painfully obvious that we should have
to abandon N for NUTS. I told the boys to get ready. England was not
more than 40 miles away – so near yet so far. I thought of trying to reach
the Channel and land in the sea, hoping we would be picked up in the
morning. I learnt later that both aircraft and launches had searched for
us, apparently thinking we had come down in the sea, their deduction
being made from the last two wireless requests for bearings which we
had asked for in the hope of trying to find our exact position.

A voice from the rear turret [Sergeant Howard 'Jimmy' James] asked
whether he should leave now. "I'll tell you when" was my answer. At
3000 feet, I gave the order to start getting out; jokingly saying I would
see them in Marseille. I have an idea the rear gunner had gone before I
had finished speaking.

When it was obvious we would have to use our parachutes, the
navigator went forward to open the front turret door to let out the front

gunner, who picked up his parachute on his way back, put it on his chest, said cheerio and disappeared through the front hatch.[2] The navigator [Ray Glensor] went next, passing some remark about missing so and so's party. My height was between 1500 and 2000 feet, when a figure appeared at my side wearing a long white sweater which stretched to his knees, and enquired whether we could still reach England now that some of the crew had gone, making the aircraft lighter. It was the wireless operator. He'd only been married three weeks and I'd met his wife two days before, so I felt very sorry for him, and especially for his wife, knowing the anxiety she would suffer from the non-return. I told him that if he didn't get out soon we would both crash with the aircraft, so he went very reluctantly saying that my parachute was on the floor beside the wireless set.

My height was now approximately 1400 feet. I throttled back the remaining engine and trimmed the aircraft into a glide. I climbed out of the seat, picked up my parachute and moved back into the cockpit to put it on. For some unknown reason, it may have been pure instinct, I looked at my instruments and realised that the aircraft had its nose well up and was turning to the right. In a second or two it was diving to earth, so I dropped my parachute and climbed back into the seat. When I levelled out from the dive my altimeter was reading 600 feet. A dark mass appeared beneath me very close which turned out to be a large wood on a hill. I passed over that very quickly, then suddenly decided to try and keep the aircraft in the air. I opened up the good engine but the ground got still closer.

I personally have never been so close to what might have been death before. At the time I certainly wasn't frightened, and to be quite truthful my thoughts, fleeting as they were, concerned my past – what a hell of a good time I'd had in the RAF and if you'd got to go, well, you'd got to go, and at that moment I thought I was going to be killed.

The aircraft was slowing up so I pushed the nose down towards a hedge that loomed up, but I only clipped the top, a moment later she touched the earth and slid her belly to a stop, and although I wasn't strapped in, I only moved forward in my seat very slightly.[3] I had opened the escape hatch before she stopped, and was out in a flash, having no desire to be taken prisoner. Not only that, but being so near the coast I thought there would be lots of Germans around and anyway I might have landed alongside a gun position.

I ran a little distance from the aircraft and listened. Everything was very quiet around me, except overhead. I could still hear the luckier ones on their way home. Dunkirk and other coastal towns were by no means asleep and the sky to the west was full of gun flashes and shell bursts.

I went slowly back towards N for NUTS, and walked round her. The only damage visible was what one usually expects from a crash landing.

German Air Force Military Field Police guards watching over Barnard's Wellington DF550. Note the 'Gorget' worn on the chain around the officer's neck.

A good view of DF550's rear turret from which Sergeant James baled out. (*Monsieur Lenglet, via Joss Leclercq*)

French policemen with the German Field Police at the wreckage of Barnard's Wellington DF550. (*Monsieur Lenglet, via Joss Leclercq*)

My next job was to destroy her. I climbed into the cockpit and went to look for the signalling pistol, but couldn't find it. I had no matches either. I made certain that what secret equipment we had on board was destroyed. As it seemed that the Germans would be collecting a fairly new bomber, I thought I might have first pick as regards souvenirs, so I tried to unscrew the 8 day clock from the dashboard but couldn't.

I decided to take my parachute with me as I had a notion that if there were no parachutes in the aircraft, the Germans might think we had all jumped out and that the crew would be scattered far and wide. What I forgot of course was how on earth did the aircraft land itself without practically any damage. I discovered later that this particular field was about the only one for miles around in which it was at all possible to execute even a crash landing. Not that I had anything to do with picking this field, that had been left entirely to mother luck and she had made a somewhat good job of it.

I realised it was impossible to destroy N for NUTS, so after a last look round I walked to the end of the field. I walked out and found myself in a lane, which appeared to lead to a farm in the distance. I retraced my steps back to the field and walked along another hedge. After wandering about [for] 10 minutes I came to a wood, very likely the one I had passed over earlier. I went about 20 yards into it, pulled the rip cord of my parachute and wrapped the silk around me, and tried to sleep. I was very tired and could still hear bombers returning home. I felt somewhat lost and a little scared.

I awoke about 6 o'clock the next morning feeling very thirsty and with thoughts of returning to the aircraft to get myself a drink from one of the emergency water ration tins. It then dawned on me that I didn't know where the aircraft was, apart from that the Germans might have found her. I next decided to remove my flying kit. I still had on my black overalls, also my Mae West. The first thing to hide was my parachute and harness. The ground was very hard but was amply covered by leaves. I got out of the pack and harness and walked on through the wood, stopping every now and then to hide the rest of my flying kit. I reached one side of the wood dressed in my service slacks and battle dress top. I removed my badges of rank and wings and put them in my hip pocket. I also kept the silk gloves I used for flying.

The wood sloped away down the side of the hill, and while walking down I heard a train. At the bottom was a single track line along which I walked, not having the slightest idea where I was going. My thirst then got the better of me and I made up my mind to find a farm, so I left the railway after a while and once more took to the woods. The first farm I came to did not look very inviting so I pressed on over the road which passed by it and up another hill, still not having seen anybody. On the brow of the hill I saw another farm towards which I walked, keeping my eyes open for anything that looked German. I could hear gunfire but as no aircraft could be heard, I took it that the Germans were firing their heavy guns across the Channel.

Not far from the farm I met an old man to whom I said, "Je suis un aviateur Anglais, et j'ai beaucoup de soif." ["I'm an English airman, and I'm very thirsty."] He looked at me as if I were a German and, pointing to the farm, mumbled something inaudible. He then started to walk to the farm so I followed. He went into a shed where the cows were being milked by a man about thirty and spoke to him, every now and then pointing and looking in my direction. The young man came up to me and took me into the house where I repeated my request for something to drink. A woman about the same age appeared and they both started talking. Neither of them looked very happy and I think they were rather frightened at my sudden appearance. At that time I can't say I was feeling very brave either. The woman, whom I took to be his wife, went away and returned with some beer, rather flat and watery but very welcome. While drinking this I brought out my maps and escape aids to try to convince them that I was British. The young man then spoke to me saying "Allemand", and pointing in a certain direction, adding that I had better keep moving and go and hide in a wood. I asked how far the Germans were and he replied "Douze kilometres" and mentioned a town, this town being St. Omer, to which I partly owed my presence on the ground after last night's firework display. I got the farmer to show me where I was on the map and marked it. The woman who had left the room, returned with six eggs and a loaf of bread. I could hardly believe my eyes, but not being a bit hungry and, as I would be crossing fields etc to the wood he had recommended, I refused the lot for fear of breaking the eggs but gladly had some more beer. I could see that they were terrified of Germans, so I decided to leave. They showed me out through the back door and I left muttering "merci, merci". They were obviously very glad to see the back of me.

It was still very early so I decided to get to the wood and try to sleep during daylight. I crossed numerous fields where farm workers were starting the day, but they took very little notice of me. I eventually reached the wood and having found a secluded spot tried to sleep. This was impossible as I was continually thinking of what I was going to do. I was never lucky enough to attend a lecture on escaping from someone who had actually done so, but we were always told that farmers and priests were the most helpful people to go to. I immediately dismissed a farmer as my next objective and decided to find a church, thereby hoping to locate the local vicar.

On leaving the wood I came to a lane and as I rounded the corner I saw a man cleaning up the side of the road with a hoe. Nobody else being about, I thought I would ask him where I would find an abbé. When I reached him I started off in my best schoolboy French. However, he didn't take much notice but sat down on the bank and rolled a cigarette. He rolled another one for me and we sat and talked for about 15 minutes, or at least he did the talking and from what I could understand he had no love for the Germans.

When we had finished our cigarettes he told me to walk on down the lane and he'd follow behind. I reached a farm and was trying to find a way in when he reappeared and took me inside. The farm apparently belonged to him. He was getting on in years, and so was the farm. The farm house was very small and was badly in need of repair and paint. Various parts of it were overgrown with weeds etc and as a matter of fact so was his face – he was in much need of a shave. He took a couple of glasses and went down some steps to appear a little later with both full of purplish liquid. It was wine of some sort but heaven knows of what vintage. While we were drinking this a very pretty dark-haired girl came through another door in the room. She didn't look very surprised at seeing me. The old man said something to her and she started to prepare a meal for me. He told me that her husband was a prisoner in Germany. Every now and then, moans and groans punctuated by almost hysterical screams came from the room that the girl had just left. Noticing my look the old man said something about "Madame – tres malade". The girl brought me some soup which had more meat and vegetables in it than soup and, although I wasn't in the least hungry I struggled through it out of sheer politeness. When I had finished the farmer produced some German cigarettes which weren't bad at all. He then went downstairs again and brought up a kind of liqueur. I then realised how tired I was and he showed me the barn, which was just outside. I went to the back of all the hay and lay down.

I slept for several hours before the farmer called me to lunch. After the meal he suggested that I should go to the orchard, which was at the back of the farm buildings, where, being on higher ground, I would have an unobstructed view of anyone who approached. It was a small garden divided into plots and I spent the remainder of the day there eating unripe pears and watching German aircraft.

The evening meal consisted of slices of pork and bread which the old man cut from a large piece on the table with his clasp knife. The girl joined us, occasionally getting up to get something or to attend to Madame. After the meal we had some more wine and a German cigarette, talking of various things and finding the language problem a bit difficult. Before I went back to my bed of hay the old man gave me a balaclava helmet to keep away the crawlers, and a blanket. He also promised to get hold of the local abbé for me the next day.

In the morning, after breakfast I retired once more to the orchard and I hadn't been there long when I saw two men coming up the path. I recognised the farmer and thought that the other was my hoped for abbé but the stranger was another fugitive, a Frenchman who had escaped from the Germans, probably from a slave train taking him to Germany. He had on blue overalls and was clutching a huge loaf of bread and had been hurrying as he was so out of breath. The farmer suggested that we should hide together. While they were talking I caught the words "dogs and cars", so apparently there were lots of Germans around, and I began to fear that they might be conducting an organised search. I said to the new arrival "If the dogs have your scent and we hide together we'll both be caught so you go your way and I'll go mine." I don't know whether he understood me but a second later he dived into the hedge while I started after the farmer who had by that time left us. I hadn't gone 20 yards when I saw two Germans coming up the path, and another one coming down the ladder from the loft. They were dressed in blue or black uniforms and were armed to the teeth with Tommy guns, revolvers and truncheons. I then realised why the other Frenchman had left us in such a hurry. I don't know what happened to him and I never saw him again.

I tore back to my retreat and dived headlong over the hedge into the field. I had started to run when I suddenly spotted two more Germans, accompanied by two dogs on chains, walking down the field about twenty-five yards from me on my left. I slowed down and started to walk as naturally as I could with the collar of my battle dress turned up. I reached the opposite hedge safely and then raced on into the next field. There was a very thick hedge along one side of it, about ten feet thick, on a bank and I dived into this having first made certain that there was an exit both sides. I crouched down and waited. The searchers made a most infernal din shouting and yelling to each other. Down in the valley there was a tiny village on which they converged. They were there about half an hour, searching from house to house and eventually they spread out twenty yards apart and disappeared over the next hill. I counted about twenty-five of the brutes.

I waited about another half an hour and then got up cautiously to look around. The field alongside the hedge was slightly convex and I got quite a shock when I saw a German helmet about 50 yards away. I suffered yet another shock when a whistle blew and they started appearing from the opposite hedge and began to bear down on my hiding place. They arrived within 10 yards of where I lay. I remembered that the Frenchman had been dressed in blue overalls and that my uniform was not much darker and Germans don't hesitate to shoot anything that is French. I thought that if they saw me it would only be a matter of seconds. They were making a fearful shindig, arguing I should imagine, and certainly swearing. One of them started down the exit I had made but stopped for some reason. I saw his boots and Tommy gun hanging down not more than four feet away and I don't think I have ever looked at a pair of boots with such intense interest before (with or without coupons!). How he failed to see me I cannot imagine.

By this time the remainder had made some sort of pathway through the hedge and proceeded to crash past a bare 10 feet from me. I think the brambles and thorns had a lot to do with their language. Of this second and last lot I only counted a dozen and they were a very tough crowd by the look of them.

I waited another half an hour until they too disappeared and then made my way back to the farm. The farmer couldn't believe his eyes when he saw me. He immediately went down to the cellar and returned with the necessary with which we toasted my good fortune. He told me they'd been through every room in the house and had left nothing to chance. After we had lunch, he produced a brown coat and hid my battle dress in the hay. I then returned to the orchard.

Later in the afternoon I saw the farmer approaching with a reverend gentleman. We shook hands and by good luck he spoke a little English so I told him that I wanted to get to Marseille eventually but how I didn't know. He asked about money so I produced what I had which he kindly supplemented with a little more. I suggested that someone should accompany me on the train but he thought it unwise. When he left we shook hands and he gave me his blessing. I felt a little disappointed and very helpless, but after my adventure during the morning I had no reason to grumble.

About 5 o'clock I slipped into the barn where I stayed until the old man called me at seven for soup. When I met him he said "Allemand", and pointed to the barn next to mine. I must have looked as though I was going on another cross country exercise, because he grabbed me and explained that there was a German deserter in there who would be away by dawn the next day. It is an extraordinary coincidence that three men, a German, a Frenchman and an Englishman, should all be running away from Germans, and should all arrive at the same place on the same day.

That evening, I told the farmer I would like to leave the next day. I went to sleep wondering where the rest of my crew were and where I was going to sleep the following night.

The next morning I went to the orchard as usual. Some cattle had broken in during the night and all the fruit had gone. I had not been there long when the farmer appeared and produced a large poster which the Germans had had printed and were displaying in all public places for the population to read.[4] It contained the penalty for hiding and aiding British airmen and the reward to anyone who gave information which would lead to our capture. It also gave me some news of one of my crew, as all our names were printed at the bottom, with the exception of the rear gunner who had apparently been captured.

I then realised who the Germans had been hunting for the day before and what an idiot I had been staying so near the aircraft. I couldn't have been more than two miles away from it. The consoling thought was that, having searched the area for some distance around the scene of my landing, they were not likely to come back to it again. I could not fathom how they had found out our names and ranks. I thought at first that Sergeant James may have told them but I was not to discover how until I met my navigator, Ray Glensor. The Germans had spelt his name wrongly. I was not to see one of the posters up for some time but was lucky enough to bring one back to England as a souvenir. I had been in France for two days and from what had happened I was lucky still to be free.

I had my last meal – lunch with the farmer – and just before going, a young man arrived with a parcel which contained a beret and some food for me from the priest, which was very kind and thoughtful of him. The farmer gave me a stout pen knife and said he would come with me for a few miles so I said goodbye to the girl and we set off at 1.30.

We walked several kilometres and once, when we stopped to light a cigarette, he said something about a souvenir. I gave him my lighter and he gave me a box of matches in return and it was well worth it!

We had been travelling over nothing but fields without coming to any roads and the first we came to led into Boulogne. Once again I was tantalised by the knowledge that England was so close, yet it was utterly impossible to get there except by travelling hundreds, perhaps thousands, of miles in the opposite direction. We passed safely through a small village in which were several German soldiers. Others were driving four-wheeled horse wagons. The few civilians we saw appeared to give me and my companion more than one look. I don't doubt that they knew I wasn't French for, except for my beret and brown coat, I was fully dressed in RAF uniform. We deviated from the village a little distance and to get back onto the road meant crossing a railway line. We heard a train coming and decided to wait for it to pass, but it stopped outside the little station. We carried on which meant climbing up the railway embankment and passing along several carriages. I saw that they were full of soldiers. It was the first time I'd seen German soldiers in any quantity, but I don't suppose they knew nor cared who we were. It wasn't so bad being with someone, but the farmer would eventually leave me and, apart from being alone, I had no idea where I was going. A French car passed us full of German Officers. I made a hitch-hike sign and we both laughed like hell. Soon after this, the old man took his leave. He wished me the best of luck and we shook hands.

I hoped to reach a town called Fauquembergues before dark.[5] I got very thirsty plodding along the white dusty road so I tried sucking one or two Horlicks tablets but my thirst only increased. At the next farmhouse bordering the road I plucked up courage and knocked at the door. I had rehearsed my little speech coming down the road and when a woman appeared I spoke as quickly as possible with lots of emphasis on the words "thirsty" and "water". It worked because she immediately went in and returned with a glass of water. I drank it and tendered the usual "merci". A little further on the road forked, but there were no signposts. I felt very much braver now, either it was the water or that I had been able to ask for a drink without making a fool of myself, so I called out to a man in his garden and asked him the way to Fauquembergues. He waved me gaily on, shouting "Toute droite". At first this conveyed nothing to me, but I decided to press on and work it out. I knew that "à droite" meant to the right so "toute droite" must mean straight on. Luckily I took the right road.

I reached the outskirts of Fauquembergues about 6 o'clock in the evening. I didn't dare go into the town so turned down another road and sat down by the side to think out what I was going to do. A lot of people on bicycles and tandems passed by. I wasn't going to sleep in the open so made up my mind to look for a farm. Fauquembergues was in a valley with hills on two sides. I had come down one so started up the other, hoping to get round the back of the town and hit the road on which I had come in on. I arrived at one road which seemed to lead in a southerly direction, so started off again. A clock in the town boomed out 7 o'clock and it was getting dark. I couldn't see a farm anywhere till a bend in the road revealed a cafe with what appeared to be farm buildings behind it.[6] The road I was on went straight on and another one turned right where the cafe stood. I turned right and saw there was a farm but couldn't see anyone about. I intended to wait till somebody came out because I didn't want to have the door opened by any German who might be billeted there. In a few minutes a woman and two children came down the road and turned into the yard gates. I approached her and asked if I could sleep in the barn adding that I would be away before dawn. This was said in very bad French but she eventually understood me and said that I'd have to wait for her husband who would be returning from the fields shortly.

He arrived soon after, driving a horse and cart. I had not mentioned anything about being a British airman to his wife so I suppose she merely repeated my request to him. He climbed down and came up to me and said there was a farm further down the road about a quarter of a mile, adding that some Germans were billeted there. I then told him who I was. It made a big difference because he then told me to come inside. I thought I'd better produce my maps etc as well to help identify myself.

A chair was brought for me and he asked if I had eaten, to which I said no. His wife cooked supper and we all sat down to eat. He was a young man and had been a prisoner of the Germans in this war, but had escaped. After supper we talked and he said he might be able to help me next morning, which was Sunday. His wife gave me a blanket and I said good night to them and went across to the barn which I reached by ladder. Neither the horse stabled below me nor the crawlers which I had collected from sleeping in hay for the past two nights kept me from falling asleep immediately.

I awoke next day about 6 o'clock and the weather wasn't very good, there being lots of early morning mist and fog hanging around. While looking out of the window, I heard an aircraft and a moment later a Ju88 flashed past flying very low and very fast.

While we were having breakfast the farmer said that he knew of a man in the village who could speak English and he'd go and fetch him. He went off about 9 o'clock and left me to have a shave. About an hour later, he returned with the news that the man he'd been to see would arrive in about two hours. The suspense was rather trying as I had no idea who he was, but it was my only chance to meet someone who might be able to help.

About 2 hours later a shortish man with glasses arrived.[7] He came straight up to me and said "Squadron Leader Barnard?" I said "Yes". He asked to see my maps and escape aids. He then shook me by saying I would have to prove who I was by answering some questions. I couldn't see how he could ask me anything personal, as he knew nothing about me, or so I thought. His first question was "What happened to the aircraft before you took off from England?" I nearly answered "Nothing, why?" but suddenly thought of the wireless trouble, so I mentioned about the generator burning itself out and he said "Yes, alright". His next question was quite amazing. He asked me where I went drinking with the boys when I was in England. I thought a long time before answering. We used to go occasionally to the Kings Head in Waltham, but not a lot. I thought of the Lifeboat in Cleethorpes so I said "Do you mean the Lifeboat in Cleethorpes?"[8] He smiled so I knew it was right. I immediately burst out laughing because it seemed so funny having to prove who I was to a strange man in a farmhouse in France by being asked the name of a pub in England. I discovered later that the Frenchman had met the navigator. They had come to the conclusion that, as the rear gunner had been captured and they knew where the front gunner was, it only left the wireless operator and myself to be found.

The Germans had gone to great lengths to find out who was helping the allied airmen to safety and they frequently sent out decoy airmen who spoke perfect English in the hope that the Frenchmen would treat them as British. It was therefore most important that anyone who professed to be British should be able to prove that statement satisfactorily. The reason I was asked a question concerning wireless was that the Frenchman didn't know for certain that I was the pilot and not the wireless operator and of course the navigator had satisfied him with the necessary information, so either of us could answer at least one of the questions.

The man then spoke to the farmer who naturally looked a little surprised and later produced his best shirt and a tie for me while my RAF shirt collar and tie were destroyed in the oven fire. My interrogator, who had been an interpreter in the last war for us, now asked me if I could ride a bicycle. I said yes and he said that in an hour's time two people would arrive on bicycles, one would dismount and I was to take his bicycle and follow about 25 yards behind the other rider, adding that if my escort was stopped I was to ride on, where to heaven knows!

At last two cyclists appeared, one left his cycle in the yard and went back to the road. The French cycles are a little different from ours, having flat handlebars and they nearly all look like racing machines. I wobbled a bit at first, I think because I was very keyed up. We went in the direction from which I'd come the day before with me keeping approximately 25 yards behind. We hadn't gone far when the fellow in front slowed up and gaily waved me to his side. He was a young lad about 20 and seemed quite unconcerned about the whole business. He said I would soon see my navigator, also that should anybody stop him or me, the other would ride on and gave me more details of where I was to go. The way he was talking and whispering made me a little scared. He showed me his watch saying a fighter pilot whom he rescued had given it to him. I had already given my lighter away so did not particularly want to lose my watch as well.

As we approached the town I dropped behind and noticed at the crossroads a man was standing and as we drew closer he pulled out his handkerchief. I noticed that this happened at all corners. After leaving the town, my friend increased speed and, I had quite a job to keep up. When about 50 yards behind, I saw him turn into a gateway. As I approached the spot a man standing by the hedge on the opposite side of the road was waving me in like a policeman. No chances had been taken even over that short distance. A man was posted at all crossroads who would give the necessary signal should any Germans be about.

I had no sooner got off my bike when the man who had been standing outside took it from me and pushed it into a shed. I was hurried inside and the next thing I knew was seeing my navigator. He was sprawled on an arm chair in his shirt sleeves and looked quite at home. Needless to say we were very pleased to see each other. The room was full of people, who stared at me as if I was a ghost. I was introduced to everybody and Madame produced a bottle of wine and they all drank my health.[9]

My navigator and I had a lot to talk about. He had been rather unlucky at first as after his parachute had opened he found himself upside down with one leg supporting all his weight from a rigging line which was wrapped around his thigh. He had managed to right himself before landing but the rigging line had cut into his flesh and he found walking very difficult and painful. Unlike me he had started to walk away from the aircraft from the start and had spent every night in a decent bed. The Germans had paid him a visit as well, because one morning an officer came to the house and Madame spoke to him in one room with the navigator next door. The German had lectured her on the crime of aiding or hiding British airmen. He had been doing this at all the houses. At one time before meeting anybody the navigator had nearly given himself up as his leg pained him so much.

I also learnt that my front gunner [Ralph Forster] would very likely join us the next day. The rear gunner [Howard James] had been captured. I heard that the very first morning after coming down, he had walked into a village still dressed in his flying kit. Some French children had surrounded him yelling "aviateur anglais", with the result that the

Germans soon appeared and took him away. If this story was true, it seemed very stupid of him and I cannot imagine why he did it. There was no news of the wireless operator.

Both the navigator and I slept in the same room, which was, I believe, the sitting room. We slept in our underwear and everything else we had was put in a kit bag. The reason for this was in case the Germans appeared, we would escape through the window with all our belongings and hide in the woods. This was only put into practice once during the whole of our month's stay there.

The household consisted of Madame and Monsieur [Fillerin], Madame's mother [Madame Cadet], two daughters aged 15 and 16 and a son aged 14. They looked after us wonderfully, providing us with everything and not allowing us to pay for anything. We were each given a razor and toothbrush and toothpaste. The food was extremely good, lots of eggs and meat. I suffered very little from boredom, there being a rather good library in the house which had been there during the last war as the house had been used as an army officers' mess during that time. We were not out of touch with the news, as we rarely missed the B.B.C. broadcasts, but were always very careful to tune in to a German station and leave it on one of their wavelengths when we'd finished. This was in case the Germans searched the home and accused anybody of listening to allied transmissions.

On the 21st September, the day after my arrival, the front gunner turned up. The people we stayed with were very proud to have three of a crew of five in their charge, and we all hoped that the wireless operator had been located. He had been however most unfortunate. Like myself, he met somebody who told him to go to a certain home as the man there spoke English. Well, he went and had no sooner got inside and been welcomed by the owner, when the man went into the next room while the wireless operator was having a drink of something and phoned up the Germans. I don't think there was ever a more surprised Englishman. Needless to say, he was later suitably avenged. I was lucky in finding a Frenchman 100% loyal to us. There were one or two who played up to the Germans. All this man got for betraying the wireless operator to the Germans was 15,000 francs.

The front gunner, like the navigator, was luckier than I, not having had to sleep in barns. As it happened they were next door to each other in the same village without knowing it. I noticed the gunner wearing shoes. I knew he had started the flight with flying boots, so asked him where he'd got the shoes from. Imagine my amazement when he announced that he'd brought them with him in case we were shot down! I also asked why he'd worn the new flying suit for gunners, which was painted completely yellow for the first time.[10] "Oh, just in case we came down in the sea!" He certainly wasn't taking any chances. Admittedly it was his 30th and last trip before being taken off operations for a rest. I was a little annoyed at his lack of faith in the aircraft and remainder of the crew, but there you are – one never can tell, anything might happen.

The days passed rather slowly but it was better than being in a prison camp. We had a lot of amusing times with the family and lots of visitors. People in the know travelled far to come and see us, as it was unusual to have 3 Britishers in one house and they'd never had more than one at a time before. The front gunner was the 13th to pass through this home. One fighter pilot they had rescued was badly wounded and lay for two weeks in the bed which my navigator had, a doctor visiting him every day. [This was Sergeant Guy Lockhart – see Chapter 5.]

We shaved every other day and had a wash every morning, the soap sold in the shop bore a remarkable resemblance to pumice stone and the toothpaste was exactly like putty. A bath was only taken before a special event such as going away. The result was that we had one the day before we left – a month later. Believe me, it was not only very welcome but was a necessity.

British pilots at that time used to drop carrier pigeons for the use of people like us but sometimes the Germans got to them first and sometimes the Frenchmen. There was one of these pigeons here and we were only waiting for a clear day to release it. The three of us wrote out our messages stating who we were and that we were safe. We also said that the rear gunner and wireless operator were prisoners of war hoping their wives and parents would be informed as soon as possible. One thing we all put down was a request for our personal belongings to be safeguarded. Eventually the right day came, naturally there was much excitement. If the messages got through it would have been a tremendous relief to everyone here and those concerned at home. We had been missing about a fortnight and it would have been nice to get a message through after such a short time. The tiny container was brought out and the messages rolled up and slipped inside. I believe the pigeon was almost as excited as we were. It had been dropped some months before and hadn't had a job all that time.

We all went into the garden after making certain the wrong people weren't about. I am sure all of us offered up a silent prayer. Monsieur held the bird in both hands and threw it into the air. All went well for a minute or two, it circled the farm, gradually gaining height, but the wretched thing had been dropped in France when very young and due to its long confinement, hadn't a clue as to where it was, and it just flew round and round the village. Our hopes turned to sorrow, and our sorrow to fear, because if the Germans had seen it, they would have shot it and rounded up the whole village to find out where it had come from. To add to the trouble another pigeon appeared, obviously a male by the way he pestered the young lady. He eventually gave up and left but the messages continued their circuits the whole morning. At last, exhausted, she settled on the roof. All attempts to grab her failed and it was decided to wait till dark and blind it with a torch. As soon as it got dark, this was done. We were all very disappointed, but it was useless and dangerous to try again.

The three of us always had all our meals except supper together, as it was dangerous for us to eat with the family in the kitchen before dark, it being possible to see into the kitchen from the road. I forgot to mention another most important member of the household. This was PIPO, a massive woolly sheepdog without whom we would have had no warning as to who approached the yard gate, and many a time our conversation was stilled while investigations were made due to Pipo's barking. We were sitting talking after supper when there was a loud knock on the door and a fumbling at the latch. We hadn't heard Pipo bark, and you've never seen three frightened airmen leave a room so quickly as we did, but it was only the young fellow who accompanied me on my first cycle ride. He'd been having fun with a German guard up the road, and had pretended not to understand what the man was saying and had done the exact opposite of what was requested of him. The German was furious and all but shot him on the spot. There wasn't a Frenchman who didn't take the opportunity of pulling Germans' legs.

Gabriel, Geneviève and Monique Fillerin with 'Pipo' the family dog being patted by Ralph Forster. Note that Forster has removed his 'Air Gunners' wing from his tunic but Donald Barnard still has his pilots' wings attached to his uniform.

CHAPTER 3

DIARY – PART 2: TO MARSEILLE, AND THE SOUTH OF FRANCE

Before we could travel anywhere in daylight it was necessary to have identity cards, but none of us had photos on us and of course cameras were forbidden. However, Monsieur still had one and twice took our pictures but the results weren't good enough, not surprising really as they were taken indoors. The last lot were taken outside and proved successful. We spent one evening deciding on what names were going to be put on the cards, also our false addresses and all the necessary information. It was all very well deciding on Christian and surnames, but half the battle was could we pronounce them? We overcame this difficulty with the help of Monsieur and Madame who devoted the greater part of that evening instructing us. From that evening onwards, my alias was Jacques de Montbas.

We were of course in occupied France and to return home it was necessary to travel to the South which meant crossing what was known as "The Line", which was the demarcation line between occupied and unoccupied France. The business of crossing the line was not as simple as it sounded; it sometimes meant swimming a river at night and walking several miles after that, which in Wintertime cannot be done by men who are unfit. It wasn't easy to cross the line as the Germans guarded it as if it was one of their own frontiers and many people had been caught. We had had no exercise since coming to the farm so Monsieur said one day that we were all going for a walk after dark. We had all got rather lazy and if any excuses were made, he told his favourite story of a pilot getting caught while crossing the line because he couldn't run fast enough. I think he made it up; anyway it had the desired effect.

After supper that night we armed ourselves with sticks and the three of us including Monsieur and his young son went out. There was a single track railway line about a half mile behind the house towards which we went. The country was a little hilly but we weren't travelling fast enough to get out of breath. We came to the top of one small hill, when Monsieur said he had a machine gun hidden not far from where we were standing. He was one of thousands who had armed themselves, and was obviously looking forward to having a crack at the Boches when the allies arrived, if the occasion arose. It wasn't as if we had been walking in a straight line to reach this spot, we certainly hadn't, but he must have known every inch of the surrounding country. We arrived back a little muddy but all the better for the walk. We had several more excursions after that and they became more interesting when we started visiting neighbouring farms.

One evening after supper, we all sat in the kitchen talking and we must have been talking about the guns we carried in the aircraft, because the conversation eventually drifted round to the price paid for revolvers in France at that time, which was about 30,000 francs. That worked out at £75, the pound being worth not less than 400 francs. We then discovered that apart from his artillery piece on the hill, Monsieur had got other armaments hidden at the bottom of a small stream on the other side of the wood. We wondered how on earth it was possible to keep guns etc in working order when left lying in a river bed. Monsieur said he would go and see what he could bring us. About 20 minutes later he returned covered in mud and dripping with water. In one hand he carried a bottle and in the other a slimy mess roughly the shape of a revolver. At a glance it was easy to see that the bottle contained revolver bullets. The mystery as regards the way these things were sealed was then explained. At the back of the garden there were beehives and the wax obtained was used to seal the top of the bottle, and the revolver was encased in solid wax which was as hard as iron. It took Monsieur nearly an hour to remove the wax and, at the end, the barrel of the ·45 was as clear as a clean glass. This was not the only weapon of destruction kept on the river bed. The hives also did their share of work, as many precious articles were hidden there, amongst them the uniforms and various pieces of clothing worn by preceding RAF airmen. No hiding place could have been better, for should a search of the house and grounds take place, even a German would think twice in interfering with bee hives.

I mentioned previously that the navigator and I slept downstairs, but the front gunner had a room upstairs and even in daylight, one had to pick one's way up the rather narrow little stairway very carefully. We'd been at the farm about three weeks and had not had cause for any panics, until one day when Monsieur's mother had called round to see us, as she frequently did. Lunch had been over for some time and people were scattered round various parts of the house when suddenly the old grandmother came pattering down the corridor that separated the kitchen from the sitting room saying "Allemands, Allemands, vite, vite". That was quite enough for all of us. The navigator grabbed our kit bags and dived through the window, but no front gunner appeared. It wasn't a question of waiting for him, it was every man for himself, as we started to run to the back of the garden. I nearly beheaded myself on a length of wire that stretched across one garden patch, but the navigator being much taller than I, the wire only came up to his chest. We were about half way up the garden when the front gunner appeared, his slight figure going all out; it turned out that he'd been upstairs at the time of the commotion and must have travelled like lightning to have caught us up. We all arrived at the top of the garden together and waited behind a large hedge, puffing like steam engines. There was a small wood further on and, if necessary, we would have carried on to there.

After a few anxious minutes Monsieur appeared and called us back. What had happened was that the grandmother had been in the kitchen pottering about as grandmothers do, when through the window she saw a German car draw up. The driver jumped out and went smartly round to the side of the car and opened the door. A German officer climbed out and made for the kitchen door. Grandma had left it by then and Madame, after seeing us all safely through the window, went to see what the cause of the trouble was, while someone else tidied up our room. The German officer enquired politely whether Madame could let him have a few eggs and some butter, but she replied that she was very sorry that she had none of either in the house, but suggested he should try next door. Of course she knew very well that he would get the same answer there. However, off he went. It appears that even German officers could not get luxuries such as butter and eggs. On another occasion some German soldiers came very early one morning, before breakfast, with the same request, and as usual the cupboard was bare.

I don't think I ever saw a German during my stay in the village due to the fact that we did not venture out during the hours of daylight, but I remember hearing them one night once on our way back from Monsieur's mother's house, where we had been entertained. They were roaring out songs in some little cafe.

Monsieur's feelings for the Germans were exactly the same as they were the last war, when he had fought against them as a machine gunner. He had started fighting when he was 18. Grandma was getting on in years, I don't know if she remembered them in 1870, but she most certainly remembered them in 1914 and now again. This time they were right on her door step. In her opinion, they hadn't changed a bit. In the last war the house had been used as a mess by British Army Officers, which accounted for the library. Grandma had a photo of a group of them.

We heard from Monsieur that the night we had been shot down, we had lost 39 aircraft, but since then we had not heard any raids going over. Very likely bad weather in England had prevented them. A few nights later we all set out to have supper at another nearby farm. About half way there, we could hear our bombers coming over. There was lots of cloud so we could not see them, but above the roar of their engines we could hear the whine of the German night fighters. It was the first time I had heard German fighters attacking our bombers. In the past in England, the position had been reversed, but on this occasion no bombers were seen to come down. I have read in the papers that our pilots and crews reported that while flying over enemy-occupied territory, lights had been seen flashing the victory sign "... –", and tonight for the first time we witnessed it. Monsieur pointed his torch upwards and the beam broke the darkness with its flashes. We don't know if our bombers saw it. I doubt they did as there was so much cloud about. It was a defiant sort of gesture from people who would not give up.

We reached the farm and had a pleasant meal. Our host produced a tiny wireless set which had come down by parachute. It was a highly complicated piece of mechanism and none of us could do much with it. We returned home having spent a very enjoyable evening, to be greeted by Pipo who had been left on guard. Monsieur had obtained one of the posters which the Germans put up for our capture, so we decided to have our picture taken with it as a background. This was done and the results were very good. Before we left each of us managed to get a poster for a souvenir, but unfortunately the front gunner lost his copy later on.

After supper one evening, we got to talking about where I had landed the night I came down, and it was suggested that Monsieur should go and see if he could find my parachute. Naturally the silk would be very useful for making clothes. Next morning he set off on his bike and arrived back having been away all day. My directions had been somewhat wrong, but he saw the marks left by the aircraft and brought home a few pieces which had been left behind after the Germans had dismantled it for removal. Although he searched the edge of the wood for some distance, he could find no parachute. An interesting point was that he measured the distance the aircraft had travelled on its belly, and it was about 80 metres, roughly 87 yards, which was a very long way because at the correct landing speed those particular aircraft don't run more than 50 yards with wheels up. So it was obvious I had been doing about 150 mph when I hit the ground but, as my airspeed indicator had been put out of action, I couldn't tell exactly at the time. There was no doubt that I had been very lucky.

We had hoped to start our journey south after a fortnight, but something had gone wrong and it was not until between the third and fourth week that we heard any more. All arrangements had been completed, such as identity cards and, as I couldn't very well travel in my blue service slacks, they were dyed black. Apart from the maps and other things we carried in our escape aid boxes, there was always a certain amount of money. For example, if a particular raid took you over all the occupied countries in Western Europe, you were given money necessary for all those countries. But for some unknown reason, although the target on our last trip had been German, we had been given none of their currency, so Monsieur took all the Dutch and Belgium money and had it changed into francs at a bank for us. We were all given ration cards, but the only reason for this was in case we got separated from the party while travelling because, while we were all together, all the paying and ticket buying etc was done for us. As it was due to the priest I had met at the beginning giving me 50 francs, I actually left France with more money than was in the escape kit.

None of us had any idea then as to who was running this highly dangerous organisation of getting allied soldiers and airmen back to England but whoever they were, they were very brave men and women. We were told at last that we should leave for Paris on October 21st, which happened to be my birthday. The day before was a great day; we were going to have our first bath. A large bath tub was put in one of the sheds and when we emerged later on we all looked very different. That evening all the people who had helped us came to say goodbye. We had cake to eat and wine to drink and of course champagne, which I believe was dug out of its hiding place for the occasion. My interpreter friend was there, also the local miller without whom we should not have had white bread to eat, that being reserved for Germans only. All told there were 13 of us present. One of the mayors of a local town was there and he presented us with a poster each. The Germans had given all the mayors of certain towns a number of these posters, with orders that they were to be placed up in the most conspicuous places, but this man had a very different idea concerning three of them. Here we have this particular mayor who pretended to work for the Germans, but who fooled them all the time, and the other one who betrayed our wireless operator. The number of traitors was very small and we estimated that in occupied France about 98% were loyal. Last night we also heard what sort of treatment this mayor who betrayed our wireless operator was getting. The treatment took several months, but I only heard it bit by bit, and will tell the whole story now.

Several weeks after the incident, a fire broke out at this man's farm one night. The fire engine was called, but of course the engine refused to start and whether it arrived or not I don't know, but it was certainly too late, the whole place being burnt to the ground. Nothing happened after that for a month or two. Then another mysterious fire started amongst his crops which, to be exact, were his livelihood. The fire engine was again called but whether it started this time or kept breaking down on the way was never disclosed, but once more the fire destroyed the lot. I did not hear the finish of it until I got back to England, some time during the first half of 1943. I was on leave in London and while making my way down the stairs of a certain hotel, to the bar, an allied airman who had escaped after me was on his way up. We had returned on the same ship from Gibraltar, having met there. His journey through France having been shorter, he had caught me up. We greeted each other and during our conversation he said "I suppose you know he's dead." I didn't have to think twice who he was referring to. We said goodbye and I continued to the bar and drank a toast to my wireless operator and some friends back in another country. I believe the person concerned received a bullet in the stomach one dark night.

Another example of treatment meted out to friends of Germans concerned a young woman. At her farm was billeted a German officer. They became friendly and she married him. Some time later the farm was burnt to the ground. She was lucky not to have been destroyed herself.

So ended a very pleasant evening, It was about midnight before we went to bed. We were being called at 4 o'clock next morning for our train ride to Paris.

Madame woke us at 4 o'clock. We dressed and went into the kitchen and had some coffee but I for one found it impossible to eat anything. It was not a question of being excited, if anything we were a little scared as we were not going on a picnic and this was the first time any of us had travelled openly as Frenchmen. We must have presented a strange sight in our different garbs. The navigator and I had berets and the front gunner a cap. Each of us carried a small parcel which contained our food, razors and toothbrush etc. M'sier [Norbert Fillerin] came in from outside and said a lorry had arrived. Then came the rather sad business of saying goodbye to the people who had looked after us so well and so bravely. We all kissed them in true French style, on both cheeks. I think Madame had tears in her eyes. We promised to come back when there was peace again, and I for one will certainly do so.

We were divided into pairs. The young man who had escorted me here was looking after the Navigator and M'sieur's mother had charge of the front gunner, whilst Monsieur took charge of me. We climbed into the back of the lorry which had rather high sides so that only the tops of our heads showed. It was about 5 o'clock and still pitch dark. When everybody was settled in we drove off. We passed through the town of Fauquembergues but after that the country became unknown to us. After driving for about 20 miles the lorry slowed down and stopped opposite one solitary building which faced a T road junction. The driver produced a torch and flashed it on the wall, at the same time calling to us to look. There on the wall was displayed one of the yellow posters with our names at the bottom, and the request that all Frenchmen should co-operate in handing us over to the Germans. They were definitely co-operating alright, but with a very different object in mind. We went on once more; the lorry slowed down, this time at some crossroads where a man was standing. He had a few words with the people in front and then leaned over against the side of the lorry to wish us luck. We recognised him as one who had been at the party only a few hours before. His job had been to see that there were no Germans about and if there were to give the necessary warning.

We stopped a little way from the station and climbed down. There were a lot of people about, early morning workers, so we mingled with them and went on to the platform. It was only a small place but was full of people, including a few German soldiers. We hadn't been there long when the train rolled in and having found an empty compartment we sat down. Two strangers intruded on us but they took no notice. It was still quite dark, but dawn was not far off. The train moved off at last. The great thing about train travellers like us was not to look interested. That would most certainly have invited conversation, and that was the one danger to be avoided. The only way to combat this was to either sleep or pretend to sleep or to try reading a book or paper, but trying to read something one didn't really understand for hour after hour was very difficult, and usually ended up by one falling asleep. (These train journeys took several hours, distances being much greater than in England.)

It was now quite light and everyone looked normal, but I doubt if they were, I know I didn't feel normal. Once Monsieur nodded towards the open countryside and on looking out we saw the Canadian War Memorial, so we knew we were passing near Vimy. The train stopped at all stations until we got to Arras, where we waited for the connection to Paris. This was a large town and there were several Germans about. The bigger the place the more suspicious they seemed to look. We waited about 40 minutes for the train but it seemed like 40 years. When it arrived there was a mad rush for seats. Everybody was bound for Paris but surely they couldn't all be in the same boat as ourselves. We all got into one carriage which had no compartments but rows of seats all the way along. The journey to Paris was quite uneventful. Although we were all one party, it must have seemed strange to any intelligent person that no conversation was carried on between us. In fact, everything was done by gestures, looks and nods. I often wondered especially when I had to travel, as I did several times, with one person looking after me on a journey that took six to eight hours that not a word was spoken between us. I believe that the other occupants thought I was either dumb or crackers, as any question put to me by them was always answered by my escort.

We arrived at a station in Paris about 12.30. This particular station was choc a bloc with people coming and going. They couldn't all be escaping from the Germans. We left the station and walked to the tube in pairs. The tube trains were similar to ours, except that certain seats were permanently reserved for the forces of the Third Reich, and notices saying "Do Not Spit" and "Do Not Swear", both written in German, were to be seen in every carriage. At one station we stopped at there was a large poster describing the massacre of 165 innocent French people by British bombers in the market place of Rouen. It happened to be true, except the bombers were American and it was their first heavy bombing raid from England. I happen to remember the date. It was October 4th because we heard the raid in progress and listened to the results on the wireless. It was most unfortunate that some of the bombs had fallen in the market place, as it was market day. But I honestly believe that hardly a Frenchman took any notice of this sort of propaganda, especially the way it was worded.

Soon we arrived at our last station and on coming out of the tube we nearly bumped into a column of German soldiers. What amazed me was their age; they couldn't have been more than 16 apiece. The reason why we nearly fell over them was because they didn't wait for anybody to come out, they just charged into the compartment. One should describe them as typical Nazi Youth. We left the tube and after walking for a few minutes arrived at a cafe, went in and Monsieur had a few words with the woman serving. Whoever it was he wanted was upstairs, so we all went up. A man came in and seemed very pleased to see Monsieur. He then shook hands with all of us. We were in a small room which overlooked the street. Across the road was a well-known restaurant outside which French cars with German number plates were parked. We had a meal which consisted of pigs' trotters, which I hate and which nearly made me sick. However, everybody else ate the lot. Soon after this another man arrived with three American airmen who, I believe, had come down on the first American heavy bombing raid on October 4th. They were very nice chaps and stayed with us till we reached Marseille.

[Donald's memory is at fault as to the number of American airmen and to the date of this raid by the US Eighth Air Force. Until he got to Marseille he met only two American airmen, Technical Sergeant Erwin D. Wissenback (ball turret gunner) and 2nd Lieutenant William J. Gise (navigator) of the 306th Bomb Group, 367th Bomb Squadron, who had been shot down in their Boeing B-17F, 41-24510, on the raid to Lille-Fives on 9 October 1942:[1]]

The most notable Eighth Air Force mission in the autumn of 1942 was undoubtedly that of October 9th to the Fives-Lille steelworks in Belgium [*sic* – France]. A record total of 108 heavy bombers, plus seven on diversion, were despatched, a figure not to be surpassed for another six months… The inexperience of the 306th and 93rd [Bomb Groups] led to a poor bombing pattern, many bombs landed outside the target area causing civilian casualties.[2]

Le Vieux Port, Marseille, where Donald & co. stayed in October 1942. In the foreground is the Quai des Belges. On the far side of the water is the Quai Rive Neuve, with apartment 28A in the modern block of flats halfway along. (*Société d'Edition TARDY*)

[After coming down near Néchin railway station just over the nearby border in Belgium, the two Americans were taken care of by Frenchman Jean de la Olla, who was in charge of the northern sector of the PAT/PAO line.]

After lunch Monsieur suggested a walk through the city, so he and I along with my crew set off. The navigator and front gunner were walking a few yards behind. I had only been to Paris once before in 1938. Although the city looked the same from an outward appearance, it must have been suffering agony. There were hundreds of German soldiers and members of the invincible Luftwaffe about along with a few sailors. They had commandeered the best hotels, restaurants, in fact everything. We passed one of the places I had visited before, places where we had sat outside to drink, and hardly a Frenchman could be seen. Most of the really fashionable shops were closed down. We passed several people wearing the yellow Star of David on their backs. Most people seemed to be fairly well dressed, especially the women. They looked depressed and miserable. We bought the inevitable picture postcard outside a shop and then Monsieur took us into a small cafe where we had a couple of beers.

We strolled past Notre Dame and along the banks of the Seine. He took us to see a friend of his, a picture dealer I think, who was rather amazed to hear that three British airmen had been wandering around Paris on a sightseeing tour with a Frenchman as guide.

Before we returned to the cafe Monsieur took us into the church of the patron saint of France, called St Genevieve. A few people were in there and one or two were standing before a shrine with a little statue of the Virgin Mary on a kind of pedestal in front of it. There was also a woman selling picture postcards of different views of the church, both inside and out. We bought one or two of those, also a medallion which showed the church on one side and the patron saint on the other. It was supposed to bring luck. It now became obvious that before leaving the church one should go up to the statue of the Virgin Mary, say a prayer and cross oneself. We three were rather reserved. We were not the only people present, but dressed as we were we looked like Frenchmen and couldn't very well leave without carrying out this little ceremony. Monsieur gave me a look which as good as said "Come on Joe, have a go" and himself went up and did the necessary. I followed feeling very scared. Everything however went off alright, and I moved away for the navigator to take my place. Finally the front gunner completed his little act and we all left still feeling very nervous, but I don't think any holier. I don't remember seeing any Germans in the church.

We walked slowly back to the cafe through the Tuileries. As I have said, it was my birthday and I could not have had a better one. When we had first arrived in Paris, Monsieur's mother, who had looked after the front gunner on our journey, had gone straight to her flat to make arrangements for some of us to sleep there as she herself was staying elsewhere. The young fellow who had escorted the navigator went off to see somebody else. The three Americans had gone and we did not see them again until next morning. The only incident which took place that afternoon befell the young Frenchman in the party. He was on the way back from visiting his friend when a German policeman shouted out to somebody to stop and come back. He, like everybody in earshot, turned round at this commotion to find that the man was pointing at him. He walked towards him, but while several yards off, was suddenly waved away. No doubt the policeman was looking for someone in particular, but on a closer inspection decided that this wasn't the man he wanted.

Monsieur was taking the front gunner and me along to his mother's flat, which was some distance away, and the navigator went along with the other Frenchman. As our train for Marseille left about 7 the next morning it was decided that we should retire early that evening. A little after dark we caught a tube and got out several stations later. We walked for about 15 minutes; after that we arrived at the flat. I had no idea where we were; the flat was at the top of a house which didn't appear to have any sign of life. It was rather cold and as there was no coal, fires were unheard of. Monsieur set the alarm clock for the ungodly hour of 4 o'clock. Having spent several hours in trains that day and walking half way around Paris, sleep came, despite the excitement, without the slightest difficulty.

We awoke to find Monsieur already up and shaving. While he was dressing we shaved. We were on our way by half past four, walking briskly to the tube. Monsieur had arranged to meet the remainder of the party in the restaurant not far from the station. When we arrived my navigator and the young Frenchman were there along with Monsieur's mother. We had coffee and rolls. Madame was not accompanying us any further, so we said goodbye to her. She was over 70 years of age. We went into the station and waited while the tickets were bought. It was no easy matter trying to get seats for all of us in the same compartment, but thanks to the efforts of the man with the Americans and Monsieur we succeeded in doing so apart from one stranger.

The train left at 7 o'clock [on 22 October]. It seemed that the French trains had one thing in common with the English ones – they were packed with people. Another thing was although they left on time, they invariably arrived late at their destination. Our next stop was Dijon where we arrived after midday. Here we didn't all go into the same restaurant. The Americans were taken somewhere else by their escort. This was the first time we had been into a restaurant. After the meal, judging by the amount of money Monsieur gave the waiter, no one with money would ever have starved in France. You could eat as well as peace time. After the meal we all gathered outside and discovered our next method of travel was to be by bus. Across the road was a small restaurant which was for the exclusive use of Germans, judging by the appropriate flags hanging outside. While we were looking at this place a soldier walked down the road, I should really say shuffled, as he was a direct contrast to the youths we had seen in Paris. He was 60 years old if he was a day!

The Americans returned and we all moved along to the bus stop. Soon a smallish bus drove up and we could see the man who was looking after the Americans fighting his way to the door to buy the necessary tickets. He got what he wanted and stood by the door almost refusing to allow anyone else inside till he had seen us safely in. We went to the back of the bus and sat down. When everyone had got in there was still room for a few more. As we drove out of Dijon there was the sound of dead silence amongst us. Every now and then the bus stopped to disgorge the odd local housewife who had been into town shopping. Occasionally a passenger was picked up. We passed through a few villages and at one, larger than the rest, we waited longer than usual. It must have been the local bus junction. While waiting there a German officer and a German civilian got in and sat together on seats just in front of our party. We all looked at each other and smiled, God knows why; I suppose it relieved the monotony a little. The officer was in the Army and like all German officers his uniform was spotless, he had an ugly-looking scar across one cheek, but whether it was due to the Russians or a duelling scar we didn't know. His companion, who was conversing in German, was smartly dressed and wore a Panama hat. It looked as if he was enjoying a holiday from his native country. I wondered what would have happened if something had gone wrong with the German officer discovering who we were. I don't think the two of them would have lasted very long in the back of that bus. The rest of our journey was uneventful, and about an hour and a half after leaving Dijon we arrived at Chalon-sur-Saône, where we de-bussed.

We walked a little way through the town until we reached a little cafe into which we all went. We sat around with our various escorts while awaiting further developments. We had a glass of wine, and every now and then one of the Frenchmen would get up and either stroll outside or disappear through a door at the back of the cafe. We then noticed that the Americans had gone. What had been happening was that every so often some passer-by who was obviously mixed up in the whole scheme would cycle up to the cafe, leave his bike outside and come in for a drink. When the required number of bikes were there, certain numbers of us would be told to come outside and the escorts would nod towards a bike. All one had to do was to get on and follow him. What it amounted to was a very well organised shuttle service, and precautions were being taken all the time. We, that is myself and my crew, were left to last and instead of going out by the front we found ourselves in a room upstairs. It seemed that the navigator and front gunner were not wearing the correct clothes. Certain garments had to be changed. I did not have to change anything so went downstairs and didn't have to wait long to find myself outside and astride a rather dilapidated bike.

For the first few hundred yards the pace was normal. There were two or three others in front of me and I think one or two behind. After a minute or two it developed into a race; the man preceding me must have been at least 200 yards ahead. This went on for about 10 minutes till the people I was following disappeared around a corner. By this time we seemed to have left the greater part of the town behind, and we were almost in open country. I reached the corner and turned after them. I hadn't gone more than 300 yards before coming to a farm. A man standing in the road nodded towards the yard into which I turned. I put my bike into a barn and was taken inside, where I met the remainder, except the navigator and front gunner who had not arrived.

Although it was getting dark, no lights were lit and a few minutes later everybody had arrived. The navigator exploded a bombshell when he announced that he had left his wallet which contained his precious poster as well as his identity and ration cards in his old jacket after changing coats in the cafe. This made matters very awkward and it was finally decided to leave the young Frenchman behind to collect the articles and follow on afterwards. This of course meant he could not cross the "line" with us that night.

We had no idea what to expect as regards crossing the demarcation line, but it wasn't long before things started to move. We hadn't been ten minutes in the farm when somebody came in and took us all outside; it was nearly dark and in single file we went through a large barn to a small river, too deep to be waded and about 30 feet across. We were about to cross the line. About 200 yards away was the main road, and the Germans had guards there. They were in fact changing guard as we crossed the river.

It was perfectly organised by the people in whose hands we were in. Whether it was accidental or deliberate I don't know, but stretching across from bank to bank lay a large tree trunk. To cross we had to sit astride this and work our way to the other side. The actual crossing didn't take more than a minute or two but when once on the other bank there were about 200 yards of fairly open ground to cover. Luckily there was a field of wheat or something between us and the Germans. We all bent double and moved as quickly as possible. If the guards had seen something suspicious all we could have expected was a hail of bullets, but thank goodness we all arrived safely at the other side of the field. We were then taken to a place that looked like a country house. After waiting for some time, it appeared that the French lady who either ran or owned it couldn't provide beds for more than a certain number of us. An argument didn't exactly take place but she wasn't very agreeable.

Eventually everybody had a bed because the navigator and I were taken to a home further down the road. We were received by a couple approaching middle age with whom we sat and talked for a while. Then the man produced a bottle of real cognac and we celebrated having completed the most difficult part of the journey. He also dragged out from a cupboard a parachute such as our paratroops wore that was entirely camouflaged and which had been used by either a French or British agent that landed nearby. He was extremely proud of the parachute and the part he had played in collecting it. It was then after 11 o'clock so we went to bed. The navigator and I shared a huge double bed and the next thing we knew was when we were called just before 6 o'clock the next morning.

The fact that we were in unoccupied France must have been a great relief to everyone, especially to those whose care we were in. However, even though officially no Germans were supposed to be within the zone, there must have been hundreds in civilian clothes, so really it didn't pay to relax completely.

Our host made some black coffee and we had a cup before leaving. We were being taken by car to a railway station a few miles away. This man had a car, a small saloon, and six of us got into it. The rest were going in another car. When we got on the open road, the driver put his headlights full on. Forgetting where we were, several of us muttered "black out". Of course we had forgotten that unoccupied France was free from any lighting restrictions. We arrived at a small station and found a train waiting at the platform. It must have been the first train of the day and was practically empty. We got into a carriage that had a corridor running down the middle and sat either side and proceeded to make ourselves thoroughly at home, there being nobody else there but our friends. The train moved off about 7 o'clock and about two and a half hours later we arrived at the large town of Lyon where we changed. The train to Marseille did not leave until 1.30 p.m., so from the station we went to a cafe about a hundred yards away and sat there drinking coffee.

After that we boarded a tram and were taken into town where we went to a small restaurant. By this time we were all very hungry and it was getting near the rush hour. While we seated ourselves one of the Frenchmen organised the meal and about half way through this he left the table to speak to the proprietor. He got what he wanted because, a few minutes later, two bottles of wine appeared. It was Châteauneuf-du-Pape, and as none of us had had anything alcoholic for some weeks, this wine had the same effect on us as on a teetotaller. By the time the coffee stage had been reached, we were all decidedly happy and some of us were a little pickled. Luckily there was no one else lunching in the restaurant, but occasionally somebody would come in to buy something at the other end of the room which had a few shelves stocking the normal commodities. Normally only French was spoken but it seemed that most of us were gaily carrying on a conversation in English. In fact it was a very enjoyable luncheon party, and we prepared to return to the station feeling on top of the world. When the bill was tendered, the two escorts put the required amount on the tray but the waiter refused to take certain of the notes, his argument being that some of the bills were not valid in unoccupied France, whereupon a furious argument began with the waiter and the two wine-fired Frenchman. In the end the matter was settled amicably and we left.

We went back to the station by tram and boarded our train. By now every compartment was full and passengers were standing in the corridor; we had to do the same. We had half an hour to wait and spent the time gazing out of the window. At half past one we pulled out of the station.

We were not due in at Marseille till about 5 o'clock. Up till this time luck had been with us regarding seats, but now there was no doubt that we should have to stand all the way, which we did. It was a very uneventful journey, and even the scenery was dull until we reached the Rhône Valley where we got some pleasant views from our window as the train wound its way around the sides of the valley. At one station at which we stopped, I believe it was Avignon, there were some Vichy air force boys on the platform, the first we had ever seen. As we neared the coast the sea stretched inland forming several oblong bays, and on one of these we saw some huge six-engined flying boats at their moorings, and several hangars on the edge of the shore. The train was late of course and we didn't arrive in Marseille till after half past five. It was late October and the weather down here was perfect, almost midsummer, and everybody was dressed in summer clothes. While we were waiting to pass through the barriers we saw an awfully pretty French girl, quite the prettiest we'd seen. We all looked at each other and sighed; unfortunately we weren't on holiday. It was nearly 6 o'clock when we left the station and walked down the very wide flight of steps that led to town.

At the bottom of the town we walked along the harbour filled with yachts and motor boats all moored together. We entered a house which was right on the edge of the harbour; after going up several storeys by lift we walked, after the prescribed number of rings had been given on the bell, into a very pleasant flat. It was here that we met the big white chief [Pat O'Leary].

The trip to Marseille had taken three days and two nights; we had travelled by truck, car, tram, bus, bicycle and tube, and on our own two

'... we left the station and walked down the very wide flight of steps that led to town.'

feet. Monsieur and his partner had safely delivered us. The owner of
the flat lived there with his wife. He was a tallish man with grey hair,
and spoke English fluently. Soon after we had arrived he brought out an
ordinary-looking book which contained the names, rank and squadron
number of all airmen who had passed through his flat. He took down
all our details which, like the previous ones, were written in the margin
on different pages. When the last one had been put down the number of
names just topped the hundred mark; in fact it was no ordinary book.

We had supper a little later and some of us were rather surprised to
see on the table things that even in England it was impossible to obtain.
Anyway no questions were asked. After supper three unknown Frenchmen
arrived and there was a long conversation between them all, I imagine
concerning our next move, which didn't take place till Sunday, October
25th. The old man discovered that I had a poster with me and did the
very best to make me part with it, mainly for security reasons. I am glad
to say I've still got it with me today. That night the new arrivals, except
two of the Americans, slept in the living room, on the floor, cushions and
blankets being supplied. We spent the next morning being fitted out with
new clothes. If we were going to travel with men who frequented such a
luxurious flat, we would have to be well dressed. Anyway, we were in the
south of France and one could not very well frequent the Riviera looking
like a tramp. I got a pair of grey flannel trousers, chequered in black,
almost a little too flashy, and a blue coat.

During the morning the young Frenchman who had had to return to
collect the navigator's wallet just before we crossed the "line" arrived,
bringing the wallet with him. After lunch Monsieur and the young man
went into the town and brought us each back a little present. Mine was
a wallet, which I still have, also postcard views of Marseille. From where
we were we could see a great deal of the harbour and the bridge affair
that connected the harbour mouth. It wasn't really a bridge, there being
a lift apparatus that travelled horizontally from one side to the other.

[Donald's 'bridge affair' was actually a transporter bridge, which had opened on
15 December 1905. Together with most of the port facilities, it was destroyed by
the Germans as they left Marseille on 22 August 1944.]

The next day, Sunday, we were all being split up. The Americans were
proceeding to Nice, the navigator, I believe, was being transferred to
another part of Marseille [see section on Ray Glensor in Chapter 5],
while the front gunner and myself were going to live in Monte Carlo.
The reason for all this was that things were becoming a little hot, not
on account of the Germans but of the French Police who had already
detained the odd member of the amazing organisation. Apart from that

'... the bridge affair that connected the harbour mouth.' – as Donald would have seen it.

if a particular place was to be raided, not more than one or two would be caught, so dispersal was the only solution.

The Americans had already left when the front gunner and I were due to go. Before they went we arranged to meet them in London, naming some well-known bar in which to celebrate, but we never saw them again.[3]

We said goodbye to Monsieur and the young friend, and friends they truly had been. The farewell was very touching, lots of kissing on both cheeks in true French fashion. Our escort this time was a man about 32. His English was more than my French which is saying something, and it gave me an opportunity of improving my scant knowledge as we conversed solely in his native tongue. We set off for the station looking very different to when we arrived due to our new clothes.

After getting our tickets we boarded our train, but had to stand in the corridor as it was full. It was nearly lunch time by now, and we began to eat our sandwiches soon after the train pulled out. The first stop of any importance was Toulon, but we didn't pass close enough to see the French fleet lying in harbour. The compartment opposite which we were standing was reserved, and only contained three people, a man and two women. Nobody else appeared to be joining them so our escort went inside to ask if we could all come in and sit down, which seemed very logical. He came out a minute later and told us that the man was a doctor and one of the women was slightly crazy, and that the other women was a nurse. The doctor didn't think it wise to come in and would rather we didn't. The crazy one looked quite young and was English. I must admit after looking at her and the way she behaved, I believe the doctor was right.

Soon after this the Mediterranean came into view. It was a lovely day and the water looked just as blue as it's made out to be. We stopped at all the famous Riviera resorts and at one of these the doctor and his charge got out. We then had the compartment to ourselves and were enjoying a very interesting local geography lesson from our escort. This lasted for a short time as at the next stop, which was Nice, several people got in and put an end to it. About tea time we arrived at Monte Carlo and from here the Italian frontier was only 6 miles away. Our first impression of this famous Riviera town was that it didn't look like a place where people came from all over the world. Monte Carlo is on the side of a hill and to get from the bottom of the town to the top was done by climbing flights of steps which were all over the place.

There again we had no idea who we were going to stay with or for how long, although we were getting used to not knowing where we were going or why. The thought kept one constantly keyed up because we had no clues as to what to expect. So far, in the short time we had been travelling we had met the most amazing people doing the most extraordinary things. Before leaving Marseille, we were told that we were going to stay with two English ladies but beyond that we knew nothing. This in itself sounded pretty good especially if our stay was to be a long one. But I regret our luck was definitely out as regards two nice young things! We walked along the main, or one of the principal, streets until our escort stopped outside a little cafe which was called the Scotch Tea House. We went inside and our stay in Monte Carlo had begun but, instead of being ten to fourteen days, it was increased to a month due to the Germans deciding to occupy the remainder of France, and the Italians, as Mr Churchill put it, "being allowed to promenade along the Riviera as far as Nice".

The British colony in Monte Carlo numbered 210 persons, whose average age was over 70. The total population was a little over 20,000 of whom 11,000 were Italian and 9,000 French. Practically every nation was represented there. When France fell, a number of British people returned home by boat, but a lot of those left behind did great work in co-operation with the French in helping to look after allied soldiers and airmen by helping them to escape.

We were greeted by a tallish English woman about middle age. A little later her companion came in. These two ran the tea house which was well known in Monte Carlo. The elder of the two, who was head of the business, was a slim woman past middle age. She was a distant relative to a very senior and famous RAF officer, who funnily enough had visited the squadron shortly before I went missing and had stayed to lunch, the two flight commanders being invited to sit at his table. While we were talking, a very distinguished-looking man came in. He was known as the Colonel and had been in the British Army for 60 years. He must have been about 80 years of age but he certainly didn't look it.

[Vincent Brome wrote that the 'tea-shop ... in Monte Carlo was owned by the Misses Trenchard – Grace and Susie – two angular, grey-haired Scots ladies thrilled to be involved in underground work...'[4] The 'very senior and famous RAF officer' was none other than Marshal of the Royal Air Force Hugh Montague Trenchard.[5] With her companion (it is not clear who Susie, or Suzy, was) Eve Sarah Trenchard, a spinster, had been running the Scotch Tea House in the Villa Flor Palace apartment block since 1924, and it was she who was to look after Donald and Ralph Forster, as she had already done for several others.

When the Germans occupied the whole of France in November 1942, they set up their headquarters in Monte Carlo – opposite the tea house. Eve was later to comment that the Germans regarded her as a harmless old Englishwoman stranded by the occupation. Little did they know that she helped an estimated 27 airmen to escape. According to Sergeant Derrick Nabarro, RAF, who had escaped from a German prisoner-of-war camp, she spent 'three months in prison for assisting escapers'. In May 1946, Eve Trenchard was awarded the King's Commendation for services to the Allied cause.[6] She died in 1977, aged 93.]

Our home was to be in the flat which the two Englishwomen shared. We waited till it was dark before walking over to the flat and then walked a little way through the town and came to a normal-looking row of street houses. Their flat was on the second floor and consisted of two bedrooms, a sitting room, kitchen and bathroom. The front gunner and I shared the other bedroom which was at the end of the building and overlooked the main street and side street. Life here was very much the same but we felt much safer, although it was not advisable to walk around in daylight. During the day we played cards and from the front gunner I learnt many new games of patience, and the little wireless set was a constant companion. Miss T[renchard] brought us our lunch every day from the Scotch Tea House and considering the great difficulty in obtaining food, we fared very well. In the evening Miss T's friend usually set course for the famous casino. If we had had passports we could have gone as well, but with the amount of money given to us in our escape kits we wouldn't have lasted two minutes.

Members of the organisation visited occasionally and from them we learnt that our stay might be prolonged owing to the possibility of the Germans moving down south to occupy the whole of France. The invasion of North Africa had already taken place and Montgomery was making a spectacular dash across Libya. The Germans therefore wished to move troops to the south of France to protect its shores against invasion. In a day or two we heard that they were on the move. We heard also that the Italians were to occupy the coast as far as Nice. Very soon the Italian columns were marching through the Principality of Monaco. Their equipment was painted in desert camouflage and from scraps of conversation that the inhabitants had had with the troops, it appeared that they had been stationed in Northern Italy for a very long time and were somewhat brassed off with the war. Most of them were concerned about their families in such towns as Milan and Turin, which were being heavily bombed, and some had not had leave for 3 years.

About that time we could hear our bombers on their way to Italy. We use to stand outside on the balcony and listen to them going over. From where we were they seemed to have little trouble with Flak.[7] Before the Italians marched in, we used to visit the cinema now and then. Our escort in charge of this operation was a member of the police force. He was an Australian and naturally knew everything that concerned the right time and place. The films were in French of course and the newsreels were entirely German, showing the Russian battle front. One scene showed an enormously long line of prisoners which the Germans said were Bolsheviks from the Stalingrad battle. Actually they were the remnants of Von Paulus's 6th Army, which had surrendered, being marched away by the Russians themselves.

After the shows our party, which numbered anything up to eight, usually stopped at a bar on the way back. On one occasion we stopped at a place which only contained two people, but while we were there two more came in. Of the dozen or so in there, they consisted of a German girl and an Austrian refugee, who I believe were married, and a red-haired American girl and an Austrian, who were trying to get married but couldn't find anybody to undertake the responsibility. Two friends of ours, Madame and Monsieur G, who kept a branch of their shop in London, the Australians, and of course ourselves from England and the West Indies. The most amazing personality there was the barman, a youth of perhaps 20, who by rights should have been in the British Army. He spoke French fairly well, but what he was doing behind a bar in Monte Carlo god only knows.

[The Australian policeman was Inspector Tony Friend, who was employed at Monaco Police Headquarters. He played a key part in the mass breakouts from Fort de la Revère in August and September 1942.[8] "Madame and Monsieur G" were husband and wife Marcel and Simone Guiton. They ran a high-class hairdressing salon called Maison Française, and had sheltered some of the escapers from the Fort de la Revère breakout.]

Madame and Monsieur G were constant visitors, and she spoke English almost perfectly. They were both very kind and entertained us in every way possible. Their firm has a large hairdressing concern in Hanover Street and both had made frequent visits to England before the war. He had been a prisoner after the capitulation but had been released, I believe owing to ill health. The Australian took us to his house one evening prior to visiting a friend of his for dinner. On the way through the town we passed in the darkness a woman and small boy. He told us she was the countess who had flown over from England two days previously on a visit to see her small son, but was returning the next day.[9] We both quite naturally asked and hoped what the chances were of getting a lift back, but of course nothing could be done without it being fully prepared and sanctioned. We certainly envied her. To reach the house meant climbing numerable flights of steps and we arrived quite exhausted, despite our fitness, due to the lack of alcohol. The dinner party was in the other man's flat and several people were there including Madame and Monsieur G. Our host was an Englishman who was obviously conversant with the organisation. At that time he was in the process of growing a beard, and one or two of his friends who had come to dinner got quite a shock. Before we left, both the front gunner and myself memorised a message to be delivered for him in London. Apparently events weren't progressing too well for him and I should imagine the beard had something to do with it.

One of the first things the Italians did was to surround the American Embassy and they managed to lay their hands on most of the official papers, which should have been destroyed, and proceeded to hold the Yanks as prisoners inside, but I don't know for how long. Rumour has it that the Americans thought they couldn't be touched.

We heard one or two amusing stories here. Goering used to visit Monte Carlo and apparently a trap to net him was engineered, but unfortunately it never came off. He would undoubtedly have lost much weight had he been in Monte Carlo as any prisoner would for any length of time. Danielle Darrieux, the French film star, had been seen around, and was said to have been the mistress of Otto Abetz, the German ambassador to France, but we heard she had married a Frenchman. Baroness Orczy, the famous authoress, was also living in Monte Carlo at the time but was rarely seen.

[Danielle Darrieux, born in Bordeaux in May 1917, has had a successful career as a film actress which, at the time of writing (2010), is still ongoing. Otto Abetz, aged 40 at the time of Donald's stay in the south of France, had married a French woman, Susanne de Bruyker, in 1932, when his politics were leftist, and he was a known pacifist. He left France when the German armies withdrew in September 1944, but was arrested by the Allies in 1945 and sentenced by the French in 1949 to 20 years' imprisonment for war crimes, not least assisting with the deportation of French Jews to the 'death' camps. Released in April 1954, he died in a car crash on a German autobahn on 5 May 1958. Inevitably, there was a suspicion that the crash was not an accident.

Baroness Emma ('Emmuska') Magdalena Rosalia Maria Josefa Barbara Orczy, born in September 1865 into a noble Hungarian family, moved to England where

in 1894 she married Henry Montague Barstow. She was a writer, and in 1903 her
play *The Scarlet Pimpernel* opened in Nottingham but failed. Reopening, this time
at the New Theatre in London in January 1905, the play became a huge success,
and in the same year the book of the play was published, and became an instant
success. Soon after the end of the First World War, from the profits of *The Scarlet
Pimpernel*, the Barstows bought the Villa Bijou in Monte Carlo, and another, later,
in Italy. In 1943, Henry died in Monte Carlo and, broken-hearted, Emmuska died
at Henley-on-Thames, Oxfordshire, in November 1947.]

Events became somewhat serious and preparations to leave were being
made. Owing to the Germans moving in, travel and communication
became dangerous and strained. For several days we heard nothing.
All the English people had to report to the Italians and were told that
virtually they were interned and must behave like internees. It also got
around that a house to house search might take place. We talked about
getting a boat which had been left behind by its owner, but the difficulty
was obtaining fuel, which could only be had at a hearty price. Our
intention was to slip away one night and sail to North Africa. We even
went so far as to work out courses for such places as Oran and Algiers
which had been captured by us already. Luckily one of the organisation
arrived and said we would leave the following Sunday, three days' time.
It was also decided to move us to an empty flat at the bottom of the town,
the owner having gone to England at the outbreak of the hostilities.

That evening, we moved our residence, escorted by Madame G. This
was the famous flat in which a dozen or so of our boys had lived after a
mass escape had been planned and executed from the mountain fortress
just inland from Monte Carlo. About 53 should have got away but,
owing to a slight hitch, only 30 or so escaped. The reason for this we
were told was that the senior officer of the party failed to pass on to all
of them the various addresses which our boys should have gone to, with
the result that many were caught wandering in the woods. The officer
concerned received the Military Cross and is now holding Air Rank,
besides being a millionaire.

[The 'officer concerned' was Squadron Leader Whitney Willard Straight, a famous
prewar racing driver, who had been shot down on 31 July 1941. He was born on 6
November 1912 in the United States to banker and diplomat Willard Dickerman
Straight and Dorothy Payne Whitney, a rich heiress. He moved to England in 1925
with his mother, sister Beatrice, and younger brother Michael[10] after his father had
died of pneumonia in 1918, and after his mother had remarried Leonard Elmhirst,
an Englishman. They lived at Dartington Hall, Totnes, South Devon. With a rich
family behind him, Whitney took to motor racing and to aviation, flying solo
without a licence in 1928 at the age of fifteen, and gaining his private pilot's licence

in the following year. In 1931, he went up to Trinity College, Cambridge, the year in which he began motor racing. He became a naturalised British subject in 1936.

Early in 1939 he joined the Royal Auxiliary Air Force, and flew with the somewhat exclusive 601 (County of London) Squadron (it had the nickname 'The Millionaires' Squadron') but, because of his knowledge of airfield construction, he was sent to Norway in 1940 to find suitable landing sites for the RAF. He was awarded the MC (gazetted on 1 January 1941) for the work that he had done in laying out a runway on a frozen lake in Norway, during which he was seriously wounded, on 25 April 1940.

On 8 August 1941 he was awarded the DFC:

Acting Squadron Leader Whitney Willard STRAIGHT, M.C. (90680), Auxiliary Air Force, No. 242 Squadron (missing).
This officer has participated in many engagements against the enemy throughout which he has displayed excellent qualities of leadership and zeal. He has destroyed at least three enemy aircraft, one of which he shot down at night.

Squadron Leader Straight was indeed 'missing', having been shot down in his Hurricane on 31 July 1941 whilst attacking heavily armed German E-boats off Le Havre, France. He managed to make his way almost to the Pyrenees, but was arrested by Vichy French police before he could cross into neutral Spain. In 1942 he was rescued by the PAT line from the hospital to which he had been sent for an 'illness' to be treated. He was evacuated by boat to Gibraltar in the clandestine Operation Bluebottle I from the south of France in July 1942, and was flown back to England from Gibraltar on the night of 24/25 July 1942, six months ahead of Donald.

The mass escape to which Donald referred took place on the night of 5/6 September 1942 from Fort de la Revère, a Napoleonic fort built high in the hills above Monte Carlo. Thirty-seven British soldiers and twenty-one airmen managed to escape through a tunnel, having been given addresses in the area to which they could go for temporary shelter. One man was injured during the getaway, which Donald mentions below. Unfortunately, the response of the Vichy police to the outbreak was so swift that, in the hue and cry that followed, thirty-four of the fifty-seven who got away were recaptured (nineteen soldiers and fifteen airmen). The rest had to be cared for in 'safe houses' along the Riviera, even as far away as Marseille, some 225 kilometres to the west. Such was the intensity of the police activity that it took one party of airmen six days to get to their safe house in Nice, only a dozen kilometres away. Twenty-five of the escapers from the fort had been shipped off to Gibraltar by 13 October.[11]

It was the strong reaction of the police to the breakout that was the reason why Donald and company had found things a little hot when they had arrived in Marseille.]

The people who were responsible for the escape were looking after us at the time and took a very dim view. During the escape one of the boys slipped and fell into the moat, breaking both legs. Although in intense pain, he remained absolutely quiet until the next morning. If he had cried out, the whole party would have been caught, but his silence enabled them to get many miles away.

The building we had arrived at was practically alongside the railway line and very near the shore. There were several flats but not all appeared to be occupied, ours being on the ground floor. It seemed as though the people who had lived there before had left in a hurry, and numerous sets of razors and odd articles of clothing had been left behind by the boys from the fort. There were numerous books to read, and we looked forward to our meals which Madame G always brought. The constant waiting if you thought too much about it brought on fits of depression. We were only there about three or four days when one of the organisation arrived with Madame one morning. It was Sunday morning and within half an hour we were all back in the Scotch Tea House.

The Italians had posted sentries at the entrance and around the station. Unfortunately our official identification cards which we had been given for use in France did not actually state we were Frenchmen. It would have been very awkward if we had been asked to produce them to the Italians. It was decided to issue to each of us another card to state that we were French. However, when we arrived at the station there was hardly an Italian to be seen. Certainly not at the entrance. Our tickets were as usual bought for us and we wandered onto the platform.

The train duly arrived and we climbed aboard. It was as normal very full but we managed to find seats. We had an uneventful trip to Marseille. The Italians had moved as far as Nice and one could see that they were trying to improve the defences. There were groups of them on the beaches lounging around. At Nice, where Italian control ended and German control began, they passed each other on the platform but one could see the way the Germans paid no attention to them whatsoever and even despised them openly.

We arrived at Marseille about 5 o'clock and it was quite dark by the time we reached the house we were staying at for the next two nights; a doctor and his wife lived there, and by the way we were received we certainly weren't the first customers they had. I think he was a Greek and his wife French.[12] Anyway they were very pleasant and the food was good. Our meals weren't what we had been used to – rather formal with a maid waiting on us – but there were no recorded faux pas.

We left very early on the second morning for Toulouse. It was with the escorts who brought us to Marseille, and the front gunner was with a young lad that I had seen before. The whole trip took about 9 hours.

During the last half, my escort got caught talking to a couple of men and a girl. He told me afterwards they were talking about the war situation, after making certain amongst each other that no one was pro-German. He also said that he would have liked to tell them who I was but thought better of it. We arrived in Toulouse about 3.30 after a very long and monotonous journey. I don't think I left my seat or opened my mouth for the last six hours, and trying to read a French book when you only know one word in three made the trip even worse.

We walked about one and a quarter miles through the town and turned into a side street opposite the canal.[13] We stopped at a house which was one in a row. After a number of calculated knocks a slim blonde girl opened the door. We were, as normal, expected and Madame, as she turned out to be, led us inside. There were several people there. Two young fellows, another woman who was not so slim as the first, also known as Madame, and a small thick-set man about 40 years old. The two young men thought we were Frenchmen, which said something for our make up. They were Americans who were both from the same Eagle Squadron but who were not shot down on the same sweep. The elder man had been in France before Dunkirk, but obviously had not made any strenuous efforts to return to England. The large Madame had fled from Paris. She told us the Germans took exception to Jews. The girl who opened the door to us was American, her husband a Frenchman who was away working and wouldn't be in till the evening. Tea without milk was made and after that we related our various experiences to each other. Early in the evening Monsieur P arrived. He was a man about 30, above medium height, slim and had black hair. I think his ears stood out a little. I can't really remember. After meeting us, the first thing he did was to switch on the radio. It was apparently a routine thing for him whenever he entered the room.

[Donald and party were in the hands of Paul Ulmann (the man whom Donald called Monsieur P) and his American-born wife, Imelda, at 39, rue Pierre Cazeneuve, Toulouse. It was a 'safe house' for the PAT/PAO line, the organisation that had been looking after all the airmen for so many weeks. The two Americans were Pilot Officer R. S. 'Bob' Smith, and Flying Officer Eric Doorly, both of 133 (Eagle) Squadron RAF. They had been shot down on 26 September 1942 and on 6 September 1942 respectively.]

This was our last stop before crossing the Pyrenees into Spain. It was in the last part of November and getting quite cold, and therefore essential to be equipped with warm clothes for crossing the mountains. The projected date was the 7th December. We passed the time by playing chess and occasionally took part in some weird, wonderful and violent gambling game organised by the Americans. One day the lead man came in and distributed scarves, socks, gloves and coats to those that needed them. One or two people were short of identity cards so he calmly opened his suitcase and produced bundles of blank identity cards. Then followed various stamping machines and inks. In a few minutes he had manufactured the necessary. His suitcase also contained the odd revolver and various incriminating articles. He would have been shot on the spot if caught.

The next day the head man arrived with an immaculately dressed young man carrying a suitcase. He was introduced to everyone and spoke French and English perfectly. We received nothing short of a violent shock when we discovered the reason for his visit. The suitcase contained a wireless receiver and transmitter and our house was to be his headquarters for a few days. We found out that the men doing this job, and a highly dangerous one, usually moved every three to four days. The reason for this was that German or French patrol cars picked up the area which the set was in within two days. On the third day they reduced it to the block and then on the fourth day to the house itself. That evening the whole paraphernalia was set up on the table and he took the table outside and tied it to the neighbour's fence. Needless to say we were quite scared. After having got so far we didn't wish to be caught, so we took great pains to remind him day by day how long he had been with us. On the fourth day he left, and it was as if the Germans had gone. He was an English Army captain who had only just entered France from Gibraltar. I was told by a captain on the Intelligence Staff when I returned to England that he had been caught red handed with all the codes etc in front of him. We've all heard of the German method of extracting information so there is no need to say what happened to him.

[The radio operator was not English but Australian Thomas Gilmour Groome, who had landed in France only on the night of 3/4 November 1942. He was caught in the tower of La Tourelle, a house in Montauban, in the act of transmitting messages to England on 11 January 1943. Contrary to Donald's understandably pessimistic view, Groome did survive Gestapo interrogation and subsequent deportation to the concentration camps. He was appointed MBE in March 1946.]

We had very few visitors these days but there was one who dropped in occasionally. He lived across the road and for all intents and purposes we regarded him as a Frenchman. He also spoke English very well. It turned out he'd come to France with the B.E.F. in 1939 and missed the evacuation like many others. His home was in Jersey and French being the common language spoken there he had no trouble in France. He had got a job and a house and was only waiting for the day of Liberation. Jersey had been overrun by Germans anyway.

CHAPTER 4

DIARY – PART 3: DEPARTURE FOR THE PYRENEES, SPAIN, AND THE UK

At last the great day dawned, the 7th of December.[1] Extra care was taken with the razor, not knowing when our next shave would be. Dressing seemed to take a little longer as well. Throughout the morning sandwiches were being cut and skins filled with wine. Extra cigarettes were handed out. We had an early lunch and left for the station. There was lots of kissing and handshaking and "we'll come and see you after the war" etc. Our party numbered seven as far as I can remember. We left Toulouse for Narbonne where trains had to be changed. While our tickets were being bought we were introduced to a man who spoke French, English and Greek perfectly. He was a Greek apparently and was carrying valuable information which had to be taken to our authorities immediately. His wife was coming with him. I didn't envy her for the walk across the mountains.

[The party of seven were Donald and Ralph Forster; Leading Aircraftman A. V. Bromwell, RAF (the airman who confused Barnard by his constant change of rank, but who was not, as Donald wrote, an Aircraftman 2nd Class); Bob Smith and Eric Doorly (the two American Eagle Squadron pilots); and Mario Prassinos (the Greek guide who had been working for the PAT/PAO escape line, and who was using the alias 'Captain Forbes'), and his wife. They were joined later by a French tank officer known as 'Frost'.]

Once more it was a question of corridor standing. On the way to Narbonne a well-built man stood alongside us and as we neared the town he turned and said "Here we are" and something about seeing us later. He spoke so quietly that we concluded he must have known who we were. As usual we kept silent. We left Narbonne station and adjourned to a cafe. The most important man in the party, whom we hadn't set eyes on to date, was our guide. He had been seen to board the train at Toulouse but not to get off at Narbonne. The stranger who spoke to us on the train joined us in the cafe. It transpired he was a French tank officer also trying to get to England.

We had a green salad for our meal and started back for the station. The train was due to leave about 5.30. We had about half an hour to wait and found a compartment occupied only by two old and dirty men who frequently spat out of the window. At the same time efforts were being made to locate our guide. The train pulled out and we could only hope he was on board. The nearer one got to the Spanish frontier the more numerous became the German Frontier Guards. At each little station, there seemed to be more guards than passengers. The Gendarmes seemed to be more numerous too. Soon darkness enveloped us. Although our faces betrayed nothing, we were nevertheless extremely keyed up and excited, and were very glad when daylight was left behind.

Our jumping off place was the village of Port Vendres. The station was dimly lit and people were peering out trying to find out where they were. The train laboriously dragged itself alongside the platform, by which time we were all up and loaded with our various items of kit but, instead of our escorts making for the compartment door on the platform side, they remained in the corridor on the other side with no platform. As soon as passengers began to descend they opened the door whispering "Vite, Vite". They clambered down into the darkness with us following like sheep. They might have warned us to say the least of it! We crossed another set of tracks in a flash and dived over the ensuing embankment. One or two of us including myself rolled right to the bottom, several yards down. My hands and knees were covered in cuts when I picked myself up. Just prior to our departure from the train, I noticed 2 or 3 people in the same corridor as ourselves. Heaven alone knows what they must have thought at the sight of several men and a woman who were obviously intent on getting out the wrong side of the train.

We lay where we had fallen or rolled, in absolute silence and pitch darkness. Occasionally there was a muttered curse as another stone or thorn touched a tender point. Eventually the train moved on and we crawled in search of one another. This was the pre-arranged spot where we were to meet our guide, so we moved on about 50 yards and waited. It was a lovely night, the moon being partially obscured by thin layers of cloud; a perfect night for crossing the Pyrenees. The thought of having to go back crossed our minds and after an hour it was obvious he had missed the train or got out at the wrong place. There was nothing for it but to search for one of those small stone erections built by the wine growers for storing tools etc. They are about 8 feet square inside. Two of the Frenchmen went off to search for one and they returned after a few minutes. They had located one a few hundred yards away. We trooped off in single file, very dejected and low in spirits. When we had all squeezed in, the food was brought out and after satisfying ourselves, the skins of wine were passed around and cigarettes. Several suggestions were brought forward to try to clear up the mystery concerning our guide. He was Spanish but spoke French as well. The root of the trouble in arranging for a guide to escort us over the mountains to Barcelona was that they demanded to be paid before the trip started. As guides were few and far between, one had no choice but to agree. It was not an enviable profession for, if caught, it meant life imprisonment, most certainly so in Spain.

Very little sleep was had by any of us that night. It was certainly impossible to lie down. Soon after dawn broke we made our weary way back to the station of Perpignan. Few people were about at that hour which was fortunate because we must have looked a queer sight. The train rolled on and we made our way back to Toulouse with frequent halts, arriving after lunch. Madame nearly had a fit when she saw us. That evening it was decided to try again the next night, but next morning our departure was put off till the next day, December 9th.

Once more we set off. The arrangement with the guide this time was that we should meet him at Narbonne. We boarded the same train at the same time and arrived at Narbonne about 4 o'clock. Our "jumping off" spot had changed, to avoid arousing suspicion. The time between trains was spent by walking round the town and waiting in the station for the wretched guide to show up. A German brass band was going full blast in one of the streets, but only a few people stopped and listened. Very likely they had been paid by the Germans to do so. The time for the train drew nearer but still no guide. It was obvious by now he'd given us the slip again. Several hours later found us back in Toulouse, but the disappointment was not so acute the second time as the novelty of the trip had died down. It was thought that the guide was averse to having a woman in the party, which accounted for his non-appearance the first time. When questioned about the second attempt, his story was that the police had surrounded the block he was living in due to a house search and that he thought it unwise to leave till they had finished.

Our third, and successful, attempt took place on the 13th. This time there was no excuse. The guide travelled in the same coach. The lead man decided to come along and I was lucky enough to be in his charge. The woman did not accompany us this time, and needless to say a watchful eye was kept on the now famous and elusive guide. The destination that night was Perpignan and everything ran smoothly until nearing the frontier. Two or three stops from Perpignan the Gendarmes came aboard. Tickets and identity cards had to be shown. Our compartment was full and amongst the other passengers was a Spanish lad who was living and working in France like many others. The Gendarme had examined two identity cards and was now looking at the one the Spaniard had given him. After a moment or two he began firing questions at the lad but didn't appear to be getting the required answers. After about two minutes of this he appeared to quieten down. I was reading, or rather pretending to read, a paper and still doing so I handed him my card. For the next 10-15 seconds I concentrated on my paper meanwhile keeping an eye open for the return of the card.

It suddenly dawned on me that he was talking. I looked up and he was glaring at me and speaking at an impossible rate. I simply couldn't understand a word. The next thing I knew was that my escort, the lead man, had been quietly answering all the questions. The only words I understood from his answers was something about "Sa tante est tres malade". Hell, I thought, now I've got a sick aunt. This little drama lasted about 3 minutes and we were very thankful when the Gendarme had gone. We came to the conclusion he was either drunk or very bad tempered. That little incident goes to show how the men who undertook the dangerous work of helping us to escape had always to be on their guard, never relaxing, making certain of doing and saying the right things. If I had been alone at the time I would have been helpless, and in no time at all would have been on my way to the nearest French prison. I will be forever indebted to my escort's timely intervention.

When we arrived at Perpignan, the same unorthodox procedure of getting off was adopted. We moved off silently and stopped several hundred yards from the railway tracks. Those who were crossing the mountains had been given a pair of puttees each. These we put on, and they proved invaluable against the country through which we travelled. We all set off, and for the next hour the country was fairly flat, but this didn't prevent the less agile members of the party from occasionally falling flat on their faces. At the base of the mountain range, we took leave of our escorts and handed over all money and souvenirs which might incriminate us, should we be caught. Several of us retained our money and other souvenirs. Both the front gunner and myself kept all our money etc including our posters in a wallet each, so if necessary the whole lot could be disposed of at once.

It was not long before we started to climb, with the guide leading and the remainder, numbering seven, behind in single file. Our party consisted of the Spanish guide, the two American fighter pilots, the Greek, the French tank officer, the RAF man who claimed to be anything from a flight sergeant to a squadron leader, who in fact turned out to be an aircraftman 2nd class, there being no lower rank, the front gunner and myself. There didn't appear to be any track or recognised path, it just being a question of climbing over boulders and up and down gulleys or through scrub sometimes shoulder high. Despite the fact that the guide had evaded us a couple of times, we just followed him blindly, thankful at last to be on our way. We climbed steadily for two hours up the side of a mountain. On one occasion we passed under a stone bridge and on coming out the other side saw that there was a perfectly good motor road which passed over the bridge. I suppose the road was patrolled otherwise we would have followed it.

At one particularly dangerous spot the Greek fell heavily and badly bruised his shin. We made frequent halts to regain our breath, and during one of these rests we were told a story by the guide. A member of the party fell and broke his leg so it was impossible for him to continue and certainly out of the question for him to return to France. He was given food and water and placed in the most conspicuous spot and left there!

About midnight, one of the shoulders of the mountain was reached, and according to the guide a height of approx 3000 feet had been climbed. There was a fairly wide grass track along the top where he said there was an empty house, the idea being to rest awhile. We plagued him continually as to whether the frontier had been crossed and if not how much further was it. According to him, it was only a few hundred yards away and he suggested we should all get a little sleep and start again at dawn and, all going well, the Spanish town of Gerona should be reached by 8 o'clock the next morning. As a result of this statement a silk escaping map was produced and the town mentioned located. From the distance scale it appeared to be at least 30 miles in a straight line. When queried, he said that most of it would be done by train. If only we had known what was going on in his mind, there's no doubt that he would have been pitched over the side of the mountain. It was practically impossible to sleep because of the cold and terrific winds which frequently reached gale force in violent gusts. In fact it was well nigh impossible to stand up outside.

At dawn, we were on our way. The grass track was followed and a good speed was maintained; then for some mysterious reason, as the track disappeared round the side of a small rocky hillock a little way ahead, the guide left the track and led us round the side of the hill. It was a question of moving mostly on hands and knees and creeping along ledges. It took us about 10 minutes to crawl round the side of this seemingly harmless lump of rock that stood by the side of the track. Imagine our amazement when we climbed back onto the path barely 100 feet from where we had left it. None of us could understand why the guide hadn't kept straight on. From then on, we began to distrust him and before midday our fears were unfortunately justified.

The grass track soon became a rough stony path, and it continued to curl itself upwards round the side of the shoulder, until we found ourselves outside a circular concrete tower, very much like a Martello tower, perched on top of the mountain. Our height was at least 4000 feet and it was bitterly cold. The clouds were skimming over and around us but were slowly lifting. From this position the Mediterranean could be seen and behind us stretched France. Various wisecracks were made to the effect that if the clouds persisted we should have to make a blind approach into Spain.

Returning down the path, the guide led us down the mountainside. The descent took a long time, as it meant clambering over boulders and wading through low scrub. We eventually got onto a track which, as far as could be seen, wound its way up and around another mountain range. The going was very weary and frequent stops were made, partly to allow stragglers to catch up. The frontier had been left behind, but it was necessary to keep our eyes open for roving patrols which were rumoured to be attempting to prevent the ever increasing flow of refugees and escapees into Spain.

The sound of deep toned bells arrested us for a moment, till it was discovered that several mountain cattle, with huge bells hanging below their throats, were just below the track trying to eke out a meal from the almost barren countryside. It became colder as we climbed and our thirsts increased. A spring was found a few yards from the track, and from it bubbled the coldest, cleanest and purest water we'd had for months. Our water bottles were replenished and we carried on. None of us had any idea where we were, but faint hopes were still pinned on the guide. At the top of the climb, the track turned sharply and we passed into a tunnel. It was pretty dark inside and necessitated stooping. Half way along there was a hole on one side that let in a little light. The tunnel was about 100 feet in length. On emerging the other side we ran into cloud that added to our difficulties concerning our position. For some unknown reason, we sensed we were completing a vast circle and that we were actually heading back to France. We commenced a violent argument with the guide, who asked if anyone had a compass as he wished to return through the tunnel and orient himself. There was only one compass, which I believe Ralph Forster had. Had we but known it, we were making our greatest mistake by letting him have it. The guide disappeared the way he'd come, and in fact he really did vanish as he was never seen again on the trip. Later on, when one of the American pilots, Robert Smith, and I were put in prison for the second time, in Barcelona, who should we see a few cells away but our onetime worthless guide, who was terrified out of his wits that we should give him away.

While waiting for the return of the guide, the clouds broke and we found ourselves looking down on the plains of France. It then became obvious that the wretched man didn't possess a single clue or else he didn't wish to risk being caught by taking us to Barcelona. After searching for him, we realised he'd left us high and dry and had bolted with our only compass. Most of us had given our compasses away as souvenirs before leaving France. He must have been in a hell of a hurry because he left his suitcase behind, and it was immediately robbed of any food, which was precious little, and shared around.

The party was now reduced to seven, and we began to discuss our next move. From our position, the East coasts of France and Spain were not very far away and the Mediterranean could be easily seen; so it was decided to retrace our steps and strike due South with all speed, as we had no desire to spend the night in the mountains. A steady pace was maintained until we saw that three members were somewhat far behind. We waited for them and realised that Mario, who had fallen down the previous night, was having trouble with his leg and said it was impossible to keep up with us. We others, that is the French tank officer, Robert Smith, the RAF man who claimed to be anything from an AC2 to a squadron leader, and myself, were all for pressing on down the other side into Spain. The remaining three were content to stay with Mario at whatever speed he could do. The four of us decided to go on and the remainder were for staying the night in a nearby goat or sheep pen. The time was about 3.30 and, after readjusting our already meagre supply of food, we set off.

Soon after leaving, the going became very tough, it being necessary to climb to the highest point nearby to discover where we were and the best route for the descent into Spain. About 5 o'clock, the top was reached and after resting a little we began what was thought to be a comparatively easy downhill trip. It was exactly the opposite. The undergrowth was extremely thick and before reaching the plains our clothes were badly torn. A fairly large stream had been our objective and this we reached about 7 o'clock. We took our shoes and socks off to wash and cool our already sore and tired feet. Our intention was to walk through the night and hide during daylight hours. We struck a narrow lane with a good surface and walked along in pairs. About 7.30 we reached a small stream which could only be crossed by stepping-stones. The American, Robert Smith, was leading and was about half way across with us behind him when suddenly a voice yelled out something.

We discovered afterwards it was the Spanish for HALT, and a rifle went off. Smith immediately put up his hands and yelled back "Ingles, Americano". This had the desired effect and the firing ceased. There was a building on the opposite bank and from it emerged two ragged-looking soldiers with rifles. We were taken inside and they began to search us. The only lighting was from a couple of hurricane lamps, supplemented by the flames from a fire. They were a shocking example of Franco's soldiery; one was a corporal and very pro Franco, the other had lots of time for the Americans and British. Their method of searching was to hold out a hand and wait till something was put into it, with the obvious result that the incriminating souvenirs, such as identity cards, remained in our pockets. We explained that we were prisoners of war and as we were now in a neutral country, they should take us to the nearest British Consul, but the corporal was all for handing us over to the police. For the next hour and a half we tried bribing them to release us. Their terms were 1000 pesetas, equal to £20.

Between us, we didn't have the right amount. Smith had two English £5 notes and to this we added our French francs. They still insisted on 1000 pesetas. Our next offer was a watch apiece. I gladly gave mine, which was losing anything up to 2 hours a day. This appeared to satisfy them and about 9 o'clock we started to leave after the corporal had given us directions as to the right road. When we got outside, the other man came out and told us exactly the opposite, explaining that the corporal was very anti the allies.

The two soldiers were on Frontier guard attempting to stop refugees etc who were pouring into Spain with obviously little success. The first 25 miles into Spain was guarded like that and we discovered later that the civil police, known as the "Guardia Civile" patrolled all crossroads. We decided to take to the fields but got hopelessly lost and about 11 o'clock it began to rain with intermittent breaks. During one of these we lay down in a field. About a hundred yards back we had passed a concrete shelter about 4 feet square, used for storing tools like the French do. All vineyards in Spain possessed one or more. I must have been very soundly asleep and was lying on my back because when I woke up it was pouring with rain and I was entirely alone. I nearly lost my head, for the sudden thought of being entirely by myself in a foreign land thoroughly frightened me. I started shouting for the others wondering where on earth they'd got to when I remembered the store shed. I found them there still squeezed in so they'd only just left me apparently, shouting to me to wake up and at the same time saying where they were going. There was barely room for four and it meant taking turns on leaving one's legs outside to make room. We spent the remainder of the night like that and, just before dawn, set off again.

Unfortunately, while jumping a ditch, most of the food supply in my haversack fell out, but it wasn't noticed until sometime later on. Needless to say the rest of the party took a pretty dim view of me. Our intention of hiding during the day went by the board as we decided to keep to the fields and avoid all main roads. The town of Figueras was where we were making for, but we didn't intend to enter it as it was a garrison town from all reports. As the day wore on we got bolder and walked along the roads until a man on a bicycle came up to us. He said it was obvious we weren't Spanish and advised us to make for a clump of bamboo further along and he'd meet us there at 3.30 with some food. He appeared quite genuine and true to his word arrived on time. He said it was impossible to obtain bicycles but there was a chance of getting a taxi! But the snag was that all traffic was being stopped at the various controls along the roads. The taxi idea appealed to us immensely as already our feet were blistered. He also said that if we were likely to repeat our trip a supply of watches would be ideal for bribing.

Before leaving he gave us directions as to the best way of avoiding Figueras without too much of a detour. But without our compass, and our maps not being in detail, it wasn't till the next morning about 10 o'clock on the 15th that we chanced to hit upon the main road to Gerona. We must have spent the night walking in circles. Each of us had our own ideas as to the right direction with the result that half the time was spent in arguing. After making certain that this was the road to Gerona from people on the road itself, we moved off in pairs. Robert and I decided to walk together, and the A.C.2 with the French tank officer. The party had become much bolder and the pace was pretty fast, about 5 km per hour.

About midday, an incident took place which very nearly resulted in the other pair being locked up. They were about a ¼ of a mile behind us and a truck containing some soldiers, a sort of mobile patrol, passed us and stopped them. Their argument was they were Canadians. This satisfied the soldiers who drove on. Both Bob and I were wearing berets. These are worn as much here as in France but the tank officer had on a soft felt hat and the A.C.2 had nothing. This may have accounted for the fact that we looked like Spaniards and weren't stopped.

We had lunch following this incident under a bridge. After climbing back onto the road to resume our journey, a couple of Spaniards who had been working nearby came up to us and warned us that there was a patrol at the entrance to the town and one at the far end. The tank officer and the A.C.2 were all for walking straight through and taking a chance on it. Bob and I decided to take a detour saying we'd see them at the other end of the village. That was the last we ever saw of them. As far as we know they were caught and taken to the grim Miranda internment camp.

[Bromwell and 'Frost' were stopped by guards on the road to Barcelona on 16 December 1942. When they told their guards that they had neither money nor revolvers about their person they were allowed to proceed. They were stopped a second time further on and sent back to Figueras, where Bromwell, having been told by one of his party that it would go better for him if he said he were an officer, promptly promoted himself to captain. Though Frost's fate is unknown, he may have followed Bromwell to the prisons at Barcelona and Saragossa before enduring a spell at the Miranda concentration camp. 'Captain' Bromwell was sent to the officers' camp at Jaraba on 14 January 1943, being released from there on 24 April. On 10/11 May he was flown back to England.]

Our detour was only successful in that we spent a considerable time fording a river. We found a lane and before we reached it, found ourselves walking onto the very main road we were trying to avoid. We must have given the impression that we knew about the patrols, because several villagers gave us the thumbs up sign and, through various means, explained that the patrols had gone. We walked through the village but saw no sign of our companions.

Our legs began to give out around teatime. We estimated we had done around 20 miles that day. It was decided to try and get a lift. A lot of the transport had been taken over by the government but they were always marked in a certain way. It wasn't worth thumbing there as the drivers might be very pro Franco and therefore anti British. We stopped one dilapidated truck, which was not marked in any way, but the cabin already had four people in it. Anyway the driver rearranged the cabin and said he'd take us to Gerona. He could speak about three words of English and we about two in Spanish, but Bob had an English-Spanish book. The driver informed us that there was a representative of the British Consul residing in Gerona. When we heard that it seemed our troubles would soon be over, instead of just beginning. Owing to the road patrols he said it would be dangerous for us to come into the town so he'd drop us this side of the river, also suggesting that we swim across instead of keeping to the road.

The river was soon reached and after thanking him we set about finding a way across. We were extremely grateful for the lift, which must have saved about 10 miles of walking. The river was about 50 yards wide and looked very cold and deep. We walked along a lane by its bank trying to find a boat. We asked one old man how deep it was and he told us it was possible to wade most of the way across. It was decided to abandon the crossing and we started towards town. On the opposite side was a derelict tank that reminded us of the civil war. No guards were encountered on the outskirts of town. It was about 7 o'clock and getting dark so we decided to turn off the main road and try to find a haystack to sleep in. After a while a farm was reached and clustered around it were numerous stacks. Spanish haystacks are quite unlike our own, being conical in shape, smaller, and raised slightly off the ground, thereby making it possible to crawl underneath.

After selecting one hidden by several others, we crawled under it. Bob soon fell asleep and I lay awake for a while and eventually followed suit. About an hour later I awoke and thought I had been dreaming of being crushed. The realisation soon dawned on me that the stack was slowly toppling over. I grabbed Bob and both of us got clear as it crashed down. One consolation was it made no noise. Another was soon found and for the remainder of the night we were undisturbed.

We awoke a little before dawn and set out through the town. Few people were about and the street lamps were still lit. Following the main street for about a ¼ of a mile we came to a fork – the signpost said turn right for the main part of the town. Suddenly we saw a sentry box and a guard stopping and examining all forms of transport. We decided to wait until the next truck was stopped and while the guard spoke to the driver try and get past. As soon as one appeared we started to stroll casually past. This was done far more easily than had been anticipated. Having no idea how far it was into the town, we decided to " jump" the next truck. Bob showed me how to get on and off the American way without breaking my neck. The town was nearer than we thought so we jumped off the back of the truck and continued on foot.

At the back of our minds, we had an idea we would soon be riding to Barcelona in a taxi; so we made straight for a garage. They informed us such a thing was impossible, simply because there were no taxis to be had. At the rear of the place appeared to be looms and bales of wool, and girls and women began coming in to start work. Soon, our predicament and who we were became known. They gave us a little something to eat and directions of how to reach the representative of the British Consul. He lived in a hotel and about 9.30 we entered the building.

We spoke to the clerk behind the desk, mentioning the consular name and that we wished to see him. The clerk placed his hands on the side of his face and bent his head sideways, meaning the gentleman in question was asleep. We clenched our hands and rocked them backwards and forward meaning he was to wake him up. Before the clerk left, we wrote our names, rank and number on a piece of paper for him to take up. A minute or two later he appeared and beckoned us to follow him. On entering his room we beheld an oldish man with whitish hair hauling himself out of bed. We got the impression that this personage had had a fairly heavy night with a bottle or two. His only apparel was pyjama trousers. The remains of his breakfast lay on a tray. We explained who we were and our precarious position, also telling him we had walked nearly 150 miles in 4 days and 5 nights with practically nothing to eat, if one can call a piece of bread and a sardine a meal, and that we had not washed or shaved for 4/5 days. We said this having noticed a basin with hot and cold water taps. We had both run out of cigarettes after the second day and asked him for some. He was extremely reluctant to let us have any and produced 30 Woodbines for the pair of us. We explained our financial position, that we'd only French notes, which were quite useless in Spain. Again very reluctantly he let us have £1 each in pesetas. He said it was quite impossible to have a meal, but could tell us where to get one, at the expense of a Frenchman living in the town and that he didn't have time to do anything for us as he was responsible for 100 or so more people interned in a camp nearby.

Owing to the state of our health neither of us realised what sort of rogue we were dealing with. I might add his parting words before we left for our meal were that it was "98 kilometres to Barcelona", about 60-70 miles. If he treated the wretched internees the way he treated us, then God help them. We later discovered that all he had to do was to ring up the consulate at Barcelona and say that he'd received two cases of Scotch whisky or some important documents from the U.K., or anything of that nature, and in less than two hours a car would have picked us up. The road to Barcelona being of concrete surface and in first class condition, with a fast car it would have taken less than two hours.

We left the hotel without really realising what had happened, and being very hungry made our way to a cheap-looking hotel not far away. We saw the manager, who gave us a glorious steak and a bottle of wine. We asked about the possibility of obtaining bicycles, but without any luck. Our host gave us directions out of town and after thanking him we set off to Barcelona, with the last words of "our gallant English gentlemen" ringing in our ears as to the distance we had to cover. The time was about 10.30 and we hoped by Saturday night, the 18th, to be in Barcelona, it now being the 17th December.

We walked steadily all morning, only stopping once to tear my one and only handkerchief into strips to bind the blisters on my heels, which were now quite raw. The road was hot and dusty and by midday we were sweating freely. Once a large car bearing the official markings of the "Corps Diplomatique" approached going the opposite way. We nearly stopped it but as it got nearer we realised it was German! Another time some labourers shouted encouragement to us in French. It seemed obvious we were refugees of some description escaping from France, as in fact we were. On the whole the Spaniards were most helpful, always warning us of patrols farther ahead. About 2 o'clock, we decided to rest and if possible sleep.

A little off the road was wooded country into which we went. Both of us desired to relieve ourselves. As we had no paper, leaves had to suffice. After that, I had the worst agonising pains in the lower part of my anatomy due I suppose to the excessive walking with very little to eat, but after about 15 minutes they passed off. It was really too hot to sleep, so after about an hour we pressed on. We walked through the afternoon and just before dark decided to visit a farm and try to get something to eat. Only once during the afternoon did we manage to obtain water. A man in a signal box on a level crossing gave us some. I think we drank about ½ gallon each.

On approaching one farm, all the dogs came out barking furiously. The senora came out too and, after explaining what we wanted, all they could give us was about ½ pint of milk, quite hot, as it had been milked on the spot from the cow which, like the family, lived inside plus the odd horse etc. I am quite certain it was the milk that kept us going until 5 o'clock the next morning, at which time we fell by the wayside. The milk was supplemented every now and then by tiny pieces of dry bread. Believe me, when you're hungry even dry bread tastes good.

We continued through the night along the seemingly endless white road, stopping now and then to rest. By about 10 o'clock, it was terribly cold, and when we rested the cold made sleep utterly impossible. Several cars and trucks passed in the night but took no notice of us. About 3 o'clock in the morning we came to a bridge under reconstruction, which meant taking the left fork and making a detour. It now became necessary to rest about every mile. We passed through a small town but didn't see anyone. Soon after that we hit the coast road to Barcelona and could hear the sea. The coast railway ran alongside the road and we decided to ride the railroad in true hobo style. Accordingly we crossed to the embankment and waited for a train. A goods train came along but was travelling too fast. While waiting we ate our last scrap of bread. By this time we could only walk a few hundred yards before having to sit down. Around 4.30 we saw red lights ahead which meant a patrol was on duty, and came to the conclusion that the road leading over the bridge must join up with the one we were on at the red lights. It later turned out this was so and that was the last road block before Barcelona, about 58 kilometres away along the coast.

We decided to rest before attempting to pass the patrol, which appeared to be about 400 yards away. Leaving the road we lay down about 10 yards between two clumps of tallish scrub. It was bitterly cold and we just talked. About 5 o'clock two men walked past towards the patrol. No notice was taken of them and soon after we decided to move on. We started towards the patrol then suddenly out of the darkness two men passed. In passing, one of them said something. We answered "Si", which meant yes and, turning round, saw the two men had stopped. Both had on three-cornered hats and long black coats underneath which protruded their rifles. Before we knew what had happened we were all standing opposite each other and they were slowly getting their guns out. Under normal conditions, we would have hit them and run but Bob and I just looked at each other and said, "Well I guess we've had it." By this time they'd removed their guns from under their coats. The point is we were so exhausted that neither of us had the energy to do anything. We now realised that the first pair who had passed us were on their way to relieve the pair on duty at the crossroads.

They mentioned the word French so we shook our heads and said "Ingles". They motioned us to follow them and with one on either side we retraced our footsteps. I remembered my two identity cards and decided to destroy them, because for all intents and purposes I was French and could have been sent back to France. Mixed up with the identity cards were souvenir postcards of various places I had visited. It was impossible in the dark to sort them out so I pulled out as many cards as possible until I was certain the identity cards were amongst them and managed to pass half to Bob and while walking back tore them into little pieces and threw them by the side of the road. Bob was not so fortunate. He bent down on the pretence of doing up his shoe lace and dropped them on the ground. Luckily neither of the identity cards was amongst his lot, because one of the guards flashed a torch on him and found only torn up postcards. They took us back to the last town we had passed through, called Malgrat, and into the local police station.

We waited a few minutes in a room under guard, all the while cursing our luck. A little later the O.C. police station came in, a little man of middle age. The first thing we had to do was empty our pockets and remove our shoes and socks. Particulars were taken down of every article. When my poster was examined, it caused great consternation. About 2 hours later we were taken through the town to a block of offices. There were certain forms which had to be filled in. I think the reason we were taken there was because there was a man who spoke English fluently, having spent a long time in Chicago. By this time a lot of people were about and we must have looked a sorry sight. Leaving the offices our next stop was the local jail. God, what a place. Luckily we were the only inmates. Massive keys were produced to open a huge iron door, behind which was another wooden door. There were two articles of furniture which resembled beds; one was iron, the spring mattress of which had great holes in it. The other was wooden with a few boards. Both were covered in filthy-looking straw. The walls were covered in writing and, frankly, the place resembled a dungeon. The only window was a tiny hole a foot square right up near the roof overlooking the street. The solitary electric bulb was worked from outside.

Since our entry into the police station we had clamoured for something to eat. Soon after, a meal of bread, fish, bananas, oranges and some wine or other was brought in. In the early morning of December 18th we began our first stretch in prison. Later in the morning we both had a shave and a haircut. I might add that they knew we had £1 each in Spanish currency on us and when we left Malgrat all our meals etc came to £1. Pretty good accountancy, almost as good as RAF accounts. After lunch, the commandant, he really was a corporal, came to see us and allowed us upstairs on to the balcony overlooking the street, the outer door of the building, which we had to ourselves, being shut. This resulted in scores of people coming to view the prisoners. We were told that 3 weeks previously the prison held a German officer who had escaped from France. The corporal made us give our word not to escape.

One day a lad of 16 spoke to us in perfect English. He had lived in America most of his life and his father had only in later years moved to Spain. He managed to obtain about a pound of very good chocolate for us and any small things we wanted. We asked permission to walk around the town, so one evening the corporal came in and, as Bob was asleep, he and I strolled round the town sight-seeing. He was most insistent on pointing out buildings that had been damaged in the civil war and blamed the entire lot on the Russians. He also described how they had tortured him.

The days were very much the same until the evening of the 20th. We left Malgrat with two plain clothes policemen as escorts for Barcelona, to a place, they told us, which was much warmer, cleaner etc. How right they were. Barcelona was brilliantly lit of course, and reminded us of peacetime London. We went into a very official-looking building and after filling in certain forms were taken downstairs. Neither of us had any idea where we were or what was going to happen. We were soon enlightened in the first room we went into. It was the prison guard room, our belts, knives etc were removed and pigeon holed, and a few minutes later we found ourselves in a cell with about eight other people. The cells were 8 feet by 10 feet and about 15 feet high. The entire cell was of concrete with a solid concrete bench along two sides. A small skylight window was the only ventilation and through this it was possible to see a tiny portion of what appeared to be a street pavement. There were between 20-25 cells, the first two or three filled with women, including one who was the daughter of a republican (government) general. He had been captured by Franco's forces and his daughter imprisoned. Poor girl, she'd been here since the civil war had ended at least.

Regards our meals which we received twice a day, anyone who was not Spanish that is French, Belgium, and German etc were fed by the Red Cross, but if you were a Spaniard your family had to provide meals for you daily. If you had no relations at all you lived solely on what was given to us, which was a small loaf of bread and as much water as you liked daily. I for one have eaten the loaf of bread in about half a dozen mouthfuls. Usually your fellow countrymen shared the meals if you had no relations.

We had not been in the cell more than a few minutes when one of the meals appeared, and it was very welcome. Both of us ate bones and all of the fish we had. Our cell mates were various types, Spaniards (anti Franco), Belgian, French etc and were most helpful, lending us a coat or something to lie on and rolling the odd cigarette for us. After our meal we hammered on the grilled iron gate for the guard. There were about six of them, and we asked to be let out to go and get a drink at the end of the corridor. Quite naturally in passing each cell we looked to see who was there, especially for our last companions, but imagine our amazement when we saw our wretched guide peering through the bars. He lost no time in being let out so as to see us in the toilet. He appeared very agitated and kept on repeating "Fermez la bouche", which means shut your mouth or don't say anything. Apparently he had a horror of being exposed. It doesn't say a lot for him being caught in his own country especially being able to speak both French and Spanish and, secondly, it looked as if he had been caught before us. He was definitely a rogue of the first order, and I expect he's still in prison.

Despite our bed of concrete we slept quite well and around 8 o'clock next morning a Spanish girl came round selling café con leche (coffee with milk). We spent the morning getting to know the others and listening to each other's experiences. There was a Belgian lad in our cell who, owing to his age, he was 17, should not have been in prison at all. He spent 40 days in prison before being set free, and that afternoon he was on his way to the Belgian Consulate. We gave him a note with our particulars on it and asked that he tell his ambassador to get in touch with our consul as soon as possible. The results were very heartening because next morning our names were called out and we were taken upstairs to see the consul who had come round on receiving our note. He had been notified that our party had left France but he had no news of our companions and told us that the other party, which included my navigator, Ray, had arrived by train in Barcelona as planned. We naturally informed him of the conduct of our gallant English gentleman in Gerona and he was simply furious. Sir Samuel Hoare, the British Ambassador to Spain, was informed, and we heard later that he got the sack almost immediately. The consul also told us that the dark-haired beauty who came round the cells with the coffee etc was working for the British, and she was the one to give notes to etc.

An amazing thing happened when our names were called out by the guards. Apparently, when this is done, the second name given is always used. It makes no difference how many Christian names one may have, so they always called my second Christian name out, being Beausire, and as none of the guards could speak English the result was practically unintelligible. Bob normally put himself as Robert E. Smith so the Spanish pronunciation was the result and it sounded pretty odd.

The next day two parcels arrived for us from the consul, containing cigarettes, chocolate, a pair of pyjamas, a towel and shaving outfit. The cigarettes and chocolate were most welcome but the pyjamas were somewhat incongruous, and it seemed a shame to soil them by wearing them as we hadn't had a bath for five weeks. It looked as if we would spend Christmas in prison and tried to make the best of it. On Christmas Eve we both wandered down the corridor to stretch our legs and on returning to the cell door got talking to one of the guards and a woman from one of the cells. The guards made no attempt to send us back to the cell. We wandered around talking to various other people. In one cell was a solitary man. He apparently had just arrived and was wrapped in a blanket as he possessed no clothes. From our conversation with the guard we got the impression he was English but, for some unknown reason, he refused to say a word. During the night what little hilarity there was seemed to increase, most of the guards having had something to drink, and very early in the morning screams and hysterical laughter seemed to come from the women's section. Most of the women had been arrested for not being in possession of the necessary pass for the trade in which they were engaged. The guards used to let them go after a few days on payment of a certain sum. Those not so well off normally remained for 5 weeks.

On Christmas Day we received a very pleasant (Christmas) present. About 9.30 in the morning our names were called and we were told to pack. It was certainly a surprise and we thought that the consul had acted very quickly. Before leaving we gave all our chocolate and most of our cigarettes away to those that were left behind. It wouldn't surprise me if some of them are still there, as the majority of them were anti Franco and, while he remains in power, there they stay. They told us that when the civil war ended the prisons held 2,000,000 people, and even in 1942 there were still 1,000,000 locked up. Their theory was that the war would end where it began in Spain.

After picking up our belts etc from the guard room, we went to a sort of reception room, and after a few minutes a captain of the Spanish Air Force came up to us. He told us we were going to Saragossa, about 300 kilometres away. The whole business seemed very mysterious and we wondered whether the consul had a hand in it, but it was later realised that the Spanish Air Force authorities had been responsible for our release, because on arrival at Saragossa I phoned the consul at Barcelona and he was under the impression we were still in prison, so obviously the Spaniards had told the army people that Air Force personnel must be looked after by the Air Force. It was very sporting of them.

Outside the prison was a Ford V.8 with a driver at the wheel. The captain got in beside him and Bob and I in the back. Driving through Barcelona we saw it for the first time in daylight. Leaving the city behind us we drove in a north-westerly direction till lunchtime. Luckily the captain spoke a little French so the drive wasn't a silent one. About 1 o'clock we stopped at a small town and went to a hotel. We ate a magnificent meal consisting of roast beef and salads, then chicken and various salads, biscuit and cheese etc. My stomach was not very strong and I only just managed to keep it all down.

We reached Saragossa about 1 o'clock that evening, it being quite dark, and went straight to the H.Q. of the Air Force Unit or Group for that area. A Spanish Air Force major, or commandant, with the help of an interpreter called Luis san Pio, a lawyer who had spent many years in London and spoke English fluently, interviewed us. From the conversation we learnt we were virtually on parole and would live in a hotel at the expense of the Air Force. About an hour later we were taken to the hotel. After signing the register the commandant escorted us to our room. It was good to see a bed with clean sheets again. He left us saying good night and asked us to call at H.Q. next morning. Bob and I had a quick wash but I decided my stomach could wait a little longer while I had a bath. After my bath I saw that my skin peeled off in several places partly through not having a bath for weeks and the lack of vitamins, I suppose.

We then went downstairs for dinner. Everyone gave us one or more looks, owing I think to the state of our clothes. We had a good dinner washed down with a bottle of wine. Usually we had one or two bottles of wine for lunch and dinner and then it came to paying the bill at the end of the week. They informed us that, though the Air Force were paying our bill, it didn't include our liquor bill or such things like baths and laundry, which were extra. From then on our drinking was seriously impeded. We slept like babes that night and next morning I phoned the consul at Barcelona. He was amazed to hear we were out of prison and were in Saragossa. I told him we had no money and no clothes. He said he would telegraph us 500 pesetas immediately and advised us to buy warm clothes and overcoats. The money arrived before lunch, so after the meal Bob and I went shopping. We divided the money, which was equal to £25 each, the pound being worth 50 pesetas then.

We returned to the hotel before tea and the clerk behind the desk smiled wistfully at us. Both of us had on new clothes and looked totally different from when we arrived. We went round to H.Q. the next morning and saw the commandant. There was no interpreter there this time. The commandant spoke the most unintelligible French and after half an hour we gathered we were going to the camp for interned airmen north of Saragossa. The men lived in a hotel taken over especially for them. In peacetime it was a famous hot springs resort. The senior officer there at the time was S/Ldr Wyatt, who had crash landed a Stirling near Barcelona as he was unable to recross the Alps after attacking a target in Italy owing to engine trouble.

[Squadron Leader M. Wyatt DFC and his seven crew were on their way in Stirling BK595, 15 Squadron, to bomb Turin, north Italy, on the night of 20/21 November 1942 when an engine failed as they were nearing the Alps. They nevertheless pressed on to the target and bombed it, but when it was reckoned that they would not get back to base (Bourn, Cambridgeshire) the decision was taken to head west to Spain. Just after midnight on 21 November they came down on the coast a few kilometres south of Palamós (and several north of Barcelona), and all eight were interned by the Spanish.

It seems that Donald's memory may be a little at fault with regard to where and when he met Wyatt and crew. Donald and Bob Smith had arrived in Saragossa on 25 December, and stayed there until they were taken, on 3 January 1943, to the spa town of Alhama de Aragón, just over 100 kilometres south-west of Saragossa. It was here that they met Squadron Leader Wyatt and crew, staying the night at the hotel Balneario Termas Pallarés, the one customarily used by the hospitable Spanish Air Force for Allied evaders and escapers on their way to Madrid.

Soon after lunch on 4 January 1943, the RAF party, some nineteen strong, left for Madrid in what Donald called the 'Embassy ambulance'. They arrived in the Spanish capital, after a journey of just over 200 kilometres, later that evening.]

A little later our friend the interpreter came in and told us that the commandant wished us to answer several technical questions relating to aviation, merely a formality, to substantiate our statements that we were really RAF pilots. A few questions were asked and we both passed alright. It was near lunchtime when we left and the commandant left the building with us. He was a very pleasant man, being most helpful all the time, always extremely courteous, this last we noticed when he left us on the street corner by saluting us.

On New Year's Eve Bob and I decided to go out and see the New Year in. We went across the road to a large restaurant cafe and sampled the Spanish beer. Upstairs a band was in full swing and a cabaret in progress. A Spanish dancing girl was whirling round the floor with castanets. As midnight drew near we wondered what was going to happen. Just before the hour the band stopped and everybody stood up. The band started as the clocks chimed out the end of the year and at the same time everybody's right hand shot out and remained in the Franco salute style until the music stopped. Luckily both of us were standing at the back of the room against the wall. We looked at each other and shook our heads, having no intention of saluting Franco. Weren't we fighting against fascism?

Incidentally, Bob and I nearly had a disastrous fight that night because, during the evening, we naturally got to talking about the war, and during one conversation I repeated the words of Churchill who said "Give us the tools and we'll do the job." I think Bob thought I meant that America should keep out of the war altogether. Anyway, he insisted on a fight when we got back to the hotel. The fight didn't last very long, and that night I demanded another room which I got. I believe the hotel people thought that the allies had split.

[Another version of this fight was that Donald had lost control of himself, and threatened to kill Bob Smith for no apparent reason. And it was Bob Smith who had to calm down the angry squadron leader. Donald again became uncontrollable, so it is told, when the two later got to Madrid where their host, a British chemical company representative called Bob Gilliland (see below), had to summon someone from the British Embassy. Donald was apparently taken away by an air vice-marshal, and Bob Smith never saw him again.[2]]

One curious thing attracted our attention one day. There was always a man sitting in the hotel hall. We thought he might be a detective looking after us, so decided to find out. We both left the hotel and turned back after a few yards. Sure enough he was on his way out. After making certain he was obviously keeping an eye on us, we both one day separated at a corner as arranged. Poor man, he must have been in a state of flux. One night we went out and after making certain he was on the job went back and asked him to come for a drink. Strangely enough he accepted and we had a glorious night, not getting to bed before 3 or 4 in the morning.

One morning we realised we had run out of money, so I phoned the consul and told him, explaining the liquor and bath situation which we had not been told about. I think he was rather annoyed with us, but let us have another 1,500 pesetas. A day or two later the commandant came round about 8 o'clock one morning and told us we were moving to the internment camp, also saying the two of us and some others already there would be released and be taken to the British Embassy in Madrid. He said a car would be arranged and our escort would be a captain. Before he went I begged him to let me have back my poster which had been confiscated among other souvenirs by the prison authorities. He said he would try his best and, I am grateful to say, he kept his word. We said goodbye and thanked him for all he had done for us. A few minutes later an official car arrived and we climbed in and set off for the camp.

We arrived in time for lunch and met the air attaché there. What we had been told about going to Madrid was true, and after lunch nineteen of us squeezed into an Embassy ambulance and left for Madrid. The reason I believe for that type of transportation was that ambulances were not likely to be stopped. We arrived at the Embassy about 9 o'clock that night, and arrangements were made with members of the British colony to put us up. Bob and I went to stay with a Mr Gilliland.[3] He had a lovely flat and a spare one next door. We had a couple of Sherries before dinner and sat down to a grand meal. Meal times in Spain are a little different from ours, especially dinner in the evening. One usually eats around 9 or 10 at night and then thinks about going out for the evening or rather for the rest of the night. I think the journey or excitement of everything must have upset my stomach once more because, about half way through, I felt very ill and looked quite green. I felt very embarrassed, but our host was extremely understanding and good about it all. I gave up the meal and lay down for half an hour or so, after which I felt much better.

Bob and I had a room in the spare flat and we turned in fairly early. Mr Gilliland's servant was a tiny Spanish girl who was called Modesta. She had instructions to bring in breakfast in bed every morning at 12 o'clock, which consisted of two boiled eggs and coffee. When one has dinner at 9 or 10 at night, then goes out for the evening, breakfast at midday was very much appreciated.

During the nine days we were in Madrid we went to numerous parties. I recommend the Spanish Sherry, but after nine days it began to tell on us. One evening, with Mr Gilliland's approval as he was dining out, Bob invited an American naval pilot to dinner. He had been shot down from a carrier and had been wandering around Madrid for 6 weeks. By the time dinner was over we were all pretty tight and during the conversation our guest's words became more and more slurred. He mentioned a girl's name I thought I knew and, as he was practically beyond speech, I got him to write it down. Next day I went round to the Embassy and asked the Air Attaché whether there was a Mrs Shillitoe working there. He said there was, so I asked if I could see her in his office. He gave me a queer look but agreed. Sure enough, in she walked. I knew her in London exactly a year ago and I never expected to see her again. The world is certainly a small place. Needless to say we went out to the nearest bar to have a drink.

The British Colony in Madrid never failed to entertain us and we had the most terrific parties, one of the last being given by the Air Attaché. The Chief of Staff of the Spanish Air Force, Vinber, was the chief guest with his wife and aides. Sir Samuel and Lady Maud Hoare were also there. During the evening two bouquets of flowers were to be presented to Lady Maud and the Chief of Staff's wife, this last to be done by S/Ldr Wyatt and I had to attend to Lady Maud. The Chief of Staff had been given one of the highest German decorations just previously, but this evening it was missing from his chest.

Soon after the party began the Air Attaché formed us into a semi-circle and introduced the Chief of Staff to each of us. My navigator had noticed in an old copy of an aviation magazine that I had been awarded the D.F.C. a few days after being shot down. The Air Attaché told the Chief of Staff, who congratulated me in English. As regards the bouquet of flowers, roses I believe, I was in a somewhat jittery state, partly due to the night before. The presentation was to take place very early on in the evening, which barely gave one time to have a few much needed cocktails. When it did take place I'm quite certain that, despite the fact I only had to walk a few yards, several petals flew off owing to the instability of my hands. After my short speech, Lady Maud murmured her thanks. The Air Attaché then came up and offered to release her of her cumbersome burden, but she wouldn't hear of it, and when I last saw her she was still clutching them.

One of the best parties given (it certainly equalled an RAF mess on a party night for the amount of liquor consumed) was given by the American Telephone Company. It was due to start around 7 in the evening. No sooner had one entered the room when a waiter pushed a tray under your nose, and if one of them saw your glass so much as half empty, he was after you in a flash. This continued throughout the night, and when we left at 7 the next morning some diehards were still at it. It would have been a remarkable thing if anyone had managed to get through to New York by transatlantic phone the next day. Bob's father was connected with the A. T. Coy and of course he had no trouble in getting through to him the day before the party.

Each block of flats in Madrid was guarded by a man known as a "Serrano", who was really a day and night watchman. He had the keys to all the outside doors, and once you left the flat it was impossible to gain admission without him. When returning from various parties, everybody used to stand outside and yell "Serrano" until he came. In the early hours of the morning it often took up to half an hour to get in after finding him asleep in some dark doorway!

Mr Gilliland took us to one quiet party, and it was there that we met for the first time what I suppose would be the Spanish nobility. These particular people were very charming and very pro British. One interesting incident occurred as midnight struck – everybody stood up and drank a toast which was "To all those flying over Germany tonight, a safe return." Apparently this was done every night by a lot if not all of the British people in Madrid including many Spaniards. I must admit it was very touching. On the other hand, I wish they'd said it a little louder the last night I was up.

On the morning of January 14th [his MI9 report says 15th] we all left Madrid by an embassy bus for Gibraltar. Robert Taylor and one of the secretaries (male) took it in turns to drive. After travelling all day we arrived at Seville and spent the night at the Majestic Hotel. Next morning we set out on our last lap to Gibraltar.[4] On the way down in the morning we stopped in a place called Jerez, where of course the famous Humbert and Woof sherry is brewed.[5] This particular place boasted a British Consul and he also ran the sherry factory. We were all invited inside and from a barrel about 10 feet up on a platform, the consul poured sherry from a tiny cup with a very long handle into our waiting glasses below and never spilt once. He told us that such famous people as King Edward VII and the Queen of Spain etc had drunk out of the same barrel. The names of these personalities were on a brass plate on the barrel. Before we left he gave us each a half-size bottle to bring home.

We rolled on through Southern Spain, the country being far prettier and greener than the mountainous north. On one occasion we passed a herd of the famous bulls used by the bull fighters. They were young bulls, not ready for the ring yet, and looked magnificent creatures. We arrived at Algeciras in the afternoon and waited for the necessary formalities to be got over. We were, I believe, described as members of the Embassy staff. When we drove over the frontier into Gibraltar a great cheer went up from us all. After being medically examined we went off to the officers' and sergeants' messes. As usual no warning had been given to anyone concerning our arrival and some difficulty was encountered in obtaining a meal.

We had been allowed to write letters whilst at Saragossa, and I had written one to England and one to my brother in Gibraltar. In the one to my brother I had mentioned I was carrying a 4000lb bomb on the raid. I also mentioned the follies of mountaineering without the proper equipment. Apparently a dim view of these remarks was taken by the Intelligence Staff and I was informed so. What infuriated me was that I was told I would not be able to see my brother. As it happened, a few hours before we sailed for the U.K. he came on board to see me. It transpired that although the RAF still refused permission for us to see each other, the Army, which he was in, had heard about it and had given him a car and a driver. He drove round Gibraltar until he discovered I was on board the "Ville D'Oran" in the harbour. Then the navy produced a launch and crew and so, despite the RAF, I saw my brother who, by the way, was a lance corporal, I hadn't seen for at least 2 years.

We spent about a week at Gibraltar and during that time made several attempts to get passage home by air. The authorities said we would have to sail, but we obtained permission from the station commander to fly if there was room, so on several evenings we packed our bags and went down to the airstrip and waited, but without any luck.

It took a week to reach Scotland. Our convoy consisted of fourteen ships, six were liners. The "Ville D'Oran" had been lying in Oran harbour since 1940 and she had not been de-gaussed against mines. It was impossible to get more than 14 knots out of her. Her bottom was, according to the crew, covered in barnacles, so, being the slowest ship, she was at the back of the convoy.[6]

At that time all troopships were dry, but we managed to obtain the odd bottle or two before sailing. We arrived in [Gourock] Scotland on the 27th [*sic* – the 26th] January and left for London the same night. Very strict security measures had been taken over us, and not only was a carriage reserved for us but we were locked in. On arrival in London we went to the Charing Cross Hotel.

[Though, curiously, Donald makes no reference to his navigator being with him aboard the *Ville d'Oran* for the voyage to Scotland, it was usual for all RAF evaders returning from Gibraltar to travel aboard the same ship.]

CHAPTER 5

THE FILLERIN FAMILY –
THE PAT/PAO LINE – THE CREW

The Fillerin family

During the Second World War many Allied aircrew – Donald Barnard, Ray Glensor, and Ralph Forster among them – were given help when they most needed it by hundreds of brave families living in occupied Europe under the yoke of their evil oppressor. One such family lived in the village of Renty, in the Pas-de-Calais department of northern France – Norbert and Marguerite Fillerin, and their three children, Geneviève, Monique, and Gabriel.

Norbert was born on 17 June 1897 at Enghien-les-Bains in the northern suburbs of Paris, the son of Louis and Jeanne (née Martel). Old enough to fight in the First World War, he saw action at the beginning of 1916 with the French 8th Infantry Regiment, before transferring to the 208th Infantry Regiment. He was taken prisoner in April 1917 at Chemin des Dames, during the Second Battle of the Aisne, and thereafter tried unsuccessfully to escape on two occasions.

At some point he learnt to speak Hochdeutsch (literally 'High German'), which suggested to anyone hearing it spoken that the speaker was an educated person, and therefore of some standing and to be respected. This linguistic ability was to stand Norbert in good stead in the grim years ahead when his country was occupied by the German Army.

On 15 February 1925, Norbert married Marguerite Cadet (born at Renty on 26 June 1897), and Geneviève, Monique, and Gabriel were born on 15 February 1926, 19 April 1927, and 8 August 1928 respectively.

When war came anew in 1939, Norbert's services were not required by his country, being considered, at the age of 42, to be too old. But, fiercely patriotic and an ardent Anglophile, his time would come when the Germans invaded France in May and June 1940. The family house in Renty had already played a small part in the First World War when it was used as a British Army officers' mess, but his first act of defiance, after Renty had been quickly occupied in force by soldiers of the Wehrmacht's 1st (Mountain) Division, was to help a number of French soldiers to escape.

The die was cast, and Norbert and others, especially his friend and local farmer Vincent Ansel, were determined to do what they could for any other deserving cases. In midsummer of 1940 two British soldiers who had been left behind after the retreat of the British Expeditionary Force had arrived in the area and were being sheltered by Vincent Ansel. Norbert helped Gunners S. J. Hall and E. F.

Norbert Fillerin with his daughters, Monique and Geneviève, and his son, Gabriel, 1942.

The extended Fillerin family at Renty.

Smeed, Royal Artillery, on their way back to England at the end of the year. They went to Paris, where Norbert sought help from an old friend from Renty, Ulysse Debas, at his Café Ulysse. Norbert's intention was to get further assistance from the American Consulate in Lyon, but instead he met a British agent there who suggested that he, Norbert, might like to become a contact for them in the north of France. The agent also gave Norbert the address in Marseille of a certain Revd Donald Caskie, who was running the Seamen's Mission, but which in reality, as everyone knew, was a sort of clearing house for stray Allied personnel trying to get back to Britain.

By June 1940, Norbert Fillerin had formed a local network ('réseau') of trusted friends in villages near Renty, such as Fauquembergues, Matringhem, Verchocq, and Wicquinghem. In due course an alliance was formed with a similar group, the réseau Didry, based on St Omer some 20 kilometres to the north-east. Named after its chief, Désiré Didry, it was undoubtedly one of the earliest French Resistance groups, having been formed in May 1940. There were other, small groups around but, so far as the Barnard crew and other early visitors were concerned, the réseaux Didry and Fillerin were the key ones.

For the Didry and Fillerin groups, there was at first little 'trade' in Allied aircrew, with the Battle of Britain being fought across the English Channel and RAF Bomber Command making only pinprick raids on Germany. Apart from Hall and Smeed, it wasn't until March 1941 that Norbert took another British person[1] by train to Marseille in unoccupied France, 1,000 kilometres (625 miles) or so to the south.

Norbert's journey was not speculative for, as previously seen, he had already established contact with a group in Marseille that was run by British officers. Rather than try to get home themselves, these officers had remained in Marseille doing what they could to help other British servicemen who had escaped from occupied France get back to England. That they were able to do so was largely thanks to the tolerant attitude of the French police in Marseille and to the financial assistance that came from generous local residents and from the British government via the American Consulate in Marseille. Without the large sums of money they could not have paid for such necessities as railway tickets, food, and official (or fake) passes for leaving the country. Travelling long distances, either from the Pas-de-Calais to Marseille or from Marseille to the Pyrenees (another 370 kilometres [230 miles] or so), was an expensive business, and well beyond the pocket of men such as Norbert Fillerin and Désiré Didry, whose financial burden was eased by the British in the south.

With sufficient funds, therefore, and with an organisation that was growing stronger each passing month, all went well for the Didry and Fillerin groups for over a year. Several RAF airmen shot down in the Pas-de-Calais were successfully sent home via Marseille, including, in 1941, fighter pilot Flight Lieutenant F. W. 'Taffy' Higginson and two wounded pilots, Sergeant W. G. Lockhart, and Pilot Officer A. E. J. G. Nitelet, a Belgian in the RAF.

Guy Lockhart came down at Aix-en-Ergny, half a dozen kilometres west of

Renty, on 6 July 1941, and was quickly found by Michel Péroy. With the assistance of a young girl, Guy was spirited away from the searching Germans to Monsieur Ansel's house in Renty, and then to the Fillerins, where he was treated by Dr Delpierre from Fauquembergues. Lockhart stayed almost three weeks in Renty, most of the time lying flat on his stomach with a bullet near the base of his spine. He had recovered sufficiently to help retrieve a new type of gyroscope from a crashed German aircraft, which found its way back to England, as did Lockhart, who left Renty at the beginning of August 1941.[2]

Alex Nitelet's aircraft, shot down on 9 August, overturned on landing, and Alex suffered severe head injuries, including the loss of his right eye.[3] He was rescued from the wreckage by farmer Louis Salmon, who took him to Vincent Ansel. He was then taken in by the Fillerin family for two months while his wounds were treated by doctors Delpierre and Houzel, from Boulogne.

There is a rotten apple in every barrel, and the Didry group was to suffer a severe blow on 8 December 1941 when, as a result of the treachery of a British Army thief and deserter, Sergeant Harold 'Paul' Cole, Désiré Didry himself and Alfred Lanselle, another key member of the réseau Didry, were arrested by the Abwehr at St Omer station.[4] On that same day, in a co-ordinated drive against the resisters, Didry's wife and daughter were also arrested. Others, too, in the area were caught, and after eight months in Loos prison Désiré and half a dozen fellow resisters, also betrayed by Cole, were deported to Germany. On 16 April 1943, Didry was executed.

Norbert Fillerin, untouched by these awful events, continued to provide help to Allied evaders and escapers. He was lucky – for now. Some aircrew, however, who also came down in the Pas-de-Calais were not always so lucky. On 17 June 1941, Czech fighter-pilot Flight Lieutenant Josef Bryks, 242 Squadron RAF, was shot down and hidden by villagers in Serny. Apparently denounced by a Polish worker, he was captured on the following day. A similar fate befell the legendary Wing Commander Douglas Bader DSO, DFC, who, wounded when brought down in August 1941, was being clandestinely treated in St Omer hospital but was given away by a civilian under questioning.

Barely five months after Donald, Ray Glensor, and Ralph Forster had gone in October 1942, Norbert was arrested. He was in Paris in March 1943 with Jean de la Olla and Alex Wattebled, both of whom also worked as *convoyeurs* for the Marseille escape line, which had now become known as the PAT or PAO line after its chief Pat O'Leary. Jean de la Olla, who was one of those to escort Donald and Ray to Marseille, had been put in charge of the northern end of the PAT line in January 1942 after Cole's treachery had been exposed the previous month. Alex Wattebled was Pat O'Leary's right-hand man. He, Jean and Norbert were horribly tortured by the Gestapo but, extraordinarily, all three were to survive the war, though in varying degrees of bad health. Jean de la Olla was left with one lung, and two fingers missing from his left hand. Alex Wattebled suffered, but recovered from, a severe breakdown. Norbert survived his torture in the rue des Saussaies,

The Fillerin family at Renty. Sergeant Forster is standing between the sisters, and on the far left is Madam Marguerite Fillerin with an unknown local resistance member.

the Paris Gestapo HQ, and final imprisonment in Hradisko, in Czechoslovakia, where he was liberated by partisans on 8 May 1945, but returned to France a shadow of his former self.

Following Norbert's arrest in March 1943, Marguerite and her three children continued as best they could to help evading airmen, but were uncertain of how to move them on down the line. A solution was found in September 1943 when two men, supposedly of the réseau Bordeaux-Loupiac, intervened and three convoys of evaders were successfully completed by the end of the year. The two men were the highly unlikely combination of Sergeant Bob Merlin, RAF, shot down on 16 August 1943, and Joe Becker, a naturalised German, who worked for the Germans under the cover of Staubach Transport Enterprise. Their theatre of operations was Frévent, Arras, and Paris. Whether or not Marguerite knew anything of these two is a moot point, for Merlin makes no mention of her, or of Renty, in his long MI9 report.[5]

At this time, with the Resistance growing, the Renty-Fauquembergues group, now affiliated to the long-standing OCM (Organisation Civile et Militaire), maintained contact with the Havet group in Lumbres, and with Raymond Boulet in Verchin. But on 30 December 1943, the Lumbres group was infiltrated by an agent, believed to be called Streift, from the Abwehr's department IIIF in Lille. Arrests followed swiftly, and on 8 January 1944 Marguerite Fillerin's turn came. Taken to Arras and placed before a tribunal, she was condemned to death. From there she was taken to Loos and then to Germany. Happily the death sentence was never carried out and she was liberated by the Americans on 11 April 1945. She was officially credited with assisting another nine airmen from March 1943 until her arrest.

With their father and now their mother arrested, the three children, nothing daunted, did what they could when they could but, with the various organisations around them having been decimated by the arrests, it was never easy. One immediate problem following their mother's arrest was what to do with Flight Lieutenant R. G. Crosby, RCAF, who had been shot down on 3 January 1944 and who was staying with the Fillerins when Marguerite was arrested.[6] With Monique's help he escaped from the house and was taken to Paris, where he joined up with another evader, Flight Lieutenant D. Goldberg, RCAF. The pair of them reached Spain in time, and were flown back to England on the night of 5/6 May 1944.

With occasional help from their grandmother (Cadet), the children did what they could, including looking after three more Canadians, shot down in their Halifax whilst attacking Arras on 12 June 1944, who remained in Renty until they were liberated in September.

Norbert died in 1977, by which time he was blind; his wife Marguerite died in 1980 and then, only a few months after her mother, Geneviève also passed on.

* * *

The PAT/PAO line

The 'big white chief' whom Donald and Ralph met (see page 85) was Albert-Marie Guérisse, a Belgian Army doctor, better known by his *nom de guerre* of Pat O'Leary or simply as 'Joseph'. Stranded in France in April 1941 after landing two agents on its southern coast, he was arrested by the Vichy French. Interned with many British soldiers, sailors, and airmen at Nîmes, he discovered that the officers among them were in contact with a number of British officers in Marseille, led by Captain Ian Garrow, who were running an escape line to Spain. A determined man, Pat O'Leary easily escaped from prison in June 1941 and went to Marseille. The authorities in England allowed him to remain there to assist with the ongoing escapes. When Captain Garrow was himself arrested in October 1941, it was upon the broad shoulders of Pat O'Leary that the mantle of leadership fell.

He inherited a working organisation with helpers based, as already seen, in the north of France, in Paris, and at several points along the escape line to Marseille, for example in the Dijon area. One of this army of helpers was Louis Nouveau, the owner of the large apartment at 28A, Quai Rive Neuve that overlooked Marseille's Vieux Port. He and his wife Renée kept an 'open house' for evaders and escapers. Ray Glensor, who was to stay there briefly with Donald and Ralph, provides a snapshot of the accommodation:

> When we had leisure to examine the flat in the light of day and with the curtains drawn, we were able to appreciate its grace and charm. It … had a commanding outlook over the Vieux Port and the old quarter of the city of Marseilles on the opposite side of the water, while to our left we could see the weird overhead ferry … Beyond the ferry we could see the old fort guarding the entrance to the harbour, and opposite it the solid structure of one of Napoleon's palaces.
>
> The lounge in which we spent most of our time was really two rooms knocked into one. The front one had windows round the sides which gave the wonderful view and allowed the entry of unlimited sunlight. The third side of the room had been knocked out, while the fourth side had bookshelves built in from floor to ceiling and was packed with a mass of beautifully bound classics jostling with paper-jacketed current works …
>
> The second room … was slightly larger and had a fireplace and lounge suite on one side while, tucked in the other corner, was the table with its chairs tucked neatly underneath. The only other noteworthy piece of furniture was a large all wave radio which was turned on avidly at six o'clock each evening for the news from London … There were only three or four pictures in the room, all of them oil paintings and all bearing the initials "L.N.".[7]

The book in which Louis Nouveau used to write the names of his 'guests' was 'Volume 44 of the Complete Edition of Voltaire's works, in 70 volumes, published by E. A. Lequien, Paris, in 1823'. The names of many of those who were to stay with Louis and Renée are listed in the book *Safe Houses Are Dangerous*,[8] with Donald, Ray Glensor, Ralph Forster, and the Americans William Gise and Erwin Wissenback being visitor numbers 148-152 respectively.

As for Gise and Wissenback, having joined a small group of evaders and escapers, they were taken by their guide to Perpignan on 25 January 1943, where they met up with Pat O'Leary and Captain Ian Garrow. Also in the party were a young Frenchman and a Belgian major, who were unknown to O'Leary and who had been added to the party by the guide, and the one-eyed Belgian erstwhile airman Alex Nitelet who, following his evasion in 1941, had returned to France by Lysander aircraft on 28 May 1942 as a wireless operator to fill the urgent need of the PAT line. He made his way to Marseille with his set and transmitted from there and from Nîmes over the coming months. Another of his roles was to act as courier for the PAT line. But he was arrested by Vichy French police in ridiculous circumstances on 1 September 1942 whilst attending a supply drop by an RAF Halifax near Nîmes. The noisy aircraft circled the drop zone three times, and woke up everybody. Interned at Camp de Chambaran, Nitelet was released by an understanding camp commandant, Colonel Malraison, along with several other

SOE agents and 'British' officers, on 27 November. Fast-tracked once in Spain, he was flown back from Gibraltar on 7 February.[9]

Meanwhile, back in France, they all caught the train to Banyuls, where Pat O'Leary left them. Though it was around 8.30 p.m. when they arrived there, the guide immediately led them off through the Albères hills and across the frontier into Spain. After walking a fair distance, Garrow sent a guide to Barcelona with a letter for the British Consul explaining their situation. The guide returned with the message that only the two British and one of the Americans were to be picked up later that day. Wissenback and Gise rolled dice for the seat, and Wissenback won. At about 4 p.m. Garrow, Nitelet, and Wissenback were driven away by the Vice-Consul, Mr Dorchy, to Barcelona. The others followed next day.

Gise was arrested by the Guardia Civile on 30 January, but was released from prison in Gerona after consular intervention had had his status changed from 'civilian' to 'military'. He was in Madrid on 7 February and, a fortnight later, at Gibraltar. Both he and Wissenback would successfully return to England, Wissenback on 20 February 1943 and Gise on 5 March 1943, though Gise was fortunate to do so. He had hitched a ride back from Gibraltar in a B-24 Liberator, which was attacked by German aircraft whilst crossing the Bay of Biscay, before landing at RAF St Eval at 3 p.m. after a 7½-hour flight.

As for Louis Nouveau in Marseille, he was forced to move to Paris not long after Donald Barnard and Ralph Forster had stayed there, but was arrested later in November 1942, having been betrayed by Roger le Neveu, an abominable Frenchman who also went by the alias Roger le Légionnaire.[10] Deported to Buchenwald concentration camp, Louis survived the war, and was to receive the George Medal from a grateful British government. His wife Renée also survived the war and was appointed MBE.

Another husband and wife pair of stalwarts for the PAT/PAO line were Dr Georges Rodocanachi and his wife Fanny (née Vlasto), who lived at 21, rue Roux de Brignoles, Marseille. Georges was born a British subject in Liverpool in February 1876, though of Greek parents, and qualified as a doctor in 1903. As a loyal British subject, he tried to join the Royal Army Medical Corps in the First World War but was refused permission. Renouncing his British citizenship he became a naturalised Frenchman. One of his tasks in Marseille in 1940-41 was to sit on Mixed Medical Boards, a repatriation scheme for sick prisoners that was organised under the terms of the Geneva Convention. Needless to say, a few borderline cases were given the good news that they were 'fit' for repatriation!

Georges's luck ran out on 26 February 1943, and he was arrested. Eventually, on 17 January 1944, he was sent to Buchenwald concentration camp in Germany, where he died on 10 February 1944. His wife survived the war and moved to London, where she died in her 75th year.

Shortly before Norbert Fillerin and the others were arrested in Paris, Pat O'Leary and Paul Ulmann were betrayed, on 2 March 1943, also by Roger le Neveu, and were arrested in a set-up in a Toulouse café. Pat, too, was deported to Germany, and also survived several concentration camps. He was awarded the George Cross (1946), having already received the DSO (1942), and was appointed Honorary KBE (1949) for his outstanding leadership, courage, and fortitude.

With the arrests of so many key workers the PAT/PAO line was hard pushed to survive, but such was the courage and resilience of those who remained free that the line was maintained. The centre of operations had to be moved to Toulouse, where the redoubtable Marie-Louise Dissard, but always known as Françoise, took over in May 1943, and the line now became the réseau Françoise. She had been involved with the PAT line for a year, even though she was then in her sixty-second year.[11] Briefly arrested, with four airmen, she was forced into hiding in January 1944. It is reckoned that she helped some 250 evaders and escapers to cross into Spain. For her services she was honoured by France, Belgium, Britain,[12] and by the USA with the Presidential Medal of Freedom, the highest civilian award in that country. She died in 1957.

* * *

The Crew

Pilot Officer Raymond Glensor (navigator)

Pilot Officer Raymond Edwin Glensor, RNZAF, was the first man to bale out of the stricken Wellington DF550: 'It was quite a pleasant sensation on the drop away from the plane. I fell gently away beneath the plane, like a bomb, keeping pace with it so that I remained beneath the escape hatch in the nose. I was so fascinated that I almost forgot to pull my rip cord.'[13] When he did remember, he was somersaulting head first, with the result that when the parachute opened its shrouds caught round his left knee. No sooner had he managed to sort out his predicament than he saw that his arrival on terra firma was imminent.

He landed on a hillside, on stony ground, near the village of Alquines, hurting his back and left leg in the process: 'My back felt awful while my leg was terribly stiff and the parachute cords had burnt through my trouser pants and left a series of painful grazes on the back of the knees.' It was around 1.30 a.m. when he pulled himself together. The 'countryside was as still as a grave' and in the distance he could see a cone of searchlights accompanied by the sporadic crump of flak. Deciding that it was high time that he moved away from the hill, he buried his parachute etc. in a hedge as best he could and, getting his bearings from the Pole Star, headed off in what he believed to be a southerly direction.

He staggered across country for over three hours until, exhausted, he hid in some bushes and tried to get some sleep. He woke up late in the morning, 'cold and stiff ... When I rolled over and attempted to straighten out my legs I was forced to let out an agonised groan. My left leg was badly cramped and the muscles were absolutely in knots.' It took him a while to get everything working, and he set off once again, feeling very sorry for himself, tired, hungry and in pain. Eventually he came across the odd Frenchman and woman until, knocking hopefully on the door of a house in the village of Bayenghem, he was let in and welcomed by the occupants, Paul Cucheval, apparently a teacher. They proved to be entirely loyal, for twice while he was there Germans came into the room next to the one in which he was hiding and asked if an 'English pilot' had been seen in the neighbourhood. Ray was not betrayed.

For members of the Resistance, though, it always paid to treat every so-called airman evader as suspicious, and when Monsieur Havet appeared asking him for proof of identity, Ray was unable to produce his identity discs. Instead, he showed him his RAF maps, which proved satisfactory. After lunch on the following day, 18 September, another man appeared and asked Ray if he had any passport photos with him. 'When I replied in the negative he said it didn't matter as he had come to fix me up. He then dived his hand into the bottom of the sack and produced a roll of canvas which he unrolled to exhibit a very nice "Exakta" camera.'[14] A couple of snaps were taken, and the man left, to be replaced a while later by Monsieur Havet again. It was, so he said, time to move on and, after goodbyes had been exchanged, Ray departed by bicycle with M. Havet. A young lad of 16 scouted ahead, while a young girl followed on behind. Along the route French 'sentries' had been posted at the various crossroads to let them know that it was OK to continue.

The journey was without incident until they had just passed through a quiet village and were cycling along beside a little river 'when my guide came to a corner and motioned hurriedly for me to stop. As I pulled up, keeping my distance behind him, I saw a German strolling round the corner towards us. I got off my cycle and proceeded to make an imaginary adjustment to the chain.' Without knowing it, Ray's destination, the Fillerins' house, was also just around the corner. There he was given 'a grand welcome'.

On 20 September Norbert Fillerin told Ray: 'I think we have found your Squadron Leader.' As the French who were looking after Donald needed to be sure that he was an RAF airman and not a German agent, Norbert asked Ray for a couple of questions to be put to Donald who, hopefully knowing the right answers, would thus prove to be a genuine RAF airman. Discounting one possible question, Ray suggested asking 'him the name of the pub where he goes drinking! It was a pub in Cleethorpes, miles from Waltham [their airfield], but the favourite haunt of the squadron and called "the Lifebelt" by the boys (its true name was the "Lifeboat Hotel").'[15]

Ray recalled the moment when his skipper appeared:

… I got up and dressed and waited for breakfast. I had my breakfast but was almost too excited to eat. Then about eleven o'clock I heard voices talking rapidly outside and a moment later my door opened and with a yell in burst Bertie [Donald].

He was looking a bit of a wreck but not really too bad under the circumstances. He had on his uniform trousers and a very non-descript coat and vest as well as a civvy shirt and tie. He was looking quite well but even more nerve-shattered than ever.[16]

The days passed, and in the confined quarters the three airmen became irritable as nerves started to fray. There was some light relief, though, when they tried to launch the wretched carrier pigeon (see Appendix II). This is Ray's version of events:

Just before we had arrived at the house Norbert got hold of a container holding 2 RAF pigeons which had been dropped one night by a plane apparently on the off chance that they would fall into the right hands. Before we arrived he had sent off one of the birds loaded with information. Since we came he had been promising to send off the other bird and include our names among the information which he could put in his message containers.

When we got up in the morning he came in with the message flimsies and asked us for the details and any messages which we wanted added. We just gave him our ranks, names and numbers and asked him to request recipient to advise the Squadron that we were safe and well and that Buck and James had been caught by Gerry. He added our note to the flimsies and really the papers, which were not very large, had an amazing amount of information on them.

After breakfast Norbert came in with the pigeon and attached the message containers to its legs. Then, after the girls had had a look to make sure that the coast was clear, we all went out into the garden and, with a few love pats, Norbert released the pigeon. It fluttered away to a poor start and after a small circle of the estate, it settled on one of the chimney pots. We were not unduly worried as it had been in its coop for some days and we figured that its wings were a bit tired. Sure enough, after a minute or so, it took off again and after climbing, it started to circle the house. However, its heart was not in this "pigeon post" game, for it soon spotted another pigeon and flapped over for a chat. They winged around the countryside for quite a while and we had just about figured that we had had it, and were on the point of going inside again, when we heard some billing and cooing coming from above us and there on the ridge were those two -- pigeons!! And ours with his message containers showing like a couple of red flags in the face of a bull. We threw stones at them, but nothing we could do would persuade that so and so of a pigeon to do his duty and get weaving back to his nice safe comfy pigeon loft somewhere in England.

It would have been funny – if it had not been so serious. After all, there can be no fun in having enough evidence to get you shot sitting on your roof in plain view of everyone.[17]

Ray Glensor noted, on 17 October, that Norbert had fixed them up with *cartes d'identité* and *cartes de ravitaillement*, and that his new name was Raymond Jules Maes, born at Bergues (*sic* – possibly Bruges, as he was supposed to be a Flemish speaker), an *agriculteur* by profession. When the great day came to finally leave Renty, on 21 October, Ray was allocated as his escort young Michel Péroy:

> … and it was with a certain amount of disquiet that I set off with him. Not that I did not trust him, but it was his first assignment and if an emergency did arise we had no means of communication. He had no English and my French was confined to about four words.

On reaching Paris the party went to the café to which the airmen had been told to go to in the event of an emergency, probably the Café Ulysse run by Norbert's old friend Ulysse Debas. Impressed on them was the password phrase 'Tu as le bon jour de Jean Peter'. They were not to know it but they would soon be meeting the parents of Jean Peter, Louis and Renée Nouveau.

They all arrived safely at the Nouveaus' apartment in Marseille on Friday, 23 October. Two days later Pat O'Leary and another man, Philippe, appeared at the Nouveaus' flat, and a heated discussion ensued. It was clear to the airmen that there was a problem, and Ray soon discovered that he was to be taken to Pat O'Leary's flat until such time as it was possible for all of them to be moved on:

> Apparently everywhere else was full and so they were breaking their usual rule of not keeping anyone in Pat's flat. From the argument that preceded the announcement it was obvious that the plan was far from acceptable to the rest of them, but that they had been forced to agree for want of some better scheme.

Grabbing his few possessions, Ray made his farewells and followed Pat and Philippe to the water's edge. A boatman was summoned, and took his passengers across the water to the old quarter. After a 'black market' meal at a *restaurant de luxe* they took a tram to Pat's 'safe house'. As intended, Ray was confused as to where this was:

> The road in which Pat had his quarters was really two roads with a grass patch in between them. Most of the buildings were flats though there were a couple of blocks of business establishments. The block of flats into which we turned had nothing to distinguish it from its neighbours. It was built of a dull grey stone with high old-fashioned floors and an iron bannistered stone staircase up which we climbed till we got to the third floor. Here we paused while Patrick knocked deliberately three times and waited and in a couple of minutes the door was opened by a

large loose-limbed woman of middle age. Once inside, Pat led me into the back living room and lost no time in introducing me to the woman whose name was Therese.[18]

The flat was located at 12, Boulevard Cassini, near the Observatory Gardens, perhaps 3 kilometres from the Vieux Port.

Thérèse Martin, as she was then known, was an alias for Maud Olga Andrée Baudot de Rouville, who was born in Paris on 14 December 1891 of a well-to-do French father and Irish mother. They had met whilst Thérèse's mother was on a visit to France. Thérèse herself, educated in an English convent, had served during the First World War as a nurse, receiving a Red Cross certificate in 1917. She had become involved in Resistance activities whilst nursing British troops in a convent in the Lille area in 1940-41, and had moved for safety's sake to Marseille earlier in 1942. When Marseille became untenable for Resistance activities she moved to Toulouse in 1943 to work with Françoise Dissard.

To Ray 'Therese had one great factor in her favour ... for she spoke almost perfect English. It was obvious that she shared everyone's disapproval of Pat's action in bringing me to the flat, and it was equally obvious that in her eyes Pat could do no wrong.'

Ray was some 6 feet 2 inches tall, which meant that his bed, the sofa, was a trifle small at only five feet long or so. Nevertheless, after Thérèse had provided cushions and a counterpane in lieu of pillows and sheets, Ray was 'mightily relieved when it was suggested that it was time to hit the sack ... To tell the truth I was missing the boys' company and was feeling pretty miserable.'[19]

One afternoon Pat left for a few days, on a trip to Switzerland to see about opening new routes out of France. It is just as likely, however, that he was off to see the main financier for escape lines, Victor Farrell, an experienced MI6 officer who had been appointed in May 1940 as Chief Passport Officer at the British Consulate in Geneva. Pat was away for eight days, a period that seemed to Ray like eight years: 'There had been nothing to do and I had been condemned to long hours of solitude and quietness for Therese had been out for most of every day doing business for Pat.' It was up to Ray to amuse himself as best he could. His entertainments largely consisted of listening, quietly, to the radio, reading, and playing cards with a French pack (only 32 cards compared with a 52-card pack with which he would have been familiar).

After a month or so with Thérèse, Ray was moved to the flat of M. and Mme. Durier in Cassis, some 20 kilometres along the coast, where he met two other airmen evaders – Flight Lieutenant T. A. Wærner, RNZAF, and Captain Richard D. Adams, USAAF[20] – and a civilian, Walter Gosling, mysteriously referred to by Ray as 'a member of the organisation'. All four were then escorted to the Rodocanachis' 'safe house' in Marseille.

On 13 December 1942, Ray, Walter Gosling, Flight Lieutenant Wærner, Flight Lieutenant R. A. E. Milton, RAF, Lieutenant W. M. Hewit, and SOE agent

Captain Dick Cooper (these last three were among those released from the Camp de Chambaran in November 1942) were taken to Toulouse, where they were looked after by Paul Ulmann. The party, now minus Wærner, took the train on 16 December to Banyuls-sur-Mer, at the foot of the Pyrenees, where they arrived about 6 p.m. From the station the party walked up the street to a wine bar: 'We sat and waited and gradually people joined us until there were about 8 or 9 of us sitting around the table … Eventually we were told to go, and we went out and up the hillside. It was just about dark and we could see the hills rising up behind the town and knew this was the seaward end of the Pyrenees.'[21]

On the night of 16/17 December, in a large party of mixed military and civilian personnel, Ray was guided over the Pyrenees. Early in the morning of 19 December the guide led them to a brickworks near the town of Figueras, saying that he would go to Barcelona to alert the consulate there. 'We never saw or heard of him again.'

Captain Dick Cooper, who fortunately could speak fluent Spanish, persuaded a *contrabandista* (smuggler) who had earlier joined the group to go to Barcelona and notify the British Consul of their whereabouts. This the man did, and on 23 December the British Vice-Consul, Mr P. H. Dorchy, arrived in his car, 'one of those big flashy American cars. It had a rumble seat in the back and this was the value of it as he could put four of us in the rumble seat and throw a rug over us. He told us he had to go through three checkpoints before he got to Barcelona.'[22] The journey to Barcelona was safely accomplished and, after six days they were driven to Madrid, where they stayed until early in the New Year, 1943. The next stage of their journey was to Seville, where, pretending to be drunken sailors to fool the watching guards, they staggered aboard a British ship with a cargo of oranges, and were hidden down by the propeller shaft. Two days later they were in Gibraltar.

An interesting story concerning these 'orange' boats is provided by author Ian Colvin.[23] Colvin was in Spain interviewing a former German agent who had been posted to Spain in the autumn of 1942 as an officer in the Abwehr's Section II – sabotage operations abroad. This officer told Colvin that there 'was the yearly Seville orange crop, which was loaded at the wharves of Seville. Well, there was often a bomb of mine in those crates. Our object in setting the time fuses was to produce an explosion at sea, so that it would seem to have been a submarine attack.' The former Abwehr man added that the British got wise to this strategy and 'froze a cargo on the quayside, so that the next bomb exploded in Seville docks'.

It would be a month before Ray sailed for home, by which time Donald had caught up with him at Gibraltar. In June 1943, having decided to remuster as a pilot, Ray was sent to Canada to learn to fly. He was back in England by early 1945, by now a flight lieutenant, and joined 166 Squadron with their Lancaster bombers at RAF Kirmington in Lincolnshire. He flew his first operation with his new squadron on the night of 18/19 March 1945, when he went as a 'second dickie' with Flight Lieutenant Mulholland and crew in Lancaster AS-P to bomb Hanau in Germany in the company of another 276 Lancasters. Ray flew a further nine ops with his own crew of Flight Sergeants Brooks, Budden, and Pacey, and Sergeants Gregory, Howard, and Ingram before hostilities ceased on 4 May, by which time he had been promoted squadron leader and had been given command of 'A' Flight.

He was finally rewarded for his bravery and leadership with the DFC, gazetted on 6 November 1945, by which time he had been posted to 49 Squadron. This is the citation for the award:

> This officer has participated in numerous operational sorties, first as a navigator and later as pilot and captain of aircraft. During his first tour of duty he attacked such heavily defended targets as Essen, Düsseldorf, Hamburg and Warnemünde. In September, 1942, Squadron Leader Glensor's aircraft was shot down over Essen. He evaded capture and, despite great hardship, made his way through France and Spain back to this country. In March, 1945, this officer resumed operational flying with undiminished enthusiasm. Since then he has shared fully in the attacks against Germany, both in the difficult early days and in the final battles. Throughout his operational career, Squadron Leader Glensor has displayed exemplary determination and gallantry.[24]

In reality there was little time left in which to have distinguished himself on bombing operations at such a late stage of the war and, having been posted to 49 Squadron in May 1945, he did little more flying, none in anger, and ended almost six years in the Royal New Zealand Air Force on 30 March 1946. He died in his native country on 7 July 1984 at the age of 67.

Sergeant Ralph Forster (front gunner)

In 1940, Ralph Forster signed up for the RAF, going from his home town of Sunderland to Durham, where he expressed a wish to fly as a pilot. Four weeks later he was told to report for a medical examination, and a further six weeks after that he was called up, and sent to Blackpool for training as – a wireless operator. He qualified, in the lowest possible RAF rank of aircraftman 2nd class, with effect from 10 February 1941 at No. 2 Signal School, Yatesbury, Wiltshire. Further training, on ab initio gunnery course No. 32, was undertaken on 16 March 1941 at No. 7 Bombing & Gunnery School, RAF Stormy Down. Again he qualified, with effect from 26 April, his logbook noting that he was 'A very sound Air Gunner'. In May he attended a wireless telegraphy course at No. 11 OTU, RAF Bassingbourn, but was assessed only as 'Average'. Training continued into June, and by July Sergeant Forster was ready to take his place in the front line with a posting to 'B' Flight, 142 Squadron at RAF Binbrook.

The great day came on 20 July 1941 when his name appeared on the crew list for

Wellington W5395.[25] The target was Cologne. It was an ineffectual raid, but Ralph had at last 'got some in', as the RAF expression went. He did no further operations in August and September, and it was only on 31 October that he went on his second operation, to Dunkirk, completing the round trip in just under three hours in Wellington Z1245 (Pilot Officer John Nigel Tillard).[26] He flew no operations throughout November and for most of December, but on the 28th of that month he went to Wilhelmshaven, with Squadron Leader Gibson and 'second dickie' Pilot Officer S. B. Critchison, in Wellington Z1287.[27] Becoming a more or less permanent front gunner for Squadron Leader A. B. Olney, Ralph flew two more operations with him in January 1942 and two more in each of February and March. As previously seen, it was on 2 April that Ralph first flew with Donald, who was on a 'second dickie' night flying test with the very newly promoted Wing Commander Olney. Ralph then flew six more operations in April with Donald, including the one to Essen on 10/11 April when they brought their bombs back after the intercom failed. After another two with the 'wingco', his tally was now seventeen.

Though he usually flew with Donald, Ralph did go to Bremen on 25/26 June with Flight Sergeant W. F. Caldow, when they were attached to No. 1481 Target Towing Flight, a unit also based at RAF Binbrook, whose CO was Flight Lieutenant Richard Pinkham. Great news awaited Caldow on his return from Bremen, for that was the day on which he was awarded the DFM. Willie Caldow was to go on to greater things, earning the AFC in the New Year's Honours 1944, and the DSO in September 1945 when a squadron leader and 'C' Flight CO on 550 Squadron.

On his return to 142 Squadron, Ralph became Donald's permanent front gunner, completing another seven ops with him until they 'failed to return' on the night of 16/17 September.

After Albert Buckell had let him out of the front turret of the Wellington, Ralph came down on a hillside near Acquin, 4 or 5 kilometres from Alquines. Putting on the pair of walking shoes that he had thoughtfully brought with him (though Donald frowned at this lack of confidence in his ability, Ralph has to this day been unable to explain why he took them), he set off in the darkness. Wanting to get off the road in case he met the enemy he saw a barn with a door very slightly ajar and walked inside. At the far end of the barn was an elderly lady of about 90 carrying kindling. She looked very scared to see him. Ralph spoke in his best French and asked her where the Germans were. She replied that they were in Boulogne, but she looked so afraid that Ralph just came out quietly and continued walking.

With dawn breaking he hid in a wood, and stayed there all day eating Horlicks tablets from his escape box and listening to 'the Germans' dogs barking as they and their masters searched for the missing airmen …' As darkness fell, using his map and small pocket compass, he headed south with the sound of barking dogs all around him. At daybreak on 18 September he sought refuge in a haystack and watched farm workers going about their business. At dusk he approached one of these, a woman: 'She advised me to go to a village nearby, which she indicated. She said that here there was a Frenchman who spoke English well. She told me that there were no Germans in the village.'

Ralph went to the village, Bayenghem as it proved, where he contacted 'a woman and a young man on a bicycle. I spoke to them, and they took me to a house next to the church. The occupants gave me a meal and some overalls. About 1800 hrs, two men were brought to see me.' The two men were 37-year-old Roger Delannoy,[28] a garagiste, and Monsieur Syoën, an engineer for Ponts et Chaussées (the department officially responsible for French bridges and roads). They both hailed from Lumbres and were members of the group calling themselves 'Voix du Nord' ('Voice of the North').

Delannoy and Syoën returned and, with Ralph in the back of their car, a Renault Primaquatre, drove half a dozen kilometres to the house at Le Verval of a M. Rebergues[29] (an ex-soldier in the French Army and also a member of Voix du Nord) and his mother, neither of whom could speak English. There was a momentary scare when, as they were approaching a right-angled bend in the road, a German Kübelwagen was seen coming towards them, but it passed by without paying any attention to the passenger in the back of the Renault. Safely at Le Verval, Ralph was told that he would be staying there for a few days, and the Rebergues family proved to be very kind to him. He had another scare one day when, looking out of the window, he saw Germans coming down the road knocking on doors. To his great relief it transpired that they were only asking for eggs.

Ralph was collected on the afternoon of 22 September by Delannoy and Syoën and driven off in the Renault again. They stopped at a certain crossroads with a signpost where he 'met two more men in cycling kit, with a spare bicycle'. One of the two, an elderly man in a tweed suit, produced one of the many 'Wanted' posters that the Germans had stuck up in the area and asked Ralph to point to his name on it. He then asked him to name his favourite pub in Grimsby. Though Ralph didn't go there himself, he knew the name, having often heard the others talking about it. The two cyclists, both members of the so-called Hervet group, explained to Ralph that they would ride ahead and that he was to follow some distance behind. After a few miles they reached Renty and the Fillerins' house, where Ralph was reunited with Donald and Ray.

The dreaded telegram informing close relatives of the loss of their son, brother, or husband was dutifully sent to the Forster household at 11, Ashleigh Grove, Fulwell, Sunderland by the squadron CO, Wing Commander Simmons, on 17 September. But no word of their son's fate, good or bad, had been received by the time that Ralph's mother wrote to the squadron on 1 November, anxious for any news of her son. A reply was sent to her three days later from Wing Commander Simmons:

We have no news whatsoever. Like you we know that two other members of the crew are prisoners of war and, as no mention is made of any casualties, it strikes me that possibly the captain, your son and the air observer [*sic*] are in unoccupied France and have not been captured. As long as we have no news one way or the other there is always hope.

Of course, by this time Ralph and the others had been moved from Renty down to Marseille. Ralph's escort for the first part of the journey from Renty to Paris on 21 October was Madame Fillerin, Norbert's mother. Donald's was Norbert, and Ray's Michel Péroy. Ray described Ralph's appearance on the day of departure: 'Ralph himself looked about 16-17 the way they had dressed him in a suit of blue denim over a shirt and tie, surmounted by a dark brown suit coat of boyish cut … Ralph was the youngest member of the crew, and looked it, so he would easily pass as Madame Fillerin's son.'

After Ralph and Donald had spent the night in Madame Fillerin's flat – she was elsewhere – Norbert took them to the appointed rendezvous, a restaurant near the Gare du Sud, where they met up with Ray and Michel Péroy and the two American airmen and their escort, Jean de la Olla ('Petit Jean'). Splitting into their old parties they set off through the drizzle for the station, having said goodbye to Madame Fillerin. Though she had jarred on the men terribly, they were sorry to see her go, for she had meant well and was a brave lady.

Ralph was now handed over to Norbert, and his journey to Marseille and beyond, up to the crossing into Spain, is as described in Donald's diary.

In the Pyrenees, now that Donald and his three companions had gone on ahead, Ralph was left with the injured Mario Prassinos and his badly bruised shin, and with the American pilot Eric Doorly. They were some way into Spain on 14 December when they were joined by two French lads who had a map. They were about 3 kilometres north of the village of Espolla when the loud command 'Alto!' echoed across the rocky terrain. Duly halting as ordered, the three men were confronted by an officer and several Spanish regular soldiers pointing their rifles at them: 'They searched us perfunctorily, and told us to walk back to Port Bou, where the proper authorities would give us passports to enter Spain. They then escorted us to a point near the frontier, and left us.'[30]

Tired and exceedingly hungry they spent the night in a hut in the mountains, recrossing into Spain a few kilometres further along in the morning. They managed to get as far as Rabós, a dozen kilometres north-east of Figueras, where they were apprehended by members of the Guardia Civile and shown the inside of Rabós police station. Some consternation was caused when Ralph showed his captors the German 'Wanted' poster that he had brought with him from Renty, which at least convinced them that they, the prisoners, were 'genuine Service evaders'.

On 17 December Ralph, Mario and Eric were taken to the local jail in Figueras, where all their money and Ralph's poster were confiscated. They repeatedly asked to see the British Consul, but were told that he could not help them. All was not lost, though, for a Spaniard who said he was a representative of the Red Cross promised to tell the British Consul in Barcelona about them. Later they managed to persuade a Frenchman to deliver the same message.

Two days later they were moved to the main prison in Figueras, and were briefly reunited with Bromwell and 'Frost'. Here they languished for seven weeks, their ghastly stay alleviated somewhat by the appearance of someone from the Barcelona consulate on 30 January 1943. Not that it did much good, but at least Mario Prassinos was released on 2 February, four days before Eric and Ralph were taken by train to Barcelona. They were then driven by lorry to Miranda de Ebro concentration camp, where they arrived about 9 February.

On 16 February 1943, five months after their son's disappearance, the Forster household in Sunderland received another telegram: 'ARRIVES [*sic*] HERE SAFE AND WELL DON'T WORRY EVERYTHING OKAY LETTER FOLLOWING PLEASE REPLY SOON ADDRESS OFICINA BRITANICA CAMPO DE CONCENTRACAION MIRANDA DE EBRO LOVE TO ALL RALPH FORSTER.'

Time may be a great healer but Ralph can still remember the poor conditions at Miranda, including the toilet, which was nothing more than a hole in the ground. Eric Doorly only had to endure Miranda until 11 March, when he was taken to Alhama de Aragón. On 24 March, he was driven to Madrid 'and thence via Seville to Gibraltar, where I arrived the next day'. On 27 March 1943, he was flown to Hendon aerodrome. Ralph was puzzled as to why 'for some reason the Spaniards seemed unwilling to allow me to proceed to Alhama with F/O Doorly'.

Back in Sunderland, meanwhile, Ralph's family received a letter from Donald, dated 28 March 1943, which was addressed from the Royal Masonic Hospital, London:

Dear Mrs Forster,
    Please forgive me for not writing sooner, but I have only just obtained your address from my navigator, F/O Glensor, who I met at a medical board, the result of which I was put into hospital being thoroughly run down and having flu.
    He told me you received a telegram from your son Ralph who is in the Miranda camp.[31] As far as I know he went there when I left Madrid, and it should at the most only take 6 weeks to get him out, and therefore he should be home by now or very soon …
    I would be most grateful if you would let me know when Ralph comes back. If you would write to me at Lloyds Bank Ltd, Cox and Kings Branch, 6 Pall Mall, London. Please do not worry because it is only a question of time.
    Yours very sincerely, D. B. Barnard S/Ldr.

So it was, for on 6 April 1943, Ralph and Sergeant H. L. McBeath, RCAF were released and driven by a Spanish Air Force officer to the hotel at Alhama de Aragón.[32] On 11 April they went to Madrid and, after another five days in another hotel, to Gibraltar, which they reached on 17 April. Two days later another telegram arrived at 11, Ashleigh Grove from the Air Ministry: 'YOUR SON SGT RALPH FORSTER HAS ARRIVED AT GIBRALTAR.' On the very next

Sergeant Forster – back row 3rd from left – at RAF Manby air gunners' instructor course. This was taken after his escape and evasion with Donald Barnard in September 1943.

day a second telegram from the Air Ministry arrived: 'YOUR SON SGT RALPH FORSTER HAS ARRIVED IN THE UNITED KINGDOM.'

On his return and after having given all the information required of him to the relevant authorities, MI9 etc., Ralph was granted a long leave before being posted in September 1943 to No. 1 Air Armament School at RAF Manby in Lincolnshire to learn how to be an air gunnery instructor. Having qualified with effect from 8 October, he was posted to No. 7 Air Gunners School, RAF Stormy Down, again as an air gunnery instructor. There he remained until February 1944 when, after another break, he returned in May to RAF Rhoose, still in Wales, where he continued instructing until the end of July. Then it was on to RAF Pembrey in August, to No. 1 Air Gunners School.

This is where Ralph's flying logbook finishes. They asked him what he wanted to do next; he replied that he wanted to be a despatch rider, something he'd always wanted to do. Right, they said, having discovered that he had worked in the Borough Treasurer's office prewar, you can go to payroll and accounts. And that is how Ralph ended his war.

Sergeant Albert Buckell (wireless operator)

Albert Buckell's wife 'lay awake in bed, listening to a gate banging in the wind' wondering where her husband was. In the morning she went to Waltham aerodrome

Sergeant Buckell upon capture by German soldiers.

and learnt the terrible news that Albert was missing. She was told that his aircraft had been shot down, but that there was always the possibility that he had baled out.

Three years earlier, on the day before war was declared, her husband – Bert to his friends – had enlisted for the duration. Training followed at No.7 Bombing & Gunnery School, and No. 15 OTU, before joining 214 Squadron at RAF Stradishall on 4 May 1940, albeit still under training. His next postings were to 99 Squadron and 20 OTU (17 September 1940) before he was ready to go into action, with 12 Squadron at RAF Binbrook on 27 April 1942. Three weeks later he moved to 142 Squadron, and to Donald's crew.

Now, five months and thirty operations later, Albert Buckell's flying career was about to end in the darkness of that morning of 17 September 1942. He had no idea how close he was to the ground when he baled out, and landed badly, hurting his back as Ray Glensor had done. After hiding for the rest of the day, with the pain in his back lessening somewhat, Albert knocked on the door of the house of M. and Mme. Wilquin in the village of Bayenghem-lès-Seninghem 'and was given food and shelter but, against the advice of his hosts, decided to leave and try to make his way home'.[33] Three days later, on his 26th birthday, he met another Frenchman, who told him to wait in his house while he fetched help. The story goes that this man, the mayor of Alquines, traded the Englishman to the Germans in exchange for his son, whom they held as some form of hostage. Though Donald has related the story of the man's fate, a few weeks after his return to England, he wrote to Albert's wife, Grace, on 28 March 1943 (the same date as his letter to the Forsters):

Sergeant Buckell with German soldiers all keen to be photographed with the British 'flyer'.

Dear Mrs Buckell,

I am so sorry that I did not write sooner, but I have only just obtained your address.

I knew your husband extremely well from the flying side as we did many hours up at Lossiemouth and on one occasion I came down south and 'shot up' your house near Newmarket. I don't know if you remember that?

Your husband was very unlucky not to get away with us, because he was betrayed by an un-patriotic Frenchman, but you will be very pleased to hear that he has been revenged. That Frenchman will never betray anybody else again.

He was the last one out of the aircraft. I tried to follow but the aircraft got violently out of control, and I had to land it in the dark. Luckily I escaped unhurt.

I would be most grateful if you would let me know which camp he is in, & let me have his address, as I should like very much to write to him.

I hope the time will come soon when I can 'shoot up' your house with him again.

Yours sincerely, [signed] D. B. Barnard, S/Ldr.[34]

Albert Buckell was to spend the remainder of the war in the hands of the German Army either at Stalag VIIIB, the very large prisoner-of-war camp at Lamsdorf (today Łambinowice) in Silesia, or at one of its work camps. With a shortage of manpower, the German Army forced large numbers of Allied prisoners of war to work at places outside the barbed-wired and well-guarded prisoner-of-war camps. Only those below the rank of sergeant were eligible under the Geneva Convention to be made to work, and this effectively precluded any captured aircrew, who were usually of sergeant rank or higher. Certainly no officer was ever allowed to undertake work outside a main camp. The answer for an airman, therefore, if he wished to attempt to escape, was to exchange identities with an eligible soldier and to take his place on a work detail.

In May 1943, therefore, three airmen – Albert, another RAF man, and a Canadian, Vernon Bastable, RCAF – swapped identities and were taken to work at the stone quarry at Marzdorf, now in the Czech Republic. After a while, sometime in July 1943, Vernon's true identity was discovered, and he was to be returned to Lamsdorf. So, the night before he was due to go, he escaped. He didn't get far this time, and was quickly recaptured. The other RAF man decided against escaping, but Albert wanted to give it a go, and left on his own. He managed to survive for a fortnight or so but, forced to eat raw root vegetables straight from the ground, he, too, was recaptured, by a Bürgermeister (mayor) near Olmütz (Olomouc).

In October 1944, Albert had another go, this time from a sugar factory at Ottmachau (Otmuchów), but suffered the same fate again. He was taken to Gestapo HQ in a Czech town, where a German deserter he met was executed. Surviving his ordeal, Albert was then sent to another work camp, at Stephansdorf (Szczepanów) aerodrome, where he stayed for the winter of 1944-45. During the winter the Soviet Armies were fighting their way westwards, and when, by February 1945, the German guards decided that it was time for Albert and his workmates to leave, a column of cold British prisoners was marched westwards away from the Russians.

At some point in all the confusion Albert and a Welshman, having become separated from the column, met a convoy of German trucks, also heading west, with a number of German soldiers aboard. The German officer in charge insisted that he and his soldiers were now the prisoners of Albert and the Welshman! Bluffing their way through Czech partisan checkpoints, they eventually met the Americans advancing to the east. Albert was flown to an airfield in Belgium, where he remembered a camp with lots of good food, and was then flown back to England, being reunited in Birmingham with his wife on 13 May 1945, her birthday.

Sergeant Howard M. James (rear gunner)
Little is known of Howard 'Jimmy' James's life and RAF career. He had flown on several ops with Donald before they were lost on 16/17 September 1942, when his wartime flying came to an abrupt end. His capture was almost comical in its simplicity, with little apparent intention on his part to try to avoid it. We can only guess at what was going on in his mind when, so the story went according to Donald, he brazenly walked into a village in his flying kit. No wonder the Germans soon appeared and captured him.

He, too, was sent to Stalag VIIIB (Lamsdorf), where his prisoner-of-war number was 27106. Albert Buckell's number was 27125, and the two were probably in the same 'purge' from the Luftwaffe's notorious interrogation centre Dulag Luft at Oberursel. Being RAF, James and Buckell should have gone to a prisoner-of-war camp run by the German Air Force (the Luftwaffe), but the sudden large influx of shot-down RAF aircrew had caught them out, and the only place for the newcomers to go was to a German Army camp.

Nothing is known of James's time at Lamsdorf, but he survived the war, despite the awful forced march away from the advancing Soviet hordes in January and February 1945.

CHAPTER 6

RAF, 1943-46

Return to active service

Every evader and escaper on his return to the United Kingdom was required to attend a debriefing interview with an officer of MI9 (Military Intelligence section 9), the British Intelligence department with responsibility for evaders and escapers. With effect from 1 January 1942, MI9 had been split into two subsections:

M.I.9(b) and M.I.9(d), the former dealing with general questions, co-ordination, distribution of information and liaison with other services and government departments and overseas commands, the latter, M.I.9(d), being responsible for organising preventive training (instruction in evasion and escape) to combatant personnel of the three services in the United Kingdom and for the issue of evasion and escape equipment and information to units at home and M.I.9 organisations overseas.[1]

Thus, no sooner had they arrived by the overnight train in London on 27 January 1943, than Donald and his navigator, Pilot Officer Ray Glensor, were escorted to a hotel in central London, where the interviews were held.[2] Here they were given a thorough debriefing, and they told of their adventures since being shot down four months previously.

Another British Intelligence department with an interest in escapers and evaders was the much larger and more widely known MI6. Responsible for national security outside the United Kingdom, they had a man based in Gibraltar at the time of Donald's and Ray's arrival there. This was Donald Darling, codename 'Sunday', who early in 1942 had been posted to The Rock (as Gibraltar was known) from Lisbon, where he had been engaged on similar Intelligence work.

Others to have days of the week as their codenames were Airey Neave ('Saturday'), based in London after his thrilling escape from Colditz early in 1942, and Michael Creswell ('Monday'), who was at the British Embassy in Madrid. In the introduction to one of his two books, Darling wrote that he 'communicated by letter and by radio with other personified days of the week. They, with me, were concerned with the evasion from European countries occupied by the Germans, of RAF and Allied Air-Forces personnel.'[3]

With national security, as ever, paramount, it was Darling's job to 'clear' everyone passing through on their way to the UK, to ensure that no enemy spy slipped through the net. It was up to him, therefore, to question each person arriving at Gibraltar from Spain or France, as he explained:

> The day after their arrival in Gibraltar I would receive each man in turn and interrogate him in depth about his movements after baling out, the houses and the people he had stayed with, their names and addresses and all the details of his long journey … As the months passed and men from several evasion lines came through Gibraltar, I acquired a vast knowledge of the men and women working in each.[4]

Once Darling was satisfied that the person claiming to be such-and-such an airman, soldier, or sailor was genuine, that person was given an emergency certificate which they were required to present to the relevant authority immediately on arrival in the United Kingdom. Donald and Ray would have been seen, however briefly, by Darling before being allowed on their way, but he would already have forwarded their details to the UK, and it was then up to the appropriate authority at the port or airport to check Darling's details with the personnel now arriving there.

Events had already shown, however, that Darling's system was not infallible. In October 1942, when fourteen airmen evaders were suddenly landed at Gibraltar, no information about them had been forwarded to England by the time that they had landed in Poole Harbour by flying boat on 19 October. MI5, the department responsible for home security, were therefore unable to check up on them. Messages flew back and forth, but MI5 had a good point to make:

> The information which we require is reaching us in the end, but much too late to be used for the purpose for which it is intended, i.e. checking up on the individual's identity when he arrives … It is so essential that we should check up on the identity of Service personnel returning to this country. We already have conclusive proof that the Germans are attempting to use Prisoners of War to infiltrate them into this country as agents.[5]

Having established that airmen such as Donald and Ray were indeed who they claimed to be, the detailed information obtained from their subsequent interrogation, especially the identities of those individuals who had risked their lives in assisting downed aircrew in occupied Europe, was put to good use. MI9 and MI6 were able to build-up a good understanding of the effectiveness of the escape lines that were being formed, and they were also able to get a picture of the effectiveness of escape aids, such as the silk maps that aircrew carried concealed in the lining of their uniforms, the tiny escape compasses hidden in buttons, and a number of other devices deployed to assist evaders make their way across occupied Europe.

With the protection of escape line members of paramount importance, it was RAF policy that returning evaders were not permitted to fly on operations again over the same territory in which they had received assistance. To avoid the possibility, therefore, of subsequent capture and of 'talking' under German interrogation in the event of being shot down again, evaders were usually posted to other theatres of operation. There was one notable exception to this rule, namely fighter pilot Bill Furniss-Roe, who was shot down twice over France, the first time in August 1943, and again in January 1944. On both occasions he returned to England unscathed, though somewhat wiser the second time, via Spain and Gibraltar.

MI5, whose job it was to keep Britain free from enemy agents, pointed out that the Germans were using prisoners of war to infiltrate them into Britain 'as agents'. Whereas MI5 were at the end of the escape or evasion line, the German secret services, at the beginning of the line, made great efforts to break into the resistance and evasion networks in France and the Benelux countries with the sole purpose of destroying them. When they succeeded, as they unfortunately did on a number of occasions, many of those involved with the escape lines were arrested and transported to various prisons and camps, in too many cases never to return. Interrogation by the German police was always inhumanely brutal.

For returning evaders and escapers, once they had been interviewed by the interested Intelligence sections, it was time to catch up on things, and in Donald's case he was able to put up the purple and white ribbon of the Distinguished Flying Cross which he had been awarded the week after he was shot down.[6] Had he not done so, he would have been improperly dressed in the eyes of the RAF! But neither he nor his navigator Ray Glensor, nor Ralph Forster, received any award for their evasion, not even the lowest award possible of a Mention in Despatches.

Donald's health on his return, however, was not all it should have been. Ray Glensor had noted, as far back as September 1942 when they were in hiding at Renty, that Donald 'was looking a bit of a wreck' and, though looking quite well, was 'even more nerve-shattered than ever'. Only a very, very small percentage of operational aircrew could hold up their hands and say that the pressure of operations had not got to them at some point in their flying career, and it is clear that Donald's physical and mental state were well below par and that he was, in his own words, 'thoroughly run down and having flu'. All this was noted, of course, by the doctors when he went for a routine medical check-up, and he was sent to the Royal Masonic Hospital at Ravenscourt Park in London for observation and a rest.

He was discharged on 2 April and, after two days' leave, was Returned To Unit on 5 April. It is possible that he spent some of his hospitalisation at RAF General Hospital, Rauceby, 'well situated in pleasantly wooded country near Sleaford in Lincolnshire' for there is an unusual entry in his logbook for 2 (*sic*) March 1943, which bears some examination. It says that he flew in Lancaster ED490 on a 45-minute war firing exercise over The Wash with pilot Flight Lieutenant J. V. Verran DFC,[7] Wing Commander Mogg, Flying Officer J. H. Moutray DFM, Flying Officer F. T. Johnson, and four crew, a total of nine crew as opposed to the usual seven. Donald and the wing commander were supernumerary.

But what was Donald doing back in Lincolnshire flying in an aircraft when he should have been quietly resting in hospital? It is conjecture that he might have been a patient at Rauceby, which is only some 15 miles south of RAF Waddington, near Lincoln, then home to 9 Squadron (one of Donald's old squadrons), to which ED490 belonged, but there may, too, have been a link with Wing Commander Mogg.[8]

Though he has not been positively identified, he may have been Frank George Mogg GM, MRCS, LRCP of the RAF Medical Branch. If so, then it seems plausible that he had taken Donald with him on a visit to 9 Squadron and that they then both went on the short exercise with the Verran crew, Mogg possibly seeing how Donald would react to being in the air again.

Donald's logbook date of 2 March is incorrect, however. The date must have been 1 March, for on the night of 1/2 March, Jim Verran and crew went off to bomb Berlin in ED490 which, on its return, collided in mid-air with another Lancaster, R5894 of 57 Squadron. R5894, which had also been to Berlin, was a few miles the wrong side of Lincoln and had strayed from the area of its base, Scampton, into the Waddington circuit. In the collision ED490 broke up almost at once, but R5894 staggered a few miles northwards until hitting high-tension wires to the north of Lincoln. Crashing at Riseholme, all seven of its crew were killed but, amazingly, four of ED490's crew survived. Johnson, Moutray and Verran were injured to some degree, but Sergeant K. W. Chalk, in the mid-upper turret, 'blinked, shook himself and climbed uninjured out of his turret'[9] which had somehow gently deposited itself on terra firma. The other three crew were killed.

There was a curious postscript to Jim Verran's wartime flying career. Whilst serving on 83 Squadron he was shot down in August 1944 and taken prisoner of war. His German interrogator then shocked him, as was the intention, by telling him that they had a recording of his voice made while he was on bombing trials over Wainfleet Sands off the Lincolnshire coast, and he even told Jim the very time and date.[10]

Donald would not, of course, have been allowed to have flown on operations with the Verran crew, or any other for that matter, but now he was in a sort of limbo. And with two of his former crew in a prisoner-of-war camp in Germany, his own crew was never to be re-formed, even though three of them had made it safely back to England. As for Donald, once out of hospital and with his leave over, there was to be no hero's welcome, no triumphal return to his squadron, no exuberant party in the officers' mess, for the simple reason that his squadron, 142, was no longer operational in England.[11]

Furthermore, to add insult to injury, he no longer held the rank of acting squadron leader, having reverted to that of substantive flight lieutenant, and in that latter rank was posted to No. 20 Maintenance Unit (MU) at RAF Aston Down in Gloucestershire, to learn to fly the single-seater Hawker Hurricane aircraft.[12]

On 6 April 1943, Donald began the conversion course being run by the Flight Conversion training unit, but after just sixteen days was attached to No. 5 MU at RAF Kemble, swiftly followed by yet another attachment to No. 33 MU at RAF

Donald Barnard flew hundreds of Spitfires repaired at the maintenance units.

Lyneham in neighbouring Wiltshire. His piloting skills were being put to good use in checking out a wide variety of aircraft types that had been repaired and which were ready, subject to his approval, to be passed on to an operational or training squadron somewhere. On 16 May 1943, he added Spitfire Mk I N3100 to his list, while other types recorded in his logbook at this time were a Beaufighter Mk VI, JL573, various marks of Wellington, and several other marks of Spitfire (see Appendix V). But it was the Spitfire that he was regularly required to test, some days putting as many as six through their paces, usually on a 20-minute sortie.

He recorded daily life in his logbook entries which, perhaps because of having to fly different aircraft, was not as dull as it might otherwise have been. On 30 May, for example, his first test flight, lasting 30 minutes, was in Wellington N2947, immediately followed by another similar flight in Wellington DR526.[13] He was then called upon to take Wing Commander R. G. A. Vallance[14] and Flying Officer Francis in the station 'hack', Airspeed Oxford ED118, from Lyneham to Everleigh, with other trips back and forth between those airfields. Though the purpose of these visits is not known, the final flight was from Everleigh to Andover and back to base at Lyneham, which suggests that the wing commander and his aide were attending meetings at Maintenance Command headquarters, which happened to be in Andover.

The following month Donald air-tested a number of Spitfires, among them Mk Vb BM315, which he flew on his customary 20-minute 'shake-down'. No doubt he had developed a standard procedure with which he was well versed, but during that flight he found something that required adjustment or some other kind of engineering attention. He landed the aircraft, and after the required works had been completed took BM315 into the air again for another 20-minute test. The flight was successful but, on landing, the starboard leg collapsed. Fortunately, no injuries were sustained, to man at least, but BM315 was returned to the factory for further repairs.[15]

Occasionally factory engineers would be taken up for a 'spin' and, on 4 June, it was the turn of a Mr Hicks to be taken up twice in Miles Master DM135. That same day Donald flew Mk IX Spitfire MA415 on two test sorties, and also Mk V Spitfires ES197 and W3634.

Though well away from the front line, Donald's duties of checking aircraft at the MUs was of great importance. Sometimes he was testing engine modifications, other times airframe repairs, before each aircraft could be released for operational service. He frequently returned a Spitfire for additional adjustments, making several short test flights prior to the final shake-down full testing.

Life became even more interesting for Donald when, on 25 August 1943, there was a requirement for a Liberator and full crew to be flown to Cairo West. Donald went in AL559 as second pilot to a Squadron Leader Watson. They landed at Gibraltar on 26 August before flying on to Cairo West on 1 September. Donald returned to Gibraltar the following day, flying as second pilot to Squadron Leader Watson in another Liberator, arriving at Lyneham with eleven passengers that evening.

Donald was frequently detailed for transit flights, several being short trips between airfields in the regular Airspeed Oxfords HN127 and ED118, always returning to the essential testing duties that formed the bulk of his daily flying.

At the end of November 1943, the commanding officer of 33 MU at Lyneham signed off Donald's logbook. The rank of squadron leader was entered alongside Donald's signature, as he had been gazetted with that rank, albeit 'temporary', on 30 July 1943, with effect from 1 July. In December 1943, Squadron Leader Barnard was posted to No. 9 Maintenance Unit (9MU) at RAF Cosford.

There had been an RAF presence at Cosford only since 15 July 1938, after preparatory work on the new site had been started by Robert McAlpine Ltd in August 1937. On behalf of No. 2 School of Technical Training (Apprentices), a contingent under Squadron Leader A. L. Franks AFC took possession of the unfinished premises on the same day that the first sod was cut at another site not far away where an aeroplane factory was to be built – Castle Bromwich.[16] At more or less the same time, an order was being placed by the Air Ministry for 1,000 Supermarine Spitfire fighter aircraft. 'The Spitfire, Castle Bromwich and Cosford were soon to get to know each other very well.'[17]

It was not until 15 March 1939 that 9MU officially appeared at Cosford. 'Predominantly civilian manned, it was the Aircraft Storage Unit for which the station had originally been intended and its task was to store, maintain, repair, modify and ultimately issue aircraft to operational units. It also included the smaller No. 76 Maintenance Unit which was responsible for the packing of aircraft for overseas despatch.'[18] The motto of 9MU was the aptly chosen *Reddimus Tamquam Nova* ('We restore as new').

On 30 September 1942, 9MU changed to full-time production of the Horsa glider, though it had begun its involvement with this type of aircraft earlier in the year and was also, later, to handle the Hotspur and Hadrian gliders. Another massive job for the unit at the same time was the tropicalising of 470 Spitfires for use in the Middle East, together with the production of twelve Spitfires Mk Va and Vb for the Royal Navy's Fleet Air Arm. With newly built Spitfires pouring out of Castle Bromwich thereafter, there was always plenty of work to be done on them at Cosford.

It was into this hectic environment, therefore, that Donald was immediately plunged, and he had his fair share of excitement when, on the afternoon of 29 December 1943, he took up Mk VIII Spitfire JG530 for an air test. The engine cut out on overload and would not pick up, forcing him to make a landing on the aerodrome, fortunately without damage to either pilot or aircraft.

The workload increased with up to ten Spitfires a day requiring testing, and on 29 February 1944 Donald experienced another serious moment when he was giving Spitfire Mk LF VIII MD325 an air test. He had reached a height of 3,000 feet when the engine cut out. Another forced landing was negotiated at the aerodrome and, again, no damage was caused either to himself or to the aircraft. His skill in this incident brought an acknowledgment from HQ 41 Group:

> Forced Landing Spitfire MD325
>
> A reference was made regarding the above forced landing which stated that the pilot Squadron Leader Barnard was to be congratulated on his skill in handling the above aircraft under the circumstances obtaining at the particular time.
>
> Although this does not warrant a green ink entry vide A.M.C.O. 23/43, it showed a very high degree of airmanship.

Engines cutting out could happen to anyone, even to one of the greatest Spitfire test pilots of all, Alex Henshaw. His first cut out, in 1942, 'happened at Cosford in EP499 when I had completed the machine and was about to turn back to the aerodrome for the final landing. As I flew at normal power and revs the engine suddenly stopped as if the magnetos had been switched off.'[19] Henshaw was able to land in a field without causing much damage.

Donald continued over the months to excel in his role as a test pilot, and on 1 June 1944 he was assessed as 'Above the Average' as a test pilot by the officer commanding 9MU, Squadron Leader Hill [?]. His air-testing duties continued into late August, when notification of a long-awaited posting arrived. By the time that his tour of duty in 41 Group had ended, Donald had test-flown over 1,100 Spitfire aircraft, and the grand total of his entire RAF flying hours was now over 2,000.

With effect from 10 September 1944 he was posted to No. 109 Operational Training Unit (OTU) at RAF Crosby-on-Eden, 3 miles west of Brampton. The station was so far to the north of the county of Cumberland that Hadrian's Wall formed the airfield's northern boundary. Until 11 August 1944, the resident unit had been RAF Coastal Command's No. 9 OTU, with Beauforts and Beaufighters, but on that day 109 OTU was formed within Transport Command's No. 44 Group, whose Air Officer Commanding was Air Commodore G. R. Beamish CB, CBE, ADC, one of four brothers from Northern Ireland, all of whom served with distinction in the RAF.[20]

As the OTU was equipped with Dakotas, there was a call in the middle of September for seven of the OTU crews to fly south to RAF Down Ampney (Gloucestershire) and to RAF Blakehill Farm (Wiltshire), where they were required to assist in the resupplying of the Allied airborne forces that had attempted to seize the bridges over the Rhine at the Dutch town of Arnhem, and which were grimly hanging on to their little piece of Holland. This was the famous Operation Market Garden, launched on 17 September, but which had stalled in the face of strong German opposition. Allied forces were desperately in need of supplies, and Transport Command lost many brave crews as they tried to drop these supplies to the troops on the ground. Flying necessarily low and slow in their Stirling and Dakota aircraft, they were easy prey for the German anti-aircraft defences and for the much faster fighters. Perhaps fortuitously for the 109 OTU crews they were confined to the nonetheless useful task of ferrying goods and material to B.56 airfield at Brussels and to bringing back casualties.

Donald, who was still undergoing conversion training onto the Dakota, did not participate in these flights abroad, but his conversion was completed with a certificate of qualification added to his logbook on 26 December 1944: 'In the event of this Pilot requiring at any time to obtain a Civil Aircraft Pilot's Licence he should forward this Certificate with an application to the Department of Civil Aviation, the Air Ministry.' It was a qualification that Donald would find of great value after completing his RAF service.

Far East postings

With effect from 27 December 1944, Donald was attached to 525 Squadron (Wing Commander D. R. Miller) at RAF Lyneham, part of 116 Wing, RAF Transport Command. He left Crosby-on-Eden with two others from his course, wireless operator Flight Lieutenant Francis Humphrey Pole (81412) and navigator Flight Lieutenant Keyes, both of whom went with him to Lyneham.

No. 525 Squadron was equipped with the Douglas Dakota which, as well as taking supplies to the Army on the near continent, was also used on what today would be called long-haul flights, going as far as Karachi (then in north-west India). On 2 February 1945, having been posted to HQ 229 Group with effect from that date, Donald, Pole, Keyes and thirteen others duly left Lyneham for

Flight Lieutenant Keyes (seated, 4th from left), Barnard's navigator on 117 Squadron.

India aboard Dakota KJ970. After a flight of seven hours their first stop was at Elmas[21] on the island of Sardinia, then Castel Benito, Tripoli (2 hours 55 min) on 3 February, and Cairo West, Egypt (7 hours) on the following day.

On 5 February their journey continued to the RAF base at Habbaniya, Iraq (5 hours 55 min) and on to Sharjah, Oman, (5 hours 30 min). Finally, on 6 February, the group arrived at Transport Command Mauripur, Karachi (4 hours 5 min), in the Indian state of Sind.[22]

Exactly one month later Donald arrived at Chaklala, near Rawalpindi, in the Punjab, on posting to the resident Transport Support Training Unit. Here operational crews were taught not only the art of parachute supply-dropping over the jungle of Burma but also such skills as were vital for survival in the Far Eastern theatre of operations.

Whilst at Chaklala Donald took the opportunity, on 21 March 1945, to fly Tiger Moth NL946, with Flight Lieutenant Pole as passenger, on a 35-minute local flight, the first chance to get his hands on the controls of an aircraft in nearly three months.

A week later Donald, Pole, and seventeen others were flown from Chaklala by Group Captain George Donaldson DFC, AFC on a 30-minute flight to Gujrat (also in the Punjab).[23]

Flight Lieutenant Pole (seated, 4th from right), wireless operator on 117 Squadron. He flew with Donald on the unauthorised flight that led to Barnard's court-martial.

No. 1 Course Pilots Transport Command Operational Training Unit, September 1944. Squadron Leader Donald Barnard is seated 3rd from left.

Donald's arrival in Burma, April 1945

After a month at Comilla in Bengal, the time came for Donald to join an operational squadron once more. On 27 April 1945, he and nineteen other passengers were flown by a Colonel Wise (possibly an American) to Hathazari, on the coastal fringes of Chittagong, then in India but today in Bangladesh. Originally home to a detachment of one of Combat Cargo Task Force's (CCTF) units, the American 1 USAAF (CC) Squadron,[24] Hathazari was now occupied by 3 USAAF (CC), and by two RAF squadrons, Nos 31 and 117, all equipped with the Douglas Dakota.

CCTF had been formed in October 1944 specifically to keep the Army supplied. 'Throughout the campaign in Burma it had been the practice to pool the air resources for the mutual benefit of the British and American elements of Eastern Air Command. The result had been a building up of a balanced organisation known as Combat Cargo Task Force, capable of operating at an intensive rate of air supply.'[1] During CCTF's relatively short existence (October 1944-May 1945) its aircrews flew 386,283 hours, carried 332,136 short tons of supplies, carried 339,137 persons and 94,243 casualties, for a total of 379,707 tons.[26] With effect from 10 June 1945, the American 4th (CC) Group with its 100 C-46 aircraft had withdrawn from this particular theatre of operations, leaving eight RAF squadrons, with their 240 Dakotas, to carry on with the supply and evacuation duties under the control of No. 232 Group.

It was as a small but vital cog in the campaign that, on 27 April 1945, Donald joined 117 Squadron, commanded by Wing Commander William John McLean DFC, AFC, RAAF (Aus.406112).[27] No. 117 Squadron was one of the component squadrons of 177 Wing, which itself belonged to 224 Group, HQ RAF Burma. HQ RAF Burma had undergone two name changes shortly before Donald's arrival, having been 3rd Tactical Air Force (3TAF) until 4 December 1944 when its name was changed to RAF in Bengal and Burma, and then to HQ RAF Burma on 27 February 1945. By whatever name, 3TAF or HQ RAF Burma, it was subordinate to Eastern Air Command (South East Asia), which was but one part of Air Command, South East Asia.

Air Command, SE Asia, Organisational Structure

Air Command, South East Asia, was an enormous organisation whose units covered a vast area – the whole of India all the way to the Burmese border near Chittagong, and Ceylon (Sri Lanka today). Air Command's HQ was in New Delhi, with an Advanced HQ at Kandy in Ceylon. Temporary Air Commander-in-Chief was Air Marshal Sir Guy Garrod KCB, OBE, MC, who had replaced the former chief of Bomber Command, Air Chief Marshal Sir Richard Pierse KCB, DSO, AFC. Also there, on the administration side, were Air Marshal Alan Lees CB, CBE, DSO, AFC (later Sir Alan KCB) and his assistant Air Vice-Marshal Robert Victor Goddard CB, CBE (later Sir Victor KCB).

They were supported, on the Air Staff, by another air vice-marshal, three air commodores, four group captains, 25 wing commanders and an equivalent Army major, and 44 squadron leaders. In addition, on the Administrative Staff, there were a further four group captains, ten wing commanders, and 24 squadron leaders. Then came the Maintenance Staff under Air Vice-Marshal C. W. Weedon CBE, consisting of two air commodores, three group captains, 15 wing commanders, and 39 squadron leaders. There were then the various Staffs of the Services – Signals, Armament, Accountant, Photography, Medical, Dental, Legal, Local Audit, Meteorological, Educational, Aeronautical Inspection, the RAF Regiment, etc.

On a more modest scale personnel-wise, 3rd Tactical Air Force (3TAF), commanded by Air Marshal Sir Alec Coryton KCB, KBE, MVO, DFC, had an Air Staff of one air vice-marshal, one group captain, six wing commanders, and eight squadron leaders. 3TAF's other Staffs were of a similarly modest scale. At the sharp end, as it were, were the operational squadrons, among them 117 Squadron, who were flying the Mk III and IV Douglas Dakotas across Burma on supply drops and on casualty evacuations.

Donald and the other new arrivals on the squadron were left with little time for such niceties as familiarisation flights. On 29 April, two days after arriving on the squadron, Donald and two of his crew were taken up in Dakota FL516 by Flight Lieutenant Roberts for local flying. He was up again on the following day, this time in KN229 flown by Flight Sergeant Hastie between Falam, Magwe, and Comilla, the flights lasting 8 hours and 45 minutes. The high mountain peaks at Falam, and the mass of jungle beneath, no doubt gave much food for thought, and would have been a strong reminder of the natural dangers that had to be faced in the air over north-east India and Burma.

* * *

Burma (the Union of Myanmar) covers an area of some 262,000 square miles, a country generally perceived as being one covered in dense jungle.[28] The terrain fought over between 1942 and 1945 was, however, more varied, with significant high peaks and a low dry plain towards central Burma. Communications across the country were generally poor, with few roads or railways, and it was dominated by the main waterways, notably the Irrawaddy and its chief tributaries, the Chindwin, Shweli and Myitnge. Almost all routes ran north-south, following the natural structure of the country.

Between eastern Bengal and central Burma lie the Lushai and Chin Hills, which extend south as the Arakan Yomas and north-east as the barrier between Burma and Assam. They consist of many parallel sharp ridges, running roughly north to south, with many peaks rising to 6,000-9,000 feet. The highest peak of the Arakan Yomas, Mount Victoria, is just over 10,000 feet.[29] These mountains are, though, covered with intensely thick jungle and form a barrier between central Burma and

In early 1945, the Arakan offensive was sustained by 117 Squadron. Dakota 'Q' undertook repairs at Hmawbi, Burma; squadron personnel are photographed on the airframe.

the eastern Bengal and Arakan coast, with the exception of two tracks. Generally speaking, it was over this unforgiving terrain that aircrews were obliged to fly, with little chance of survival if forced down.

Besides the terrain were the challenging conditions of the heat and humidity which brought with them jungle sores, while insect bites were endured and snakes avoided. All service personnel were required to take mepacrine tablets daily to prevent malaria, the naturally transmitted disease caused by the bite of a female Anopheles mosquito.

* * *

For months prior to Donald's posting to 117 Squadron in the Burmese theatre of operations, the RAF had been heavily, if not entirely, involved in the support of the 'Forgotten Army', the famous British Fourteenth Army under Lieutenant-General (later, 1949, Field Marshal) Sir W. J. 'Bill' Slim KCB, CBE, DSO, MC. A measure of the brilliance of Slim's generalship was that he was reckoned by some to have been the greatest general of the twentieth century. In February and March 1944, Fourteenth Army's 15 Corps had decisively beaten the Japanese in Arakan, and this was followed in May, June, and July of that year by the crushing defeat of the Japanese in the Kohima-Imphal battles. The Japanese had launched their spring offensive with the object of seizing the gateway to India, but these defeats ensured that it was a total failure, their casualties being estimated at 100,000. Their subsequent retreat during the monsoon also took its toll, costing them thousands more lives.

According to General Sir Oliver Leese, appointed Commander-in-Chief Allied Land Forces, South East Asia on 12 November 1944, it was time to ensure the destruction 'of the Japanese Army in Burma, with the proviso that these operations must in no way interfere with my responsibilities for the protection and opening of the Ledo/Burma Road and the air routes to China.'[30]

* * *

After his two local flights at the end of April, Donald flew with Hastie again in KK166 on 2 May, and was then considered ready to fly his first operation. His regular crew were Flying Officer J. W. Charter, RCAF, (2nd pilot), Flight Lieutenant J. F. Cuthbert DFC (navigator), and Flight Lieutenant Francis Pole (wireless operator). Others flew with them from time to time to make up the full complement of five, but eventually the fifth crew member was usually Flight Sergeant Handley.

On 5 May 1945, therefore, Donald flew his first drop, 6,900 lb (just over 3 tons) of supplies to a spot near Rangoon. On the same day he and his crew took a further 6,930 lb to Magwe, returning with 790 lb of mail from the troops for onward despatch. Fourteenth Army required on average some 2,000 tons of supplies per day but, as the maximum tonnage that could possibly be carried over land was only 700 tons a day, the balance had to brought in by air.

It was thanks to crews such as Donald's that Fourteenth Army was able to steamroller its way south through Burma, pushing the Japanese Army before it: 'Supply by air formed a large and vital part of the whole gigantic transportation effort which the prosecution of this campaign entailed ... It is enough here to say that during the peak month of April, 1945, when Fourteenth Army was racing for Rangoon, over 68,100 tons were delivered by air, over 11,000 men were brought forward and nearly 10,000 casualties evacuated.'

According to his logbook, during his first month of operating on 117 Squadron, Donald and crew delivered a gross total of 216,120 lb of supplies, in addition to carrying 76 passengers and casualties, in just eighteen sorties. And during May 1945, 117 Squadron flew the truly astonishing total of 4,936 hours, and carried 9,230,000 lb of freight to many destinations, which is believed to be a record for any transport squadron in any theatre of war. General Leese wrote:

Air transport was used on a scale hitherto unprecedented in modern war ... [To] get the true measure of the effort, it should be remembered that the air-crews who delivered the goods often made three or four journeys a day over hazardous jungle country, often flying in appalling conditions of weather; many casualties were caused by these fearful conditions, but the risks were unflinchingly faced. The ground crews worked unceasingly by day and night in the open, sometimes in torrential rain, to keep the aircraft in commission and to enable the very high rates of service to be maintained.[31]

Though the Dakota was performing well in the prevailing conditions, and RAF groundcrews managed to maintain high levels of aircraft serviceability, there was apparently one feature of the Dakota's reliability that was beyond even the groundcrews' ability to overcome. This was 'an epidemic of main bearing failures in Dakota aircraft engines which had caused an appreciable drop in serviceability; one squadron needed 26 new engines.'[32] On 6 August, for example, Donald flew to Barrackpore to 'collect new motor for [Dakota] "C" '.

It was usual for Dakota crews to have to fly two sorties each day, sometimes three but rarely four, with payloads being delivered mainly to airstrips. Where that was not possible they were dropped by parachute, helped on their way by the despatchers. Loads were stacked in the Dakota's fuselage close to the doors and in order to despatch as many loads as possible, one despatcher would position himself on the floor with his back to the aircraft. Facing the open door he would kick the load out, his fellow despatchers replacing the load as fast as it left the aircraft. A year earlier, on 26 May 1944, one Dakota of 194 Squadron, also one of 224 Group's squadrons, nearly came to grief on a drop when its load of bags of rice shifted suddenly, upsetting the centre of gravity to such an extent that the pilot was fortunate to be able to regain control of his aircraft before hitting the deck. Loading was, therefore, a precise science.

Over the dropping zones it was Donald's practice to bank the aircraft and lift the tail slightly, thus ensuring that the parachutes – known locally as 'statichutes' – would not become entangled on the airframe as they left the aircraft. But before being able to drop the supplies, a crew had to find their allocated Drop Zone (DZ). Over thick jungle this was easier said than done, but those on the ground learnt to mark the DZ with smoke fires in the form of a large letter 'L', with the pilot of the supply aircraft then flying along the long arm of the 'L' dropping the supplies as he went.

As well as carrying supplies and mail, the Dakotas also ferried passengers, and on the first of the two trips he flew on 11 May Donald noted the return of 'repats 18' from Meiktila to Base. As a rule, Donald was now flying every other day, and on 13 May delivered 6,000 lb of petrol (in cans) to Zayatkwin on one sortie and a further 6,000 lb on a second to Payabyu in Dakota KK166. On 15 May, on the second trip of the day, he flew KK166 to the airstrip on Ramree Island, taking '19 passengers & freight 8,000 lb'.

Ramree Island, off the Arakan coast, was no stranger to 117 Squadron. The island – actually connected to the mainland by large mangrove swamps which are infested by *Crocodylus porosus*, the fierce saltwater crocodile and the largest of all living reptiles – had been cleared of its Japanese occupants in January and February 1945 in Operations Matador and Block. After 'softening up' by the RAF, on 21 January 1945, with the considerable help of the Royal Navy and Royal Indian Navy, the initial assault was made by the 71st Indian Infantry Brigade, and was followed up by the 4th Indian Infantry Brigade and, on 26 January, by the 36th Indian Infantry Brigade, of the Indian XV Corps. Also heavily involved were the Royal Marines.

Fighting was concluded by 22 February, and of the '1,200 to 1,500 Japanese in occupation on the day of landing, only a few escaped. The remainder were either killed in battle or drowned in the mangrove swamps. Only twenty prisoners were taken in spite of all efforts of persuasion towards the close of Operation "Block", when many Japanese troops, without hope of relief or escape, had reached the final stages of exhaustion.'[33] Operation Block, a Combined Operation to close river exits from the island in the east and north-east, lasted for the fortnight ending on 22 February.

Once the island had been taken a landing ground of sorts was prepared, though in the time available before the onset of the monsoon season Army engineers were unable to lay an all-weather strip 'for the express purpose of monsoon air supply operations'. It was to be a feature of the Ramree airstrip that it was 'often so waterlogged that aircraft could not get off'. Nevertheless, a detachment of 117 Squadron, together with Nos 31 and 436 (RCAF) Squadrons, moved in on 16 April, and were now considerably closer to Rangoon than hitherto.

Donald made another sortie to Ramree on 16 May, having to put down at Akyab due to the weather, and on 18 May flew three sorties (20,900 lb in total) in KN302. He flew three again on 19 May (20, 900 lb) in FZ612, and another three on 21 May, this time returning with twenty-five 'casualties' from Toungoo – Donald called it Tongoo – to Akyab. The demand on the squadron was now so great that Donald was regularly flying three sorties a day. On the last day of the month he noted: 'F/Lt Page & crew brought back.' Why this was necessary is not known.

With the pace of operations slowing down, on 2 June Donald amused himself with half an hour's local flying, being taking up in a Stinson L-5 Sentinel (KJ433) by a Flight Lieutenant Rogers. Next day it was back to business, though for some reason, possibly bad weather, Donald was diverted to Akyab on return from Toungoo in KN461. He later recovered to Base. On 6 June, in a change of direction, Donald flew KN303 to Alipore (south of Calcutta) and on to Dum Dum (just north of Calcutta). With him and his crew were thirty passengers, possibly personnel off on leave.

Around this time Wing Commander W. J. McLean, 117's commanding officer, was repatriated to Australia, and was succeeded by Wing Commander A. J. Samson DFC.[34] The squadron's stay at Ramree ended when it moved back to Patenga strip[35] immediately to the south of Chittagong, so that 117 Squadron could be in a position to cover the central Burma supply route. The other transport squadrons based at Rangoon provided the southern area with its supply requirements. At Patenga, the weather became their worst enemy, as the heavy monsoon rain produced difficult flying and terrible ground conditions. The personal contribution of Donald's crew to the support of the Army in June 1945 amounted to the evacuation of 84 casualties and the transportation of 56,500 lb of supplies.[36]

The 26th Indian Infantry Division had landed by ship at Rangoon just as the monsoons had started on 2 May 1945, and after the Japanese had withdrawn their troops from that city, but June and July were the worst months for the feared cumulo-nimbus cloud which, as a result of the monsoon conditions, could build up from low level to above an aircraft's ceiling. By and large the battle with the weather was won, but not without a number of casualties. Air Chief Marshal Park mentioned in his Despatch that it was 'on record that one Dakota aircraft flying over Burma actually found itself turned upside down in a storm, and it was only the skill and presence of mind of the pilot which averted disaster'.

The dangers of these clouds were highlighted in the August 1945 edition of the RNZAF's national magazine *Contact*:

Cumulo-nimbus, the thundercloud, has become known to the aviator the world over, as a stark warning of flying conditions in which the turbulence and air currents are such that there is no effective counter-measure. Terrific up currents, down currents and chaotic air masses have been known to render normal control movements entirely futile and many an aircraft has plunged helplessly to its destruction thousands of feet below in an uncontrollable manoeuvre from which there is not time to recover.

Sometimes, structural damage sufficient to completely wreck the aircraft results, as witness the miraculous escape of a young New Zealand pilot, Warrant Officer Colin Brown, flying a Spitfire between Chittagong and Calcutta. Colin took his Spitfire off from Chittagong one afternoon in the monsoon and climbed toward Calcutta …

Suffice it to say that Colin Brown was forced to climb through a thick layer of murk, which concealed the dreaded cumulo-nimbus clouds. At around 27,000 feet the Spitfire disintegrated, blasting the semi-conscious pilot into the void. He recovered his senses sufficiently to pull the ripcord of his parachute, but not before he was down to an estimated 1,500 to 1,000 feet above ground. He survived his terrible ordeal with a broken back.

At the end of June 1945, Donald's squadron was particularly exposed to the dangers of flying in the area of these 'cu-nims', as evidenced by two separate incidents on 26 and 27 June. In the first, when the port engine of Dakota KN218 failed, the pilot was unable to avoid a cumulo-nimbus cloud. The turbulence threw the Dakota onto its back with such force that it broke into four sections and crashed, killing the six airmen aboard. On the following day Flying Officer A. C. Kent and crew were killed when Dakota KN602 was lost, cause unknown. The RAF's official casualty list gives only the names of the five crew and eight passengers, but recent research suggests that a further seventeen servicemen who were aboard were also killed (see Appendix IV).[37]

Donald and crew were continuing to evacuate casualties at this time, bringing out seventeen on 20 June, twenty more two days later and, having taken ammunition to Rangoon, another twenty on 26 June.

In the first half of July the Japanese Twenty-Eighth Army was ordered to break out of the Pegu Yomas,[38] whither they had earlier retreated, and to assist with this operation the Japanese Thirty-Third Army was ordered to make a diversionary attack across the Sittang River, which they did on 3 July. But they had attacked too early, for the Twenty-Eighth Army was not able to move until 17 July and, when it did, it was ambushed by concentrations of British artillery that had been placed along the likely route. Hundreds of Japanese 'drowned trying to cross the swollen Sittang on improvised bamboo floats and rafts. Burmese guerrillas and bandits killed stragglers east of the river. The breakout cost the Japanese nearly 10,000 men, half the strength of Twenty-Eighth Army. British and Indian casualties were minimal.'[39]

Despite this battle, Donald's flying reduced considerably in the first two weeks of July, flying only two operations on 10 July, in Dakota KN254, but no cargo was noted in his logbook. A week later, on 17 July, he flew to Toungoo with 6,000 lb of supplies and 'Radio equipment'. He flew on from Toungoo to Myingyan, in KN567, to pick up, as he says in his logbook, '25 JIFFS'.

'Jiffs was a pejorative term used by British Intelligence, and later the 14th Army, to denote soldiers of the Indian National Army after the failed First Arakan Offensive of 1943. The term is derived from the acronym JIFC, short for Japanese-Indian (or -inspired) fifth column. It came to be employed in a propaganda offensive in June 1943 within the British Indian Army as a part of the efforts to preserve the loyalty of the Indian troops at Manipur after suffering desertion and losses at Burma during the First Arakan Offensive.'[40]

The day was a busy one for the crew of KN567, a further 6,000 lbs of stores being flown to Meiktila and another thirteen Jiffs taken to Myaungmya.

On the next day, 18 July, again in KN567, the Barnard crew flew 4,000 lb of barbed-wire to Toungoo, on the Sittang River, for the construction of compounds to hold the many Japanese prisoners of war following the British success against the Japanese Thirty-Third and Twenty-Eighth Armies. Then it was on to Mingaladon with three passengers, and back to Base with two passengers and twenty casualties. Not yet finished for the day, KN567 took 6,000 lb of clothing to Myingyan and brought back four Jeep motors to Base.

Donald had a day off on 19 July, and all he did on 20 July was to go up for a spin in Harvard trainer FX474 flown by a Flying Officer Jones. On the following day Donald took KN593 to Mingaladon with 6,000 lb of supplies, returning with twenty casualties and four passengers. No further operations took place for the rest of the month, but on 30 July, in FD837, Donald noted that they had to return from Agartala because of 'weather'.

On 1 August, with his crew plus Flight Sergeant Poole and two groundcrew, Donald took Dakota 'G' on an air search, but for whom or for what he did not say. On the next day, after Wing Commander Samson had selected him to lead 'A' Flight, 117 Squadron, Donald displayed his leadership qualities by volunteering to carry out an emergency evacuation of a casualty from a beach identified in his logbook only as 'George'. Donald flew a Captain Edelstone, RAMC, and three medical orderlies to the place, and made a successful, though difficult, landing. His logbook reveals that the casualty unfortunately died.

On 7 August, in KN245, he took 5,000 lb of supplies and 1,000 lb of meat for a drop at Mandalay. Later that same day, with Group Captain Stephenson also aboard, the cargo was 6,000 lb of 'Bithess', returning with 4,000 lb of gas capes.

Made of a thin, rubberised material, frequently printed in a camouflage pattern, these capes were worn like a poncho, and were commonly used as a light rain cape. Rolled or folded and secured to the webbing when not in use, they were to prove a key piece of equipment for ground troops in need of protection from the extremely wet weather. 'Bithess' was a material originally developed for use on temporary aircraft runways. It was capable of producing an all-weather surface with long strips of bituminised hessian laid directly onto carefully packed earth. Not only was it used for aircraft runways but also for miles of roads across Burma.

It was not unknown for a second coating of this material to be added during the monsoon periods.

The devastating atomic bombing of Hiroshima on 6 August 1945, and the destruction of Nagasaki three days later, forced Japan to offer unconditional surrender on 14 August. The epic supplying of the Allied armies by air now came to a close:

> The period May to August, 1945 – covering the re-entry of the Allied Forces into Rangoon and later the surrender of Japan – cannot be termed spectacular in air supply operations when reckoned against such efforts during the Allied advance down through Burma earlier in the year, when the mobility of Fourteenth Army was almost entirely provided by the Allied Air Forces whose record supply tonnage averaged 2,900 tons per day in April, 1945.

> The period ... was not only the monsoon period but the period, with the exception of the July battle in Burma, during which the Allied Forces on ground, sea and in the air were building up their organisation and strength to deliver the next blow which would have fallen upon the Japanese in Malaya in early September. Nevertheless, the R.A.F. Transport supply squadrons met the demands required of them, and the supply effort for that period may be summarised as follows:

	May	June	July	August	Total
Tactical Trips	7,998	7,211	8,258	3,779	27,246
Personnel Carried	7,795	2,321	3,017	4,651	17,784
Casualties Evacuated	3,899	2,515	2,044	1,514	9,972
Supplies Delivered	23,172	19,978	22,170	9,418	74,738
Estimated Total	23,951	20,210	22,472	9,883	76,516

With the emphasis now on the recovery of prisoners of war, an operational detachment from 117 Squadron, including Donald, and with Wing Commander Samson commanding, flew to Hmawbi near Rangoon on 18 August, standing by for the new and important task of recovering Allied prisoners of war and other personnel from French Indo-China, Siam, Malaya and the Netherlands East Indies.

News had spread of the terrible conditions that so many prisoners had endured, that casualties were very high, and were rising on a daily basis. As early as April 1945 a large white-painted message had been seen on the roof of Rangoon jail: 'JAPS GONE. RAF HERE. EXTRACT DIGIT.' It was short and to the point, and though little could be done immediately to evacuate all the thousands of Allied prisoners, on 2 May, Wing Commander A. E. Saunders, officer commanding 110 Squadron, landed in a Mosquito at Mingaladon and was taken to the jail at Rangoon to see for himself the piteous state of the 1,400 inmates.[42]

POWs message to aircraft at Rangoon jail.

In July 1945, well before the Japanese surrender on 14 August, Allied air forces, in anticipation of victory, had already dropped propaganda leaflets on Japanese forces, and one type in particular was dropped on their soldiers who were trapped in the Pegu Yomas of southern Burma. These particular leaflets not only called upon the enemy to surrender after telling them of the hopeless position of their homeland but, on the reverse side, offered them safe conduct through the Allied lines with the added assurance that they would be given food, medical attention, and honourable treatment.

Once the surrender came, however, it was imperative, given the parlous state of the Allied prisoners of war (there were almost 100,000 of them, with 35,000 alone on Singapore Island), that everyone, including the Japanese prison guards and prisoners of war, the local Japanese forces, and the local native population, were informed by leaflet of what they should do when the surrender was formally announced. To implement this, Operation Birdcage was launched on 28 August by Allied air forces operating from bases as far afield as Ceylon (Sri Lanka), the Cocos Islands, Bengal and Burma. The four-engined Liberators with their long range flew from bases in the first three mentioned places. Over the four days of 28-31 August some 18 million leaflets were dropped on 236 localities and on ninety prisoner-of-war camps throughout Burma, Siam, French Indo-China, Malaya, and Burma. All in all, thirty-three million leaflets were dropped over enemy-occupied territory in south-east Asia, and such was the determination of the crews that 'one group of towns in the hinterland of Malaya was successfully covered only at the third attempt'.

It was not only the twin- or four-engined transport aircraft that were engaged on Operation Birdcage but also the single-engined North American P-47 'Thunderbolt'. It was one of these that proved to be the only casualty of the operation. The pilot, 24-year-old 1318357 Warrant Officer George Edwin Chaney, 34 Squadron, having reported that he was having trouble with his aircraft, KJ356, was killed when it crashed in flames at Kraburi on the Kra Isthmus, Malaya, on 30 August.[43]

Air Chief Marshal Sir Keith Park noted 'that Operation "Birdcage" was carried out in very indifferent conditions. Even more important still was the fact that an all round trip of many of the sorties was equivalent to a trans-Atlantic flight.'[44]

It was a prodigious effort by all concerned, but still more was expected from the transport squadrons now that the fighting war was over. It was time to help the prisoners, many of whom were, as Sir Keith wrote, 'emaciated, gaunt and pitiful beings – some, indeed, were too weak to stand upon their legs'. All that could be done initially by way of assistance for the prisoners was to get medical supplies and food to them as quickly as possible, and this could be done only by air.

So it was that Operation Mastiff 'was planned to ensure that medical aid, comforts, food, clothing, R.A.P.W.I.[45] Control Staffs where necessary, and any other essential preliminary needs were introduced into the [prisoner-of-war] camps as early as possible'. It, too, began on 28 August and would continue 'until the last prisoner of war and internee had been evacuated from all areas by air and sea'.

Sometimes, in places where the Japanese were no longer in control, the local population protested violently at the next occupier of their land as one RAF officer, Flight Lieutenant Frederick Markham Ball, would experience for himself. He was parachuted into Java in September 1945 to see to the needs of some 24,000 'RAPWI', and was still there when fighting broke out at Semarang on 20 October between the Japanese and Indonesians. A state of anarchy existed throughout the area, and Ball was required to draw upon all his negotiating skills, tact, and diplomacy:

> In order that information concerning the state of affairs which existed should reach Batavia, Flight Lieutenant Ball forced his way past 60 barricades from Ambarawa to Magelang and then flew a Japanese light aircraft to Batavia. Here he was able to give valuable information, thus enabling troops to be sent to Semarang in time to save the situation. Flight Lieutenant Ball was then appointed to command the Rapwi in Magelang. When the town was evacuated owing to the fighting, he remained behind in order to negotiate for the safety of 2,500 Eurasians

and Ambonnees refugees. Throughout the long and dangerous period Flight Lieutenant Ball continually carried his life in his hands and his performance of his duties was an inspiration to all.[46]

A measure of the efforts made by the aircrews may be gathered from the journey of 3,400 miles made by the crew of one of the first aircraft involved on 28/29 August when they took a medical team from the Cocos Islands to Changi airfield on Singapore Island.

Operation Mastiff was summed up by Sir Keith Park in his Despatch:

With the Japanese surrender in the second half of August, there came orders for the move of six R.A.F. Transport squadrons to the Rangoon area to transport stores, and to evacuate Ps.O.W. from Siam, French Indo-China, Malaya and the Netherlands East Indies. As the result of these squadron moves, and the military situation at the time, the number of normal transport operations fell away very considerably. The majority of the trips, indeed, were concerned with moves by squadrons and the stocking up of the Rangoon airfields with provisions for the liberated territories and the P.O.W. camps.

August 28th – the historic date on which Operation "Mastiff" was launched to bring relief to the thousands of Allied Ps.O.W. in the prison camps throughout the vast territories of South East Asia – saw the transport squadrons, as well as other aircraft of the Command, including those of the R.A.A.F., take part in what was described as "one of the greatest mercy missions of the war".

Many of the flights undertaken in these operations were equivalent to a Transatlantic flight, and yet 75 per cent, of the crews succeeded in reaching their targets and dropping their messages as well as parachuting medical supplies, Red Cross parcels and teams of medical and signalling personnel provided mainly by airborne formations. Later, many thousands of Ps.O.W. and internees were evacuated from these territories by air.

It is not difficult to visualise the plight in which our Allied Ps.O.W. would certainly have found themselves after the official Japanese surrender, had not all resources, including Air Power, been used, and organised quickly, to bring relief, comfort and sustenance to these unfortunate men, many of them too weak to stand on their own legs. Only Air Power could have penetrated these vast territories throughout South East Asia with the speed required to initiate that essential relief. The pin-pointing of many Japanese P.O.W. camps, in addition to the great distances flown by aircraft and the hazards of weather encountered in these tropical regions, speaks magnificently for the navigational and flying skill of our aircrews.

Mastiff was also not without casualties. According to Park's Despatch, over the three weeks from 30 August to 19 September 1945, 327 sorties were flown on the operation, of which 25 were abortive and from which four aircraft were missing.

A Liberator of 99 Squadron, with a crew of eight, was lost on 1 September 1945. The pilot of the aircraft was flying over the Sungei Ron camp near Palembang, Indonesia, 'in the middle of the morning, and made several passes dropping containers. On the final pass, and having completed the drop, the aircraft made a steep turn at low level and its wingtip touched the ground and it cartwheeled and exploded.'[47]

It is not clear which, apart from the 99 Squadron Liberator, were the other losses but a second loss was possibly 48 Squadron's Dakota KN532, which crashed on 5 September with the loss of thirty lives. Another Dakota, KK118, this time from Donald's squadron, was lost on 6 September. All twenty-six on board were killed. This loss, as were a number of others, was attributed to the aircraft entering a cumulo-nimbus cloud which, as already seen, were to be avoided at all costs. Sometimes, when going round them or returning whence one had come was not an option, it was not possible to avoid their devastating internal currents.

Another Dakota was lost on 7 September, KN584 of 357 Squadron, with sixteen persons on board, but the cause of the accident was not established. Then, on the following day, came the devastating loss of 117 Squadron's commanding officer Wing Commander Samson, his crew and many soldiers, forty-one in total, all killed when Dakota KN593 encountered a deadly 'cu-nim' cloud (see below, page 171).

During a fortnight of waiting and filling in time, the only operations flown by 117 Squadron at Hmawbi were the transportation of various loads of medical and other supplies from Akyab to Mingaladon for storage in preparation for the reception of the former prisoners. Feelings were running high among aircrew that this procedure was producing an unacceptable delay in dealing with the grave situation of the many hundreds of starving prisoners of war who were in urgent need of help. The official history of the RAF Medical Services offers a plausible reason for some of the delays:

> There was little delay in repatriating prisoners of war from the European theatre, who were rapidly evacuated by air, but owing to the greater distances involved and to certain other factors it was some time before the Far East prisoners reached the United Kingdom and the waiting period which elapsed had some bearing on their physical condition on arrival. The Japanese Government capitulated on August 15, 1945, but because of typhoons and the heavily mined coastal waters, it was not until approximately September 15 that the American forces were able to land in any strength. The task of caring for the prisoners during this interim period was an extremely difficult one for the medical officers.[48]

The delay in recovering the Allied prisoners of war weighed heavily on Donald's mind, and the knowledge that these prisoners were awaiting collection brought him to boiling point. He was now about to make the decision that would bring about the end of his distinguished service in the RAF.

During the evening of 1 September 1945, there was talk in the squadron mess of the plight of the POWs who had been recovered from the Japanese. After a while, having allegedly drunk a couple of gins, Donald said 'To hell with Mountbatten, to hell with everyone,' and decided to take a Dakota and fly down to Bangkok to get some of these boys out. As it would be an unauthorised flight, and one for which Donald would take full responsibility, he asked his crew to go with him, but his navigator, Flight Lieutenant Cuthbert, refused to have anything to do with such a flight, and told 'Barney' that he couldn't do it. His wireless operator, Flight Lieutenant Pole, however, agreed to go, as did another navigator on the squadron, Flying Officer Norman Davies, after he had been approached by Donald. As Norman said: 'Well, when a junior officer is asked by a squadron leader you don't refuse him.'[49]

Donald told his crew to meet at 0200 hours next morning, 2 September, and they duly assembled at Dakota KN593. In the absence of any groundcrew, they had to start the engines themselves, and at 0250 hours Donald began their take-off run.

The duty officer at the airfield's control tower, which was always manned, was Flying Officer William Barons (166855). No aircraft movements were expected, but on that particular morning Barons' attention was drawn to a Dakota which was in the process of taking off. Furious instructions were issued over the radio by the staff in the control tower to abort the take-off, and Flying Officer Barons himself flashed a red signal – STOP – by Aldis lamp. In no mood to comply with either order, the pilot – Donald, of course – carried on.

Three hours later, Donald arrived at Don Muang (Bangkok) from Hmawbi airfield as dawn was breaking, and taxied up to the hangars, in which ex-prisoners of war were sleeping on the concrete floor. The Dakota crew distributed among the emaciated prisoners what few comforts they had brought with them, but were struck by how subdued they all were. Donald collected twenty-five prisoners of war in the worst condition, and two Public Relations Officers, and flew them on a flight lasting 2 hours 40 minutes to Mingaladon, Rangoon, where medical assistance was waiting. Donald then returned to Hmawbi. There is no mention in 117 Squadron's Operational Record Book of this whole business, but a suitable note must have been made of it at the time. If it was, then it, too, no longer appears to exist.

Though Donald's personal objective had been achieved, the consequences for him were to prove most serious. Sixty years after his personal crusade, William Barons wrote of the night's events as he remembered them:

> I was with the Squadron [117] at Patenga Airport (near Chittagong) and then at Hmawbi (near Rangoon). I knew S/L Donald Barnard as a Flight Commander of our Squadron.

The Dakota aircraft that Barnard flew on his unauthorised collection of POWs.

Towards the end of 1945 all the Dakota squadrons were on stand-by. We were waiting for permission from H.Q. to fly to Bangkok and Saigon to bring prisoners of war back to Rangoon for eventual resettlement and onwards journeys home. For several days this permission was not given causing much frustration among everybody.

S/L Barnard having had a few drinks one night decided to fly to Bangkok – only one other crew member went with him. I was a young Flying Officer at the time doing duty at our flying control tower. This was just a watching brief because there was no night flying at all. I was alerted to the fact that a Dakota was about to take off. I called up on our Radio/Telephone control system – there was no reply – obviously it had not been switched on [in the aircraft]. I shone a red light from an Aldis type lamp at the aircraft repeatedly but was ignored and the Dakota thundered past and took off into the darkness. I reported this and was told the pilot was S/L Barnard.

S/L Barnard was court-martialled for this and subsequently dismissed the Service. I was called to give evidence at the Court-Martial in January 1946.

A few months later I was having a drink in a hotel in Batavia when Donald Barnard came in. What a surprise!! He was in the uniform of an Officer in the Dutch air line (KLM). We had a chat together – he told me he was very happy with KLM and was in fact awaiting promotion. We did not mention the unfortunate incident which led to his Court-Martial.[50]

With plans already in place for the recovery of the Allied prisoners, the first official shuttle sorties to Bangkok and Saigon, unknown to Donald, began on the following day, 3 September.

The medical plan for evacuated prisoners of war included advanced base hospitals in Rangoon, and it was anticipated that they would be in a position to deal with the sudden influx of recovered Allied prisoners of war. A total accommodation of 10,000 beds was reached in Rangoon at the close of operations against the Japanese occupying forces. Some 16,000 prisoners of war were to be evacuated from Siam and French Indo-China by air into Rangoon, the majority being flown from Bangkok, which was used as a transit staging post.

The hospitals in Rangoon quickly became effective in processing the sick prisoners of war, the vast majority of whom were expected to recover within a three-month period, when they would be ready for repatriation to their home country. The bald figures quoted in the official RAF medical history of the war suggest that only 1,237 returned RAF prisoners of war of the Japanese were deemed to have some form of notable sickness. Of this total, five only were to die of their ailment – listed in each case as debility, deficiency, infections, pulmonary T.B., and circulatory – whereas a further 129 were classified as 'Invalids' and the rest – 1,103 – as 'Others'. As the history said:

> The problems of the returned prisoners of war, in particular those from the Far East, were unfortunately not confined to their physical condition. The privations that they had suffered had produced in many of them a diversity of mental symptoms which made it very difficult for them to adjust themselves to normal everyday life.[51]

Returning to the everyday life of 117 Squadron, Dakota KN593 was in the air again on 7 September, this time with Wing Commander A. J. Samson at the controls. He flew to Saigon, where thirty-one ex-prisoners and other passengers were loaded onto the aircraft. Having refuelled at Bangkok they were on their way back to Rangoon on 8 September when, still some 150 miles short of their destination, for whatever reason, Samson, a hugely experienced pilot, apparently flew into a developing cumulo-nimbus cloud. In what can only have been turbulent air within the cloud KN593 broke up and crashed into the sea. There were no survivors. An hour or so after midday villagers at Nuaunggangle, about 13 miles north-west of Moulmein, Burma, heard an aircraft out to sea, then an explosion. The incoming tide that evening brought with it various bits and pieces from what can only have been KN593. Low tide on the following day revealed wreckage scattered over a sandbank, and several unidentified bodies, which were recovered.[52]

One of those lost was Donald's friend and regular crew member Flight Lieutenant James Cuthbert DFC and Bar.[53] Having flown together on over forty operational flights, there can be no doubt that his death would have been hard felt by Donald.

In the first week of September, the Dakotas alone dropped or landed over 400 tons of stores and brought back 4,000 prisoners of war, while during the second week they delivered 600 tons and brought back another 3,700 men. By the middle of the month, 9,000 prisoners had been flown from Bangkok to Rangoon.

The majority of these prisoners were very sick and severely emaciated, a large number being survivors of the building of the notorious Burma–Thailand railway. The conditions on the railway were horrific, with prisoners being forced to endure regular beatings for not maintaining the required progress on daily construction levels set by the Japanese engineers. The estimated numbers of civilian labourers and prisoners of war who died during construction varies considerably. Some figures suggest that a total of some 311,000 people worked on the line – 250,000 Asian labourers and 61,000 Allied prisoners of war – and that an estimated 90,000 labourers and 16,000 Allied prisoners of war died, the vast majority being buried alongside the railway track where they had fallen.

On 12 September 1945, in a ceremony in Singapore, Lord Louis Mountbatten, as Supreme Allied Commander South East Asia Command, formally accepted from General Seishiro Itagaki the overall surrender of 680,000 Japanese soldiers, sailors, and airmen in South East Asia.[54]

Court martial

As this wretched chapter in human history drew to a close, away from the flood of human misery that were the prisoners of war, Flight Lieutenant Grant took Donald on 20 September 1945 to Chittagong. One can only surmise that the purpose of this extended visit to India was for Donald to attend some formal investigation with regard to his unauthorised actions on the night of 2 September. At this time Headquarters RAF Burma, Air Command South East Asia, was based at Calcutta.

Whatever the reason, Donald returned to 117 Squadron at Hmawbi on 10 October 1945. The squadron's days were now numbered, its magnificent services no longer required, as the Operational Record Book reveals:

> On December 17 1945 No. 117 Squadron officially disbanded. This brings to a close a series of Operational achievements, both in the Middle East and Burma campaigns, which have rarely been surpassed by any other Transport Squadron. Every member of No. 117 Squadron may

justifiably be proud of the fact that they have helped the Squadron to live up to its motto "IT SHALL BE DONE".

It would be three months before Squadron Leader Barnard resumed any flying. His great friend Flight Lieutenant Francis Humphrey Pole accompanied him in Dakota FD847 during an air test on 10 January 1946. This was the last entry written by Donald as a serving officer in the RAF, his days in the Service, as also those of 117 Squadron, were numbered.

On 17 January 1946, a General Court Martial dismissed Squadron Leader Donald Beausire Barnard DFC from RAF service. The supplement to *The London Gazette* published on 21 May 1946 simply announced, on page 2396: 'Dismissal by sentence of General Court Martial. Sqn Ldr D. B. BARNARD D.F.C. (40352) 17th Jan 1946.'

Unfortunately, no record remains of the proceedings of the court martial, despite diligent searches having been made by the Air Historical Branch (RAF), and we are most grateful to Sebastian Cox, Head of AHB (RAF), for this reply to our enquiries:

> We have consulted both the National Archives catalogue and the Director of Legal Services for the RAF.
>
> It would appear that the detailed papers relating to the Court Martial of Sqn Ldr Barnard have not survived as they are not among the courts martial papers preserved in AIR CLASS 18 at TNA. I have recalled the courts martial ledger for overseas courts martial held at AIR CLASS 21 in TNA and there is a brief reference to the charge and the sentence in the ledger. However, the charge is only recorded by Section of the Air Force Act, in this instance Section 40, Conduct Prejudicial to Good Order and Discipline. A charge under this section of the Act would be explained in greater detail as with respect to the exact nature of the offence on the charge sheet, but this is not recorded in the ledger …
>
> I regret to say that no other papers relating to the court martial appear to have survived the review process.

Section 40 of the Air Force Act states:

> Every person subject to this Act who commits any of the following offences; that is to say, is guilty of any act, conduct, disorder, or neglect, to the prejudice of good order and air force discipline, shall on conviction by court martial be liable, if an officer, to be cashiered, or to suffer such less punishment as is in this Act mentioned …

The Manual of Air Force Law[55] gives, in the notes to Section 40, 'a few instances of offences not uncommonly charged under this section' including, for example,

'Being in improper possession of public property or of property belonging to an officer or comrade (where there is no evidence of actual theft)', and 'Being in some place away from his unit on a particular date when his duty required him to be with his unit.' When all is said and done, it is extremely difficult to see how Donald's 'offence' fits under any of the listed criteria but if someone wanted to make an example of him, then it would not have been too difficult for charges to have been brought, saying that his actions were prejudicial to 'good order and air force discipline'.

The procedures for RAF courts martial were also detailed in the Manual of Air Force Law, while the punishments that may be imposed by a court martial were set out in Section 44 of the Air Force Act. Eight such punishments were listed for officers, in a decreasing scale, and fourth on that list was cashiering.[56]

There can be no doubt that Donald was foolish to have gone on such an unauthorised flight, however noble his motives may have been, but it seems harsh, to say the least, that a man with such a war record as his, and decorated with the DFC to boot, should be kicked out of the Service, having so loyally served King and Country for six long and very dangerous years. Perhaps, though, there was a problem with the Senior Staff back at HQ in Madras, hundreds of miles away from the front line and beyond any possible danger, who through sheer petty-mindedness had nothing better to do than hand out such a pathetic punishment for an action of an individual that had caused no harm to anyone, and which, on the contrary, had eased the plight of twenty-five of those poor sods who had been prisoners of the Japanese.

Another decorated serving RAF officer, Acting Squadron Leader Donald 'Dimsie' Stones DFC, was also to fall foul of some ghastly individual, a Provost Marshal, whilst on leave in Madras from his fighter squadron on the Burma front. Words were exchanged with the Provost Marshal in front of junior ranks, and they ended with Stones telling the wretched policeman to go away and multiply, or words to that effect. The decision of his court martial, that took two days, was that he be given a severe reprimand. He also lost command of his squadron, and was reduced to the rank of flight lieutenant. Stones asked his Brief what the Japanese would have done in such circumstances, and it was agreed that the policeman would probably have been sent to the front to make him more warlike! Such, though, was the so-called Madras 'Sloth Belt', where non-combatants envied those with fine war records.

For Donald, however, Section 44(e) of the Air Force Act saw to it that his RAF career was over. But just as one door closes, so another opens …

CHAPTER 7

CIVILIAN FLYING, 1946-55

Whatever his feelings following his court martial from the RAF, Donald wasted little time in finding other employment. As we have seen, early in 1946 he was spotted by an old RAF acquaintance in a hotel in Batavia in the uniform of an officer in the Dutch airline KLM (*Koninklijke Luchtvaart Maatschappij*, literally Royal Airline Company). The airline had been flying the Douglas DC-3 Dakota before the war on the service via Batavia to Sydney, and it is possible that someone with local experience and knowledge, i.e. Donald, was required to fill a temporary need in the Far East. Whether or not he was ever in the employment of KLM, however, is unclear, for by March 1946 he was in England flying for the fledgling British Aviation Services Limited. But perhaps he was with KLM for the flight to the Far East in April 1946?

By the end of the war Air Commodore Griffith James 'Taffy' Powell had already spent many years in the airline business.[1] After four years in the RAF (1926-30), he joined Imperial Airways on 1 September 1930 and flew aircraft, including Calcutta flying boats and the Handley Page H.P.42, across Africa and on Middle East routes.[2] He became a Senior Master navigator on his return to England in 1936, and flew a flying boat across the Atlantic in July of that year. On a flight at the end of the year he crossed from Eire to Newfoundland (2,000 miles) in the then record time of 14 hours 24 minutes, and with the wind behind him came back in the record time of 10 hours 33 minutes. In 1937, he became Operational Manager in Bermuda of the Imperial Airways company set up to operate between Bermuda and New York in combination with Pan American Airways.

When war came in 1939 he tried to enlist in the RAF but, having just come off the Reserve of Air Force Officers, and with the Air Ministry busily 'gathering in reservists', was not immediately wanted. Instead, he enlisted in the RCAF (service number C.1227) and became Chief Navigation Officer for Eastern Air Command in Canada in the rank of squadron leader. In 1943, he was Wing Commander Senior Air Staff Officer on the Air Staff of No. 45 (Transport) Group, whose headquarters were at Montreal Airport (Dorval). For his outstanding managerial work he was awarded the CBE (gazetted 2 June 1943), the citation for which revealed more of his wartime career:

This officer was in charge at Bermuda for over six months during which period he showed outstanding ability. Since January 1942 he has been senior air staff officer at Command Headquarters and has successfully organised the flights for the North Atlantic, South Atlantic, Labrador, Greenland and South Pacific to Australia. His organising and administrative abilities are outstanding and he has had to handle service and civilian personnel as well as to deal with the Canadian and United States of America governments. He has proved himself to be a pilot of exceptional ability and has flown the Atlantic many times.

In the early weeks of 1945 he was still serving at No. 45 Group HQ, now an air commodore back in the ranks of the RAF, 'when Air Commodore Brackley, Chief of Staff in Transport Command, thought it would be a good idea for me to finish up in an operational command. He knew that Air Commodore Whitney Straight, who commanded No. 216 Group and who was American-born, was not fit and wanted a change.'³ As luck would have it, 'Taffy' Powell was required to go to Cairo for a conference, and took the opportunity to meet his old friend Whitney Straight. As neither was keen on the change, they were able to persuade Transport Command to drop the idea.

With the end of hostilities in May 1945, Powell, now in his late thirties, had to decide what to do for a living. He had already made considerable contact with Captain A. G. Lamplugh, the head of the British Aviation Insurance Group. 'This was a formidable group and before the war Lamplugh had dominated all aspects of civil aviation insurance in the United Kingdom and a good deal in Europe.'⁴ Captain Lamplugh FRAeS, MIAeE, whose company title was Underwriter and Principal Surveyor of the British Aviation Insurance Group (BAIG), wanted Powell to join the group as chief technical officer, which he was happy to do.

In the burgeoning postwar days of passenger air transport, Powell and Lamplugh, realising that they needed to recover BAIG's pre-eminent grip on aviation insurance, hit on a scheme to provide new airlines with suitable aircraft and, having provided the aircraft, the companies would then need aviation insurance! Given that the war had only recently ended, there was a severe shortage of aircraft, but Powell heard that a number of war-surplus DC-3s were stored at Silloth in Cumberland. The plan, simple in concept but not so easy to execute, was to buy these DC-3s, have them refurbished, and then ferry them to the buyers. Powell managed to arrange their purchase, and came to an arrangement with Canadair, a company situated near Montreal, to have the former military transports refurbished for the carriage of civilian passengers. With the assistance of the Douglas company, the manufacturers of the DC-3, the necessary spare parts were made available to Canadair. All that remained was for the DC-3s to be flown from Silloth to Canada to be refurbished and then to be flown back to Europe or wherever for use by the purchasing airline. As this would in effect be a new arm of BAIG, Lamplugh and Powell persuaded the shareholders in 1945 to establish British Aviation Services Limited (BAS), through which the business would be completed, and BAS was duly incorporated in 1946.

Early in that same year Powell was appointed Air Adviser to the Zinc Corporation, an Australian mining company. They already had a number of enterprises operating under the name Silver City, including a small Lockheed aircraft that was used to fly between Sydney and Broken Hill in Australia.⁵ At a meeting 'in the company's guest house in Broken Hill … the idea of a new air company to service the mining industry was born. That it should be called Silver City was a foregone conclusion …'⁶ BAS were appointed managers and given a ten per cent stake in the company, Silver City Airways, which was incorporated on 25 November 1946. In 1947, the Zinc Corporation moved its headquarters to London.

As a start the new company operated four Dakotas and three Lancastrians: G-AHBT *City of New York* purchased by BAS on 17 August 1946 and, on 10 October 1946, G-AHBV *City of Canberra* and G-AHBW *City of London*.

BAS took full control of Silver City Airways in 1948 when it bought out the other shareholders, the decision to become Silver City's sole shareholder coinciding with BAS's strategic move to become an airline operator in its own right under the Britavia name.

It was in this new order of things in 1946, when they were attempting to secure contracts in the fast-growing freight and passenger market, that BAS required a number of suitably qualified pilots, and Donald was hired as one of them. Perhaps he was fortunate to be taken on at a time when there was a large surplus of wartime-trained pilots, and maybe his huge experience in flying the DC-3 counted in his favour; but there were many other pilots seeking a postwar flying job, as was evidenced by the number of 'Situations Wanted' adverts in aviation magazines, such as this one in *Flight* on 14 February 1946: 'R.A.F. Fl. Lt., pilot, D.F.C., 6 years' uninterrupted flying, 2,400 hours all heavies, entirely accident-free; release imminent; experienced all weathers; 500 hours as York instructor, 18 months in Transport Command; seeks position any capacity as pilot.' 'Situations Vacant', on the other hand, were largely for engineers, aircraft draughtsmen, trimmers, upholsterers, and so on. Clearly, Donald was fortunate to get his job when he did.

Continuing to use his RAF flying logbooks to record his civil employment with BAS, Donald's first entry shows that on 20 March 1946, with a Squadron Leader Uprichard as second pilot, he flew Dakota DT-970⁷ from Stoney Cross airfield in the New Forest the short distance to Blackbushe airfield.⁸ April 1946 began with a flight in a DC-3 from Blackbushe to Malta on the first day of the month, from Malta to India between 2 and 4 April, and subsequently on to Singapore, arriving there on the 7th. A strange twist of fate saw Donald returning to Bangkok within several months of his unfortunate dismissal from the RAF. Was this when Donald was seen in the bar of a hotel in Batavia wearing his KLM uniform?

Having completed the freight consignments to the Far East, Donald then returned in the same DC-3 to the UK on 17 April 1946. Employment with British Aviation Services brought with it the opportunity for him to fly a number of different aircraft, among them Lancastrian G-AHBT, which he added to his logbook on 26 August 1946, the very day on which it was delivered to the company.⁹ On this aircraft he flew several short freight transport sorties as second pilot, thus gaining the opportunity to take to the controls of this iconic aircraft.

Donald Barnard's 'Consul' G-AIRP, which he flew between 3 November and 15 December 1946.

Between June 1946 and November 1948 the company was also to acquire a number of twin-engined Airspeed AS65 'Consul' aircraft, which had been developed from the Airspeed Oxford.[10] Over 4,000 Oxfords had been produced for several air forces during the Second World War, after which 162 of them were refurbished and adapted for civilian use. With a crew of pilot and radio operator, it was able to carry up to six passengers and luggage:

> During the immediate post-war years [the Consul] gave sterling service and satisfied the demand for charter class aircraft at a time when more modern designs were not yet available. All the main Oxford components were retained, but the cabin was redesigned to accommodate six passengers. Double doors were fitted to the cockpit bulkhead, extra windows installed and luggage space provided at the rear of the cabin.[11]

Donald was already familiar with the Oxford, having accumulated over 80 hours on it during his RAF service, and in October 1946 his chance came to fly one of the Consuls. He regularly thereafter flew the aircraft on routes to the Mediterranean and beyond, with Marseille, Tunis, Malta, and Cairo being among the several destinations. A souvenir luggage label of the Nile Hotel sits within Donald's logbook, commemorating an overnight stay there on 28 November 1946. Donald's time at BAS, however, was nearing its end.

On 21 February 1946, *Flight* magazine reported, with not a little exaggeration and inaccuracy, 'Mr Whitney Straight, who spent a fair proportion of the war years getting captured and escaping from the Germans, is starting up a flying training scheme in London.' The scheme duly flourished, so that by January 1947, in yet another change to his flying career, Donald was taken on as Chief Flying Instructor at Straight Aviation Training Limited.

The founder of this company was Whitney Straight. Before the war, concentrating on civil aviation, he had set up a number of companies, including the Straight Corporation, which ran a number of airports in Britain. By 1938, he operated forty aircraft and employed over 160 people on eight aerodromes, and also ran a number of flying schools.

At the end of the war, following his appointment as Air Officer Commanding No. 216 (Transport Command) Group at Heliopolis in Egypt, Whitney Straight CBE, MC, DFC, became deputy chairman of BEA and then, in July 1947, chairman of BOAC at the age of just 34. The Straight Corporation's postwar activities were under the direction of Group Captain William Neville Cumming OBE, DFC (awarded in November 1925). Towards the end of the war, Cumming had been serving on the Air Staff of No. 222 Group (Air Command, South East Asia), Colombo. Possibly for work in south-east Asia involving him with the Dutch colonies, King George VI granted him 'unrestricted permission' on 6 July 1945 for the wearing of the decoration Commander of the Order of Orange Nassau, conferred on him 'in recognition of valuable services rendered in connection with the war' by Her Majesty the Queen of The Netherlands.

Straight Aviation Training Limited, originally formed in 1939 and a subsidiary of Straight Aviation (based at Bush House, Aldwych, London), was now able to provide up to six simultaneous classes of courses for refresher training to qualified crews, and civil conversion courses for ex-RAF pilots. Added to the company's prewar equipment was the modern, synthetic link training system connected to a cine camera which, at the time, was regarded as the most modern approach to aircrew training.

Donald was also instructing qualified pupils in flying the Avro Anson aircraft, and he recorded daily training exercises over many months to come. One logbook entry records a navigation exercise, on 22 March 1947, when instructing under-training pilots and navigators. Their course took them over Warwick and King's Lynn, but while over King's Lynn their aircraft, Anson G-AIFA, was struck by lightning and its aerial was burnt off. Donald's compass was also rendered inoperative, and the wireless operator's trousers were badly scorched. Perhaps it was fortunate for Donald that this was to prove the most interesting sortie that he was to undertake during his seven-month period of employment with Straight Aviation.

Keen to expand his flying experience within the growing civil aviation infrastructure, Donald's employment was secured by the Australian company Intercontinental Airways Limited in October 1947.[12] Between 7 and 16 November 1947, he flew the Australian-registered Lockheed Hudson VH-ASV from Croydon in London to Sydney in Australia. This long journey, halfway round the world, was flown in stages: Croydon–Rome–Nicosia–Basra–Bahrain–Karachi–Gwalior–Calcutta–Rangoon–Penang–Singapore–Sourabaya–Bali–Koepang–Darwin–Cloncurry–Charleville, and, finally, Sydney.[13]

This particular Hudson was no stranger to long flights, having been brought over to Australia in February 1940 from the United States. It then served with 14 and 13 RAAF Squadrons as number A16-30, before eventually being declared surplus to requirements and offered for sale on 20 February 1946. Four months later it was sold for £600 to Mr G. R. Broad of Sydney. It then appears to have been sold to Warren G. Penny, of Intercontinental Air Tours, and named *Aurora Australis*. It was seen at Croydon Airport, on 21 September 1947, a matter of weeks before Donald flew it back to Australia.[14]

As the aircraft had been refurbished for a crew of three and ten passengers, it is possible that Donald was carrying emigrants from Britain to Australia. This was not only a time of considerable migration from Europe but was also the time of the partition of India and Pakistan, the two self-governing countries legally coming into existence at the stroke of midnight on 15 August 1947. It was never going to be an easy process to sort out the new states, particularly as many Hindu, Sikh and Muslim communities found themselves on the wrong side of the border. It was decided to repatriate some of these communities by air, and the task was given to BOAC. Air HQ in New Delhi advised that some 7,000 Pakistan nationals would have to be flown from Delhi to Karachi, and around 1,500 Indians in the other direction. In fact, when the air operations had been completed by the end of November 1947, some 35,000 people had been repatriated one way or the other. It was a small fraction of the totals of those having to be moved, as, based on the 1951 census of displaced persons, 7,226,000 Muslims went to Pakistan from India, and 7,249,000 Hindus and Sikhs from Pakistan to India.

Donald, meanwhile, operating as captain or second pilot in Lockheed Lodestar aircraft of Intercontinental Airways, flew across many south-east Asia routes carrying freight and passengers, usually in G-AGBU, until, in early March 1948, the company's activities were suspended and he found himself out of a job. This sudden and unexpected development left him with the need, yet again, to seek other employment.

It wasn't long before the Australian aerial survey company Adastra Airways took on Donald as a pilot – on 19 April 1948. This small company, which was established in 1930, had opened a route in 1934 from Sydney to Bega (a small town on the coast of New South Wales), a flight of a little over two hours. Passengers were hard to come by, and the story goes that when Arthur Butler of Butler Air Transport wanted to buy the route in 1940, he approached Lou Pares

DH-90 Dragonfly VH-AAD outside the original Adastra hangar at Mascot. The print from which this photograph was scanned was supplied to Roger McDonald by Marie Breckenridge, who once worked for Evelyn Follett in her Air Centre. (*Graham Reddall Collection. www.adastra.adastron.com/aircraft/dragonfly/h1vhaad.htm*)

of the Adastra management. Pares spoke briefly with the managing director, Frank Follett, who suggested that Pares told him that they wanted £400. Pares takes up the story:

> I proceeded with this highly involved sale as follows:
> Pares: "We will sell it for £450."
> Butler: "I'll give you £400."
> Pares: "Sold."
> Butler: "Here's the cheque. See you later."
> Deal closed.[15]

Frank Follett explained more of the company's history in a letter of 25 September 1947 to the general manager of the Australian Commonwealth Disposals Commission:

> Later we entered the field of aerial survey, being actually the Australian pioneers of this aviation activity in a private capacity. We were the only aviation company in this State [New South Wales] to weather the depression period and apart from a small subsidy received from the Government in connection with the air route to Bega we have received no financial assistance. Our air survey activities have been conducted entirely

from our own resources and have been built up into an organisation that is well and favourably known throughout Australia. We have carried out work for almost all State and Commonwealth Departments and have surveyed in all the Eastern States, Tasmania, South Australia, Central Australia, Northern Territory and in New Guinea.[16]

Adastra Airways had recently gained a contract to survey and map over 50,000 square miles of the State of Victoria, having also secured the contract to survey the Darling River in neighbouring New South Wales.[17] Donald conducted several aerial photographic sorties in the company's de Havilland DH.90 Dragonfly, VH-AAD.[18]

It is not clear whether or not Donald was released from his employment with Adastra, but the company's situation took a turn for the worse when one of its aircraft, Avro Anson VH-BGO, was destroyed on 5 June 1948 by fire in a hangar at Nhill, Victoria, together with two other Ansons, VH-BES and VH-BET. Donald actually flew VH-BGO for its Certificate of Airworthiness inspection on 31 March 1948 on a 45-minute flight which he recorded as an air and radio test. With him during the flight were an engineer identified as E. Haynes and two radio mechanics.

Donald signed off his logbook at the end of June 1948 with a grand total of 3,496 hours 35 minutes. No further entries were recorded until September 1951, when the logbook was stamped by the Commonwealth of Australia's Department of Civil Aviation. It is presumed that some registration process was required that enabled Donald to continue flying within the civil aviation laws of Australia, for between 4 and 29 September he flew 5 hours in DH.82 aircraft VH-AVO at the Kingsford Smith Flying School, Bankstown, Sydney. The logbook ink-stamp records a logbook check with the total experience of hours recorded, duly signed by the inspecting officer.

In January 1952, he was back at work with Adastra Airways flying on surveying and photographic duties, a job that lasted only until April 1952. Shortly after this he decided to leave Australia and to return to the United Kingdom.

Return to Britain

It was to be a full year before Donald was to fly again, but on 14 April 1953 he underwent a formal, basic flying test in de Havilland Chipmunk G-AMMA, the examiner being Captain Leonard William Yard, who had also served in the RAF in the Second World War.[19]

The Air Ministry had recently adopted the scheme of releasing regular RAF operational squadrons from the general flying tasks of target-towing, calibration, and anti-aircraft co-operation, replacing them with subcontracted civilian operators and pilots. It set in place five civil units across England and Wales, taking over the various squadrons' aircraft, which included Spitfires, Beaufighters,

Oxfords and Vampires.[20] The Civilian Anti-Aircraft Co-operation Units. (CAACU) pilots were employed to tow targets across the various military ranges for all three of the Armed Services, the usual target being constructed of close-mesh netting 30 feet long and 6 feet high. CAACU pilots also flew aircraft on tracking exercises for observers and for Territorial Army anti-aircraft gunner exercises.

CAACUs operated under civil aviation regulations on contract to the Air Ministry. No. 2 CAACU was operated by the Marshall Group, a well-established aviation company which had been formed in Cambridge in 1937. Having secured the contract to supply the Air Ministry with the requirements of a CAACU, Marshalls started operations at Langham in Norfolk during March 1953, and Donald was employed as one of their pilots.

One of the main aircraft types to be flown was the Spitfire Mk XVI, on which Donald had gained an impressive amount of experience during his RAF service as a test pilot. With great confidence, therefore, Donald climbed into Spitfire TE203 for his first local flight, on 6 July 1953. He flew several times daily thereafter, his logbook entries recording sorties usually of just over an hour's duration.

With the requirement to add the twin-engined Mosquito T.2 aircraft to his qualifications, Donald attended a short conversion course in January 1954 at the

Donald Barnard at 2 CAACU, *c.* 1953/54. (*Richard Oliver*)

Mosquito T.III TV959 at Blackbushe, 21 December 1958. Donald flew this aircraft while at White Waltham in 1954. (*Robin A. Walker, www.abpic.co.uk/photo/1036878/*)

RAF Home Command Examining Unit, at White Waltham in Berkshire, flying only between 18 and 22 January.

This unit, as the name suggests, had a significant area of responsibility, one such being the training and development of pilots, for which it was equipped with a variety of aircraft. The staff carried out instrument ratings for selected pilots and visited the CAACUs and civilian flying clubs that were within the RAF flying scholarship scheme. Donald's qualification by this unit enabled him to pilot the Target Tow Mark T.2 Mosquito, an exciting aircraft to fly. He often flew target tows over the ranges at Stiffkey in Norfolk.

Then, in June 1954, came Donald's turn to enter the 'jet age' when he was required to attend the RAF's 233 Operational Conversion Unit (OCU) at Pembrey, near Burry Port in Carmarthenshire. With the reduction of postwar RAF strength, the Air Ministry had decided to continue with the development of separating aircraft types into specific conversion units, and so, at Pembrey, Donald would receive instruction not only on how to fly the Mark T.11 de Havilland Vampire jet but also on which tactics to use to best exploit its performance. This form of instruction was applied at every OCU, but varied according to which type of aircraft was being flown at individual OCUs. At Pembrey, after 2 hours 40 minutes in dual Vampires and 9 hours 10 minutes solo, Donald qualified on the Vampire,

Mosquito Mk 35 RV367 flown by Donald Barnard at 2 CAACU in 1954. (*Ken Jackson*)

and so was able to add this type of aircraft to the Spitfires and Mosquitos that he was qualified to fly at Langham. Having successfully passed his course, Donald was now cleared to fly every type of aircraft deployed at No. 2 CAACU.

In the postwar years the development of radar was making rapid progress, and one of the ways in which the RAF were involved in this vital field of aviation was for aircraft to be flown on what were called ground control interception (GCI) sorties. Playing his part in this development, Donald was required to fly many sorties and, in order that data could be collected, collated, and acted on without delay, the Air Ministry was developing control and reporting methods. The Sector Operations Rooms, GCI stations and Anti-Aircraft operations were being merged into a Sector Control and Reporting Centre. High-flying aircraft were an immediate threat to Britain's air space, with heights of 80,000 and even 100,000 feet being considered possible. It was concluded that the time required to achieve interception of a target meant detection at 190 miles for a sea-level target, 260 miles for a target at 30,000 feet, and 330 miles for a target at 60,000 feet.

In late 1954, Donald was occasionally flying the Vampire jet on tactical sorties to heights of 25-40,000 feet.[21] His logbook recorded further GCI sorties in early 1955 with RAF Neatishead, one of the developed and refurbished Second World War radar sites. Its function during that war was to carry out ground controlled interceptions with the aid of plan position radar displays, and in September 1941,

Vampire VV687 which Barnard records as flying between July and November 1954. Jack King is working on the engine. (*Ken Jackson*)

the 'first radar (Type 7) was installed and operational with an establishment of two officers and forty airmen and airwomen ... Training commenced with 255 Squadron, equipped with the Beaufighter Mk 2.' A German Heinkel III was damaged after two Beaufighters had been vectored on to it in March 1942, but it was not until 28 April 1942 that Neatishead achieved its first kill, when a 68 Squadron Czech warrant officer pilot shot down an enemy aircraft while under its control. In March 1947, the station was established as a Sector Operations Centre, and on 1 July 1953 was renamed 271 Signals Unit. In June 2004, when radar operations ceased, Neatishead had been 'the longest continuously operational radar site in the world'. Latterly it became a Remote Radar Head, its purpose being 'to provide radar, ground-to-air radio and data links coverage as part of the UK Air Surveillance And Control System (ASACS), in support of national and NATO air defence'.[22]

But, over half a century earlier, a double-level underground operations block had been constructed, accessed by a staircase in a guardroom disguised as a bungalow. On the ground, protected radar plinths had been constructed some distance away from the site. A standby generator building was constructed and designed to resemble a church, these efforts being taken in order to avoid detection as best as

Above and below: Once flown by Donald Barnard, Mosquito Mk 35 RV367 after the undercarriage collapsed on landing, 13 March 1957. (*Ken Jackson*)

possible. With the Soviet Union's first fully fledged H-bomb tested in 1955, and the advent of supersonic high-flying bombers, every second saved in warning was vital to the protection of Britain's air space, as the 'Cold War' produced seriously worrying times for the country.

Donald had played a vital role in the RAF during the Second World War, and his flying with No. 2 CAACU in the 1950s had added to the history of aviation in Great Britain. On 11 April 1955, the final entry in his logbook records an air test in Mk LF XVIe Spitfire TE330. This particular Spitfire had been taken on charge by the RAF on 14 June 1945 at No. 9 Maintenance Unit, Cosford. Taken out of storage on 6 February 1947, it served on 601 Squadron RAuxAF at Hendon, and thereafter passed through a number of maintenance units until it arrived at 2 CAACU in 1954. The aircraft was declared non-effective on 16 July 1957, and was subsequently deployed as a static gate-guard at RAF West Malling in Kent. Later secured by the RAF Historic Flight, Spitfire TE330 took to the sky again and flew during the Battle of Britain flypast celebration in September 1957.

When the Historic Flight acquired two further aircraft, TE330 was bundled into a USAF C-124 cargo aircraft at RAF Odiham and flown across the Atlantic to the United States, where it was presented to the USAF Academy in Colorado Springs on 3 July 1958. Sold to the Smithsonian Institution in September 1959, it was moved for display to the USAF Museum in Dayton, Ohio, in 1961 before being sold in 1996 to Hong Kong-based businessman James Slade. He sent it to Don Subritzky in Auckland, New Zealand, for restoration work in 1997, but in 1999 he sold it to the Subritzky family. After restoring it to an airworthy condition, the family sold the Spitfire for a record NZD$3.164 million (£1.6 million) on 14 September 2008 to Hong Kong shipping magnate Gao Yanming, head of the HOSCO Group, who donated it to the China Aviation Museum in Beijing on 4 December 2009.

So, TE330, the last aircraft flown by Donald during his aviation career, continues to be valued, albeit in faraway China, as a fitting tribute to the history of the RAF during the Second World War.

When he landed Spitfire TE330 on 11 April 1955, he had accumulated during his entire flying career, both military and civil, a grand total of 3,959 hours 10 minutes in the air. He was 37 years of age.

The family man

On 14 May 1953, the year after his return to the UK, Donald was married at the Register Office in Kensington, London, to Rosalind Mary Copeland, daughter of George and Mabel (née Segol) Copeland, who was born on 26 February 1928 in Darling Point, New South Wales, Australia.[23] It is possible that the two met when Donald was flying for the various companies in Australia. Back in England, and employed by Marshalls at Langham on the north Norfolk coast, the newly-weds moved to the Old Cottage at Wiveton, barely two miles from the airfield. It was

Donald with his son David in 1954. (*Richard Oliver*)

while they were there that their son, David George Beausire Barnard, was born on 5 March 1954 at Longacre Maternity Home, West Runton, a few miles along the coast from Wiveton.

The marriage was not a happy one, however, and divorce followed. In 1957, Rosalind left England and returned to her native Australia, taking young David with her. Little is known of Donald's movements thereafter, but on 22 October 1962 he was in Reading, Berkshire, marrying Una Taylor, who was then a month short of her forty-eighth birthday. Records show that her legal surname was O'Shea, it being likely that she had married a Laurence J. O'Shea in 1939 in Paddington, London, who had died in 1950 in nearby Marylebone.

It is probable that the couple moved to Scotland after their marriage and remained there until 1965. At some point during their stay in Scotland, Donald had had an operation on one of his eyes that effectively prevented him from carrying out any further flying. Evidence for this, and for his residency in Scotland, comes from a letter that he wrote to his sister Lesley.[24]

Life in Sussex

By the end of the 1960s, Donald and Una had moved to Hove in East Sussex, on the south coast of England. They lived firstly at Denmark Villas and then Eaton Gardens. With much housing redevelopment having taken place in the 1950s, Hove became a popular location for retiring service personnel. Donald, though, was already familiar with the town as his sister had once lived there.

After Una died in February 1985, Donald would spend his days tending the small garden which belonged to the flat he occupied, sharing stories of his flying days with friends and acquaintances. They recall a restless look in his eyes when talking about his flying, and many an evening would be spent with him reliving his fascinating account of his time 'on the run' in France. When asked about why he had left the RAF, a neighbour recalls he would furrow his brow and say: 'When you believe in something that you know to be right, sometimes you have to live with the consequences, no matter how hard that might be.' No further explanation was forthcoming, and Donald would quickly return to the tales of his evasion.

Life took an unexpected, and ultimately tragic, turn for Donald when he started to experience discomfort inside his mouth. Where once he would talk happily for many hours about his life and flying career, he was now no longer able to speak without pain. Eventually he turned for advice to a neighbour, who persuaded him to visit the doctor. After various tests, the results came through: Donald was suffering from cancer of the tongue. Where once he had been a lively, engaging talker, Donald became reserved, drawing into himself, with his health failing as time moved on. In January 1997, no longer able to fight the illness, he moved to a nursing home in Peacehaven, East Sussex, which at least was able to provide him with specialist palliative nursing care for the remainder of his days.

Squadron Leader Donald Beausire Barnard DFC, a man of integrity, conviction and strength, fought for six long years for freedom, not only for himself but for others, and his unconquerable illness would be the only time that he was to lose the fight, when cancer took his life on 17 May 1997 at the age of 79.

THE MESSAGE ATTACHED TO THE PIGEON AT RENTY

Un message envoyé de Renty par Norbert Fillerin.

Un message par pigeon voyageur en date du 12 octobre 1942:

Le Portel: travaux importants dans le Fort de l'Eure en mer, face à la ville. Ligne de chemin de fer établie entre le fort et le rivage. Elle fonctionne à marée basse. Beaucoup de ciment employé. Tous les accès de la ville sont murés et les rampes de la falaise garnies de barbelés et abris de sacs en terre pour mitrailleuse.

Rouen: Bombardement fantaisiste inconsidéré, loin de tout objectif militaire. Genre bombardement Boulogne 14 août 1941 après-midi.

Saint-Omer: Bombardement vendredi 2 octobre sur aérodrome Bruyères très réussi. Incendie; beaucoup de matériel détruit. Nombreux morts. Les ateliers sont à la place du moulin. Nouveaux hangars le long du bois de Longuenesse. Nombreuses baraques à l'extrêmité ouest du champ vers C.D. 212.

Lille: fin septembre; deux convois de recrues entraînées partis pour Russie.

Paris: Usines Talbot, Lorraine, Goodrich fabriquent pièces Renault.

Tours: champ d'aviation; aviation renforcée depuis Dieppe.

Le Mans: à Laval, fortifications. Bruits persistants de concentration de blindés. Même bruits pour Mézières-Charleville.

Nord-France: D.C.A. considérablement augmentée, disposée pour servir anti-chars. Nombreux nouveaux postes de repérage par le son: un en construction à 100 mètres au sud de la C.D. 92 sur la route de champ allant à la ferme isolée "La Forêt" à Assonval. Moral des Boches: mauvais. Des recrues de plus en plus jeunes ou très vieilles. Bluff: à Boulogne, mêmes troupes sous divers uniformes: marine, aviation, feldgrau. Les civils allemands, à Saint Omer, sont armés. A Boulogne, 250 arrestations à 4 heures du matin dont 17 agents de police; radio et journaux présentent la chose comme départ de volontaires pour la relève. Points sensibles à la circulation routière boche: le pont d'Armentières, R.N. 42 sur la ligne de chemin de fer. Dispositions allemandes, dans chaque subdivision des Ponts et Chaussées, recensement de tout matériel pouvant servir au génie militaire et formation d'une équipe de quinze hommes pour réparation immédiate des ouvrages et routes détruits ou endommagés; par ordre de l'Oberfeldkommandantur 670.

Equipage bombardier recueilli par Commando 6:

S/LDR. D. B. BARNARD n° 40352

P/O R. E. GLENSOR n° 2403442

SGT R. FORSTER n° 1053891

Save et well, returning shortly. Please safeguard personal effects.

F/SGT BUCKELL same crew. Definitely prisoners of war.

SGT JAMES safe and well. RAF

Cinq pigeons tombés à Longvillers région Berck-Montreuil ont été remis à la Kommandantur.

Lumbres: 1er octobre: sur wagons, 12 pièces de 105 court, montant vers la côte. Recueilli au sud de Lumbres: appareil émission radio de la marine du Reich; appareil cylindrique, plus batterie, le tout accroché sur ballon. Opinion: doit être lâché par sous-marin pour surveillance auditive. Pour vérification de notre identité, adressez-vous à Guy Lockart, pilote de chasse, 9, Athelstone Road, Colchester, Essex. Nous attendons accusé de réception à l'émission de 13 heures 15 et de 21 heures 15: "Avons reçu message des amis de Guy. Signé RST commando 6". Bonjour à Lockart qui se souvient des amis de M. Leblanc.

Prière à la B.B.C. de passer ceci dans les messages des forces françaises combattantes: Pour Maurice, né à Malo en 1917: les parents à qui il écrivit en juin dernier demandent de ses nouvelles.

Ceci est notre dernier message. Ne pas envoyer de jeunes bais qui se perdent ou qui, comme numéro 3, ne veulent pas partir. Pigeon lâché le 21 octobre à 11 heures, heure solaire. RST Commando 6. Vive De Gaulle.

Verso

Plan d'Aire-sur-la-Lys qui signale central téléphonique allemand situé de la chapelle du collège.

RENE EST SANS REPONSE DU SUD DEPUIS TROIS SEMAINES POUR SES TROIS FILLES. PREVENEZ A. NITELET. OEE. RAF.

Avons bien entendu accusé de réception du message n° 1, mais pas celui du numéro 2. Bulletin d'informations du 12 octobre, 10 heures 15. Très net.

N'avons pas encore trouvé de tracts Laval genre (*Courrier de l'Air*). Que la B.B.C. fasse plus peur aux collaborateurs dont garde de la chasse pour les Boches. RST commando 6.

Envoyez-nous des pigeons. Vive la France et les Tommies.[1]

* * *

Rough English translation of the message attached to the pigeon:

A message sent from Renty by Norbert Fillerin.
A message by carrier pigeon on 12 October 1942:

Le Portel: significant work at Fort de l'Eure in the sea, facing the town. Railway line established between the fort and the shore. It runs at low tide. Much cement used. All the entrances to the town are bricked up and the cliff slopes have barbed-wire and shelters of sand bags for machine guns.

Rouen: Ill-considered fanciful bombardment, far from any military objective. Type Boulogne bombardment 14 August 1941 afternoon.

Saint-Omer: Bombardment Friday 2 October on Bruyères aerodrome very successful. Set on fire; much material destroyed. Many dead. The works are at the site of the mill. New hangars along the wood at Longuenesse. Many huts at the western end of the field towards C.D. 212.

Lille: at the end of September; two convoys of trainee recruits left for Russia.

Paris: Talbot, Lorraine, Goodrich factories manufacture Renault parts.

Tours: airfield; aviation reinforced since Dieppe.

Le Mans: at Laval, fortifications. Persistent rumours of concentration of armoured vehicles. Same rumours at Mézières-Charleville.

North France: Anti-aircraft defences considerably increased, arranged to serve as anti-tank. Many new sound-locating stations: one under construction 100 metres south of the C.D. 92 on the field road to the isolated farm "La Forêt" at Assonval. Morale of Boches: bad. Increasingly young recruits or very old. Bluff: at Boulogne, same troops in various uniforms: naval, air, feldgrau. Civilian Germans, in Saint Omer, are armed. At Boulogne, 250 arrests at 4 o'clock in the morning including 17 policemen; radio and newspapers describe it as departure of volunteers for labour service.[2] Sensitive points of Boche road traffic: Armentières bridge, R.N. 42 over the railway line. German provisions, in each subdivision of the Highways Department, stores of all material which can be used for military engineering and formation of a team of fifteen men for immediate repair of the works and roads destroyed or damaged; by order of Oberfeldkommandantur 670.

Bomber crew collected by Commando 6:

S/LDR D. B. BARNARD No. 40352
P/O R. E. GLENSOR No. 2403442
SGT R. FORSTER No. 1053891
Safe and well, returning shortly. Please safeguard personal effects.
F/SGT BUCKELL same crew. Definitely prisoners of war
SGT JAMES Safe and well. RAF
Five pigeons that fell at Longvillers in the Berck-Montreuil area were given to the Kommandantur.

Lumbres: 1 October: on wagons, 12 units of 105 short, going towards the coast. Collected from south of Lumbres: German Navy radio transmitter; cylindrical apparatus, plus battery, the whole hung on balloon. Opinion: must be released by submarine for aural monitoring. To check our identity, contact Guy Lockart [*sic* – Lockhart], fighter pilot, 9, Athelstone Road, Colchester, Essex. We await acknowledgement of delivery in the 1315 hours and 2115 hours transmissions: "Have received message from the friends of Guy. Signed RST commando 6". Hello to Lockart who remembers the friends of M. Leblanc.

Ask the B.B.C. to mention this in the messages of the Fighting French forces: For Maurice, born in Malo in 1917: the parents he wrote to last June ask for news.

This is our last message. Do not send young bay pigeons who get lost or who, like number 3, do not want to leave. Pigeon released on 21 October [*sic*] at 11 o'clock, solar time. RST Commando 6. Long live De Gaulle.

Back of message
Plan of Aire-sur-la-Lys which shows German telephone exchange located in the college chapel.

RENE HAS HAD NO REPLY FROM THE SOUTH FOR THREE WEEKS FOR HIS THREE GIRLS. WATCH OUT FOR A. NITELET. OEE. RAF.

Have good reception of message No. 1, but not number 2. News bulletin of 12 October, 1015 hours. Very clear.

Have not yet found the Laval leaflets (*Courrier de l'Air*). Let the B.B.C. frighten the collaborators more which keeps the Boches on the look-out. RST commando 6.

Send us some pigeons. Long live France and the Tommies.

CONVOY MKF7, GIBRALTAR–GOUROCK, 20-25 JANUARY 1943

When Donald and the other evaders and escapers sailed from Gibraltar on 20 January 1943, their ship, the *Ville d'Oran*, took its place in convoy MKF7, the nucleus of which had departed Algiers on 18 January making for Gibraltar. Having left Gibraltar on 20 January – Donald said 'Our convoy consisted of fourteen ships, six were liners' – it arrived in home waters and dispersed on 25 January. At its largest, MKF7 was made up of eighteen merchantmen and liners, and six escorts, though only these nine liners continued to the UK from Gibraltar:

Liners	Tons	Built	Owner/cargo (where known)
Batory (Pol)	14,287	1936	Gdynia America Line
Duchess of Bedford (Br)	20,123	1928	Canadian Pacific Steamship Ltd
Franconia (Br)	20,175	1923	Cunard Steamship Co.
Monarch of Bermuda (Br)	22,424	1931	Furness Bermuda Line
Ormonde (Br)	14,982	1917	Orient Steam Navigation Co. 824 troops from Gibraltar
Otranto (Br)	20,026	1925	Orient Line / 18 troops, 234 mails.
Reina del Pacifico (Br)	17,702	1931	Pacific Steam Navigation Co.
Sobieski (Pol)	11,030	1939	Gdynia America Line
Ville d'Oran (Fr)	10,172	1936	Compagnie Générale Transatlantique 200 passengers from Gibraltar.

Escorts (Pennant No.)	Tons	Built	Type
HMS *Folkestone* (U22)	1,045	1930	Hastings Class sloop
HMS *Gorleston* (Y92)	2,075	1929	Lulworth Class cutter1
HMS *Totland* (Y88)	1,546	1931	Lulworth Class cutter2
HMS *Wear* (K230)	1,375	1942	River Class frigate
HMS *Wellington* (U65)	1,256	1934	Grimsby Class sloop3
HMS *Weston* (U72)	1,060	1932	Falmouth Class sloop

Notes:

(a) 'MKF' of the convoy designation MKF7 stood for 'Mediterranean – UK Fast', a designation first used in November 1942. The '7' signified the seventh in this series of convoys. There were altogether fifty-one MKF convoys, involving

563 ships, of which only two were lost, *Warwick Castle* on 14 November 1942, and *Ettrick* on the following day, both to U-boats. All six escort ships were with the convoy from 18-25 January 1943.

(b)   After a ship's name, (Bel) – Belgian; (Br) – British; (Fr) – French; (Nor) – Norwegian; (Pol) – Polish; (US) – American.

(c)   These ships sailed from Algiers but detached from MKF7 on 19/20 January 1943 at Gibraltar:

Vessel	Tons	Built
Bergensfjord (Nor)	11,015	1913
City of Edinburgh (Br)	8,036	1938
City of Pretoria (Br)	8,049	1937
Clan Lamont (Br)	7,250	1939
Heranger (Nor)	4,877	1930
Irénée du Pont (US)	6,125	1941
Lanarkshire (Br)	9,816	1940
Leopoldville (Bel)	11,509	1929
Orbita (Br)	15,495	1915

(d)   *City of Pretoria* was sunk with all hands by U-boat U-172 on 3 March 1943. *Irénée du Pont* was sunk by U-600 on 17 March 1943. *Leopoldville* was sunk by U-486 on 24 December 1944; 783 US troops on board perished.

(e)   Ship information from:
http://www.convoyweb.org.uk/mkf/index.html?mkf.
php?convoy=7!~mkfmain

FAR EAST DAKOTA LOSSES, JUNE-OCTOBER 1945

Listed below are several instances of Dakota crashes in which aircrew, civilian passengers, soldiers, sailors, or prisoners of war were killed. The crashes were mostly the result of engine failure and/or of flying into the dreaded cumulo-nimbus clouds, but were never the result of a direct attack by the enemy. Even when miles behind the front line the perils of the air were ever present, danger lurking in every cloud.

That so many personnel were lost on some occasions is attributable to the air-lifting capacity of the great workhorse that was the Dakota. It should not be thought, however, that disastrous losses were confined solely to the squadrons that flew it, such as Donald's 117. They were not, as evidenced by the losses of two Liberators of 99 Squadron on Operation Mastiff, KL491 on 1 September and EW236 on 6 October 1945, in which 17 crew were killed. Alas, there were other fatal crashes too.

The authors fully acknowledge that most of this list could not have been compiled without reference to *The Price of Peace: A Catalogue Of RAF Aircraft Losses Between VE-Day And End Of 1945*, one of a series of excellent reference volumes produced by Wing Commander Colin Cummings.

* * *

Dakota KN254, 215 Squadron, 7 June 1945:

Warrant Officer Peter LeRoy BOUCAUT, RAAF
Flight Sergeant Gordon Keith GIBB, RAAF
Flight Sergeant Ronald WYNNE
Flight Sergeant Andrew STEPHEN
Leading Aircraftman Leonard COYLE
Leading Aircraftman Henry Norman SANDFORD
Corporal Thomas Frederick SANDILANDS
IND/59280 Enrolled Follower DEVI DUTT, RIAF, serving with 215 Sqn
IND/58295 Enrolled Follower GEORGE
IND/58294 Enrolled Follower MUHAMMAD
IND/6682 Enrolled Follower RAMZAN
IND/6576 Enrolled Follower BIRAI
IND/8973 Enrolled Follower BISHNATHA

IND/58021 Enrolled Follower KANNAN
IND/53812 Enrolled Follower KANSHI PARSHAD
IND/58018 Enrolled Follower MADHAVEN
IND/58014 Enrolled Follower MADHAVEN
IND/58025 Enrolled Follower NANU
IND/6575 Enrolled Follower PHERAI
IND/58012 Enrolled Follower RAGHAVEN
IND/53541 Enrolled Follower RAM KRISHNAN
IND/6621 Enrolled Follower SARNAN

Note: It is believed that the aircraft entered a cumulo-nimbus cloud without warning, and that the turbulence caused a mainplane to fracture. The pilot was thereafter unable to control the aircraft, and crashed.

* * *

Dakota KN468, 96 Squadron, 13 June 1945:

Pilot Officer Alfred William CULSHAW
Flight Lieutenant James Jeffrey ALLEN DFC, RAAF
Leading Aircraftman Cyril Leonard BUNN
Leading Aircraftman Alan HULL
Aircraftman 2nd Class George HULLAH
Flying Officer William John TOLLIDAY

Note: The pilot of this aircraft, Flying Officer Bruce Douglas BANCROFT DFC, RAAF, survived the crash-landing and, although himself badly burned in the resultant fire, with the help of the navigator succeeded in pulling four other personnel from the wreckage. For his bravery Bancroft was awarded the George Medal on 2 July 1946.

* * *

Dakota KG694, 194 Squadron, 14 June 1945:

Warrant Officer II John Maynard COX, RCAF
Flight Lieutenant James Murray RICE
and an unnamed passenger

Note: The accident was caused when the port engine caught fire and the pilot tried to land on rough ground. Three others on board were saved by the navigator, Flying Officer John James Baillie, RCAF, who was awarded the George Medal, gazetted on 26 February 1946:

The KING has been graciously pleased to approve the award of the George Medal to the undermentioned:

Flying Officer John James BAILLIE (Can/J.37488), Royal Canadian Air Force, No. 194 Squadron.

On 14th June, 1945, Flying Officer Baillie was the navigator of a Dakota aircraft which crashed near Mydngyan airstrip in central Burma. The fuel tanks burst and fire soon spread to the fuselage. When he recovered consciousness Flying Officer Baillie discovered that his leg was entangled in the static line and that his clothes were burning. He freed himself by a great effort and, although he was suffering from multiple head injuries, a broken cheek bone and concussion, he dragged two Indian other ranks clear of the wreckage. On hearing screams from inside the aircraft, he re-entered. In spite of further burns which he sustained to hand and leg, he rescued the delirious wireless operator who resisted his efforts. By his great courage and complete disregard for his own safety, Flying Officer Baillie saved the lives of the wireless operator and two Indian other ranks.

* * *

Dakota KK175, 194 Squadron, 20 June 1945:

Wing Commander Robert Cree CRAWFORD DFC
Flying Officer Neil William NEELANDS
Flight Lieutenant Frank William FORRESTER
Warrant Officer Allan Oliver WALKINGTON

Note: Wing Commander Crawford was the popular CO of 194 Squadron. His DFC was gazetted on 19 October 1945, with effect from 19 June 1945. The fatal accident happened after the aircraft had descended through cloud and struck a hillside.

* * *

Dakota KN563, 435 Squadron, 21 June 1945:

Warrant Officer William Bennett ROGERS, RCAF
Pilot Officer Joseph William KYLE DFC & Bar, RCAF
Flight Sergeant Charles Peter McLaren, RCAF
Flying Officer David McLean CAMERON, RCAF
Warrant Officer I Stanley James COX, RCAF
Leading Aircraftman Cornelius John KOPP, RCAF

Note: This aircraft disappeared whilst on a supply drop to the 14th Army. The wreckage was found upside down in a deep ravine in 1996.

* * *

Dakota KN455, 62 Squadron, 23 June 1945:

Flying Officer Kenneth Herbert ROE
Pilot Officer Simon Gascoigne EDEN
Sergeant John Roland HYNE
Flying Officer Douglas Henry LODER

Note: The crash was attributed to a problem with the starboard engine that was known before take-off. The aircraft was seen to enter cloud with the starboard engine on fire, after which it crashed into a hillside. Pilot Officer Eden was the 20-year-old son of the future British Prime Minister the Rt. Hon. Sir Robert Anthony Eden KG, MC, PC, BA, DCL, JP, MP (later Lord Avon).

* * *

Dakota KN218, 117 Squadron. 26 June 1945:

Flying Officer William Stanley BRADLY, RCAF
Flight Sergeant George Peter CRAVEN
Flying Officer Maxwell Alvin RUSSELL, RCAF
Sergeant Alec Youlton DAVIES
Flying Officer Ronald Thomas William HOLT
Flight Sergeant William George STEVENS

Note: After the port engine had failed, the aircraft entered a cumulo-nimbus cloud and broke up in the turbulence.

* * *

Dakota KN602, 117 Squadron, 27 June 1945:

Flying Officer Anthony Charles KENT, pilot
Flight Sergeant Richard Beart BALL, co-Pilot
Sergeant Arthur Walvin COOPER, wireless operator
Flying Officer Harold Matthew O'REILLY, RCAF, flight engineer
Warrant Officer Edwin Anthony FAHEY, RAAF, navigator
Captain (Quartermaster) William FINNEY, 37 Field Ambulance RAMC
Private William Edward PARSONS, 2nd Battalion Welch Regiment

Lance Corporal Ronald George STRANGLEMAN, 2nd Battalion Welch
   Regiment
Lieutenant KART AR SINGH BATTH, 15th Punjab Regiment
Sepoy ASSA SINGH
Sepoy CHANDGI RAM
Sepoy SINGHALL RISAL
Sepoy TEJA SINGH

Possible additional casualties not recorded in the Casualty Files:
Craftsman ABDUL AZIZ KHAN, 17 Recovery Company IEME
Sapper ALA SINGH, 23rd Battalion Indian Engineers
Craftsman ASA RAM, 17 Recovery Company IEME
Sepoy BACHAN SINGH, 9th/13th Frontier Force Rifles
Jemedar BIR SINGH, 17 Recovery Company IEME
Sepoy DEB SINGH, 19th Hyderabad Regiment
Sepoy GULA JAN, 17 Recovery Company IEME
Sepoy GULDAD KHAN, 9th/13th Frontier Force Rifles
Lance Niak HARI SINGH, 13th Frontier Force Rifles
Havildar JISUKH, 26th Battalion Indian Pioneer Corps
Sepoy KHAN MUHAMMAD, 9th/13th Frontier Force Rifles
Sepoy MUHAMMAD SADIQ, 9th/13th Frontier Force Rifles
Sapper RAM BAHADUR, 290 IWT Operating Company Indian Engineers
Sepoy SANKARAN NAIR, 151 GP Transport Company RIASC
Clerk S N SARKAR, Military Accounts Department
Craftsman VINAYAGAM, 17 Recovery Company IEME
Pioneer YUSAF All, 3 Bengal Civil Pioneer Force

Note: The reason for the loss of this aircraft was never discovered.

* * *

Crew of Dakota KN208, 436 Squadron, 7 July 1945:

Flying Officer Alexander Ross Weir HARRISON, RCAF
Flying Officer William Jacob FRIESON, RCAF
Flight Sergeant Sidney Herbert Lodington SMITH, RCAF
Flying Officer William Crawford CAMPBELL, RCAF

Note: The crew were experiencing navigating difficulties, and the pilot accordingly
made a spiral descent through a break in the clouds but crashed when attempting
to land in a valley.

* * *

Crew of Dakota KN457, 62 Squadron, 13 July 1945:

Flight Lieutenant William Seymour HAMILTON, RNZAF
Flying Officer William Oliver DAVISON
Warrant Officer II Roy Howard JONES, RCAF
Pilot Officer John Ross MOORE, RAAF
Warrant Officer Terence William BINNING, RAAF

Note: The Dakota was on a supply sortie when it was seen to enter into a flat spin and crash. A search of the wreckage revealed that the pilot was not in his seat at the time.

* * *

Crew of Dakota KN562, 117 Squadron, 13 July 1945:

Squadron Leader Richard Neville ROWSON
Flight Sergeant Augustus Arthur SHALLOW
Flying Officer Bernard Barker STANSFIELD
Warrant Officer Granville Mundon EASON
Leading Aircraftman Stanley BATCHELOR

Note: When both engines failed shortly after take-off, the pilot attempted to return to base.

* * *

Crew of Dakota KN556, 194 Squadron, 25 July 1945:

Flight Lieutenant Thomas Leonard MUMBY DFM
Pilot Officer Ernest John GREENWAY
Pilot Officer William VAUGHAN, RAAF
Pilot Officer Geoffrey Charles Oscar POLLIE
Flying Officer Graham Henry GLASGOW, RAAF

Note: The aircraft was seen to have stalled at low altitude shortly after take-off and crashed into the sea before a recovery could be made. Flight Lieutenant Mumby's DFM was gazetted on 17 January 1941, when he was a sergeant on 75 Squadron.

* * *

Crew of Dakota KJ922, 357 Squadron, 30 July 1945:

Warrant Officer Joseph Reid MILNE
Flight Sergeant Albert BINNS
Flight Sergeant E. M. CLARKE
Sergeant Charles Raymond FRANCIS
and possibly a fifth fatality, name not known

Note: The crew were on a Special Duties flight. To reach the Drop Zone the pilot was forced to fly below cloud, but encountering higher ground he was forced to fly into the cloud and struck a hill.

* * *

Dakota KN532, 48 Squadron, lost on 5 September 1945:

Flying Officer John JONES
Flying Officer Norman KERR
Flying Officer David Fitzhardinge KlNGSCOTE
Flight Sergeant John Chatten RUSTON
Captain Ernest HODGSON, 1st Battalion East Yorkshire Regiment
Leading Aircraftman Cecil David DAVIES
Pioneer CHANDRI, Indian Pioneer Corps
Pioneer HANMAPP A BURKEL, Indian Pioneer Corps
Niak HIRA SINGH, RIASC
Pioneer MARYA, Indian Pioneer Corps
Lance Niak NARAYAN JADHAO
Sapper S. M. RAHMAN, 102 Railway Operating Company Indian Engineers
Sapper SUBUDHI SHEKHAR BOSE, 130 Railway Operating Company
Sapper N. N. BARUA, 102 Railway Operating Company
Sepoy ABDUL HAFIZ, 6 Animal Transport Company
Private Ernest John BENNETT, 1st Battalion East Yorkshire Regiment
Major William DAVIES, IAOC
Barber ISLAM, 22 Field Remount Section
Ambulance Sepoy ABDUL AZIZ, 90 Staging Section IAMC
Sapper NAZIR AHMAD, 102 Railway Operating Company
Private Patrick O'CALLAGHAN, Devonshire Regiment
Servant PHAJJU, 101 Anti-Malarial Unit IAMC
Craftsman RUSTAM, ALl 62 Mobile Workshop Company IEME
Sergeant Eric Walter Joseph SAGAR, 505 Postal Unit RE
Sepoy YAQUB, 85 Mobile Workshop Company IEME
Private Philip MARLOW, 2nd Battalion Worcestershire Regiment
Pioneer BALKRISHNA, 1489 Company IPC

Sepoy MAHAIN, 3532 Company RIASC
Sepoy PHOHNDER SINGH, Burma Regiment
Sapper BARNAN, 182 Railway Operating Company
Havildar SAJJAN SINGH, 182 Railway Operating Company

Note: The Dakota was taking hospital patients from Meiktila to Chittagong in a monsoon when the pilot attempted to climb through the cloud. He unwittingly entered a cumulo-nimbus cloud, and the turbulence broke off the port wing.

* * *

Dakota KK118, 117 Squadron, 6 September 1945:

Flying Officer Roland Henry Travis SQUIRE
Flight Sergeant Eric William TRAIL
Flying Officer John McPherson ROSS
Flying Officer Edwin Maurice SISSONS

Others are believed to be:
Aircraftman 2nd Class Joseph BROWN, RAF
and soldiers of 1st Battalion The Queen's Royal Regiment (West Surrey):
Private Douglas John AUBURN
Private Leslie BASS
Private Henry Walter CRANKSHAW
Private Leonard FINCH
Warrant Officer II (CSM) Victor James GOODCHILD
Private Joseph HILLIER
Private Bryn Ellis JONES
Lance Sergeant Richard Henry Benson KEMP
Private Reginald Lancelot MUNT
Private William Walter OLIVER
2nd Lieutenant Bryan Peter PATTIE, Royal Fusiliers attached
Lance Corporal Charles Edward PRITCHARD
Lance Corporal George Albert RACKETT
Private Stanley Joseph REED
Private William Stewart REED
Private Ernest Cyril SMITH
Private William James STOKES
Private Frederick John STONE
Private Edward James SULLIVAN
Private Alfred Charles SWINCHATT
Private Sidney George Thomas VICKERY

Note: The soldiers were on their way to Saigon for garrison duties. This was yet another instance of a Dakota breaking-up in the turbulence of a cumulo-nimbus cloud.

* * *

Dakota KN584, 357 Squadron, 7 September 1945:

Warrant Officer 1 Harold William SMITH, RCAF
Flight Sergeant Alexander Fraser CALDER
Flight Sergeant Roy Metcalfe HERDMAN
Flight Sergeant Daniel McLEMAN
Captain Alan Leslie GOLDSMITH Royal Engineers
Corporal Stanley Harold GOODWIN Royal Engineers
Lieutenant-Colonel Edgar James KENNEDY OBE, Royal Corps of Signals
Second Lieutenant Samuel McCammont LITTLE, General List ex Gordon
    Highlanders
Sergeant Archibald SMITH, RAF HQ 904 Wing
Sergeant Alfred Claude Brenton SOWDEN MM, Royal Corps of Signals
Lieutenant-Colonel Sydney Isaac WIGGINTON OBE, Sherwood Foresters
    Regiment

RAF passengers believed to be:
Flight Sergeant William Thomas Patrick DAVIES
Flight Sergeant Robert NAPIER
Leading Aircraftman Frederick John BRYANT
Flying Officer Bernard HOBART, 28 Squadron
Flight Sergeant Donald Hugh WILD, 28 Squadron.

Note: The cause of the crash was not discovered.

* * *

Dakota KN593, 117 Squadron, 8 September 1945:

Wing Commander Arthur James SAMSON DFC (218 Squadron 1943)
Squadron Leader Robert Philip Brent GROTRIAN
Flight Lieutenant Bernard BRIDGE
Flight Lieutenant James Forties CUTHBERT DFC & Bar (216 Squadron 1944 &
    September 1945/117).
Squadron 1946 awef 7/9/45)
Flying Officer Thomas Watkin HUMPHRYS DFC (117 Squadron 1946 awef
    7/9/45)

Flying Officer John Dundee LORIMER
Flight Sergeant Derek BATEMAN
Flight Sergeant Bruce ELLIS
Flight Sergeant Kenneth Harold GOAD
Major John Cooper SCOTT, The Worcestershire Regiment
Corporal Herman Robert Francis ABLITT, 198 Field Ambulance RAMC
Lance Sergeant Ernest Albert ARTHUR, 88 Field Regiment RA
Gunner James Bellingat BRYCE, RA
Signalman George Kenneth CHADWICK, Royal Signals Battery
Quartermaster Sergeant Harry COTTERILL, 6 HAA Battery RA
Gunner John James CRAWFORD, 125 Anti Tank Regiment RA
Bombardier Fred DAWES, 5 Searchlight Regiment RA
Lance Sergeant Manley Ernest DE ROUX, 9th Battalion Royal Northumberland Fusiliers
Private Horace EDWARD, RAMC
Lance Sergeant Ernest Joseph EDWARDS, 2nd Battalion Gordon Highlanders
Private James FERROW, 6th Battalion Royal Norfolk Regiment
Private Ronald Gordon Victor GADD, 2nd Battalion East Surrey Regiment
Sergeant Robert Henry HAWTHORN, 3 HAA Regiment RA
Gunner Norman Frank HENDY, 5 Searchlight Regiment RA
Bombardier Fred HIGHLEY, 80 Anti Tank Regiment RA
Gunner Bernard Owen Edward HUGGETT, 11 Coast Regiment RA
Private Lawrence JEEPS, 2nd Battalion Cambridgeshire Regiment
Sergeant Alan Ross KNIGHT, 80 Anti Tank Regiment RA
Gunner Ronald Cecil LEWIS, 6 HAA Regiment RA
Private George Edward MARSKELL, 5th Battalion Suffolk Regiment
Lance Bombardier Ronald MURFIN, 9 Coast Regiment RA
Gunner John David PAYNE, 35 LAA Regiment RA
Gunner John Dinder PEARS, 11 Coast Regiment RA
Driver Marshall PRICE, RASC & RAMC
Sergeant Horatio George RADFORD, Royal Signals
Gunner William Joseph RANDELL, 5 Searchlight Regiment RA
Signalman Leslie Frederick Noel ROY, Royal Signals
Constable SAMAD BIN PANJAR, Straits Settlements Police
Private Andrew SKELDON, 2nd Battalion Argyll & Sutherland Highlanders
Sergeant Vernon THOMAS, 3 HAA Regiment RA
Lance Corporal Francis John WARREN, RASC

Note: The aircraft, returning with former prisoners of war, entered a cumulo-nimbus cloud and broke up in the severe turbulence.

* * *

Dakota KJ902, 233 Squadron, 12 September 1945:

Warrant Officer Reginald William EVERED
Sergeant Douglas Philip SWAIN
Warrant Officer Alan Milward TYSON
Flight Sergeant Dennis John FERRIS
Corporal William Lawrence WEST, Air Despatcher
Driver Charles ELLIS, Air Despatcher
Driver Ernest LORD, Air Despatcher
Sepoy NAGA (ASR/10289), RIASC

Note: The aircraft was flying over a partially cloud-covered Drop Zone when it hit trees on concealed high ground. The starboard wing was torn off and the aircraft crashed into a gully, where it caught fire.

* * *

Dakota FL526, 233 Squadron, 26 September 1945:

Flight Sergeant John FISHER
Flying Officer James Lowden OSLER
Corporal Ronald Frederick COOPER, No. 61 Company RASC
Lance Corporal Frederick George FORSTER, RASC

Note: The crew had made their supply drop but were probably too low, with the result that the aircraft hit some trees and crashed. There were, however, three survivors.

* * *

Dakota KK123, 233 Squadron, 6 October 1945:

Flight Lieutenant Jack George MOULDER
Flying Officer Cyril James SACH
Flight Sergeant Norman William Munro MACKENZIE
Warrant Officer II (CQMS) AMNA GADGE
Sepoy BISRN BIBRANRATH
Sepoy SUKH LAL, 510 Stores Company IAOC

Note: The aircraft was making a supply drop in a valley when the starboard engine failed. The pilot had no option but to climb on only one good engine, but a stall resulted in the aircraft crashing.

* * *

Dakota KJ957, 48 Squadron, 23 October 1945:

Flying Officer Norman Charles TRIGG
Flying Officer Cyril Reginald Arthur BROWNING
Sergeant Stanley Wilfred MARTIN
Flying Officer Edward Albert SMITH
Flight Sergeant Joseph THURSFIELD
Flight Lieutenant Herbert WROE
Sergeant Edward Charles Mitchell SELLEY, 117 Squadron
ABDUL LATTIF, Civilian tailor
ABDUL RAHMAN, Bearer
CHANAH CHONNA, Dhobie (laundryman)
MUNNGOW, Dhobie
PUNA, Dhobie
RHODEEN, Barber
UNTOO, Dhobie

Note: In deteriorating weather the aircraft was seen to enter a cumulo-nimbus cloud, which was presumed to have been the cause of its loss.

AIRCRAFT TYPES (AND ENGINES) FLOWN IN SERVICE BY DONALD BARNARD

Month first flown	Type	Engine	Hrs flown
October 1937	DH Tiger Moth	Gipsy	59
January 1938	Hawker Hart	Kestrel	64
February 1938	Hawker Audax	Kestrel	½
April 1938	Airspeed Oxford	Cheetah IX	74
September 1938	Avro Anson	Cheetah	893
November 1938	Handley Page Harrow	Twin Pegasus	166
June 1939	Bristol Blenheim	Mercury VIII	17
June 1939	Vickers Wellington I	Twin Pegasus XVIII	767
July 1939	Miles Magister	Gipsy	5
September 1939	Avro Tutor	Lynx	40 min
April 1940	Vickers Wellington IA	Twin Pegasus XVIII	
February 1941	Westland Lysander 1	Mercury	5
March 1942	Vickers Wellington IV	Twin Wasp	
April 1942	Vickers Wellington ID	Twin Pegasus XVIII	
April 1942	Short Stirling	Four Hercules	½
July 1942	Vickers Wellington III	Twin Hercules	
April 1943	Miles Master III	Twin Wasp Junior	11
April 1943	Hawker Hurricane Mk I	Merlin III	6
April 1943	Hawker Hurricane Mk II	Merlin XX	
May 1943	Vickers Wellington X	Hercules VI	
May 1943	Beaufighter VI	Hercules VI	6
May 1943	Vickers Wellington VI	Merlin	
May 1943	Miles Master II	Mercury XX	
May 1943	Supermarine Spitfire I	Merlin III	578
May 1943	Supermarine Spitfire Va	Merlin	
May 1943	Supermarine Spitfire Vc	Merlin	
May 1943	Supermarine Spitfire IX	Merlin	
May 1943	Supermarine Spitfire Vb	Merlin	
May 1943	Vickers Wellington X	Hercules XVI	
June 1943	Supermarine Spitfire VIII	Merlin	
June 1943	Supermarine Spitfire XII	Griffon	
June 1943	Vickers Warwick	Twin Wasp	½
June 1943	Supermarine Spitfire IIa	Merlin XII	
June 1943	Supermarine Seafire IIc	Merlin XXXII	

June 1943	Supermarine Spitfire IV PRU	Merlin	
June 1943	Supermarine Spitfire VI	Merlin	
June 1943	Supermarine Spitfire XIII	Merlin	
July 1943	AW Albemarle	Twin Hercules	½
July 1943	Bristol Beaufort	Twin Taurus	½
July 1943	Miles Master I	Kestrel XX	
July 1943	Miles Monarch	Gipsy Major	1
July 1943	Vickers Wellington III	Hercules VI	
September 1943	Vickers Wellington II	Twin Merlin	
October 1943	Supermarine Spitfire Ia	Merlin	
October 1943	Supermarine Spitfire VII	Merlin	
November 1943	Handley Page Halifax V	Four Merlin XX	2
November 1943	Fairchild Argus	Scarab	½
December 1943	Bristol Beaufighter II	Twin Merlin XX	
December 1943	Bristol Blenheim IV	Twin Mercury XV	
December 1943	Westland Lysander III	Mercury XX	5
February 1944	Bristol Blenheim V	Twin Mercury XX	
May 1944	AW Whitley V	Twin Merlin X	6
August 1944	Percival Proctor	Gipsy Queen	40 Min
October 1944	Douglas Dakota III	Twin Wasp	772
June 1945	Stinson Sentinel	Lycoming	½
July 1945	Douglas Dakota IV	Twin Wasp	
July 1945	North American Harvard	Wasp	1
August 1946	Avro Lancastrian	Merlin	10
October 1946	Airspeed Consul	Twin Cheetah	87
April 1948	DH Dragonfly	Twin Gipsy	27
October 1947	DH 86 Express	Four Gypsy	4
October 1947	Supermarine Spitfire XVI	Merlin	
November 1947	Lockheed Hudson	Twin Cyclone	66
January 1948	Lockheed Lodestar	Twin Cyclone	100
October 1953	DH Mosquito III	Twin Merlin	116
October 1953	DH Mosquito 35	Twin Merlin	
February 1954	DH Chipmunk	Gipsy Major	16
June 1954	DH Vampire TII	Goblin	54
June 1954	DH Vampire 5	Goblin	

Total hours as per logbook: 3,959.10

Note: The hours shown against a particular type are the aggregate for all marks of that type which is listed, e.g. Vickers Wellington I, 767 hours, is the total for all Wellington marks shown. 'AW' = Armstrong Whitworth; 'DH' = de Havilland.

THE MEDALS OF SQUADRON LEADER DONALD BARNARD DFC

Distinguished Flying Cross (DFC)

The DFC was issued to officers and warrant officers of the RAF for acts of valour while flying on operations against the enemy. The lower arm of this cross configuration medal is engraved with the year it was awarded to Squadron Leader Barnard, 1942. A total of 20,354 DFCs were presented to members of the Allied and Commonwealth Air Forces during the period 1939-45, together with 1,550 First Bars, and 42 Second Bars.

1939-1945 Star

The 1939-1945 Star was awarded to personnel who had completed six months' service in specified operational commands overseas between 3 September 1939 and 8 May 1945 (2 September 1945 in the Far East). RAF aircrew qualified with two months' service in an operational unit including at least one operational sortie.

Air Crew Europe Star

The Air Crew Europe Star was earned almost exclusively by RAF personnel. This medal can be awarded only after qualification for the 1939-1945 Star. The Air Crew Europe Star was awarded for 60 additional days' service in an RAF Unit engaged in operational flying over Europe from bases in the UK, with at least one operational sortie undertaken prior to 5 June 1944.

Burma Star 1941-1945

The Burma Star was awarded for one or more days' service in Burma between the above dates. Those serving in Bengal and Assam in India, China, Hong Kong, Malaya, or Sumatra between certain other specified dates also qualified. RAF aircrew engaged on operations against the enemy also qualified provided that at least one operational sortie had been completed.

Defence Medal

Awarded to service personnel for three years' service at home, one year's service in a non-operational area (e.g. India), or six months' service overseas in territories subjected to air attack.

War Medal 1939-1945

This medal was awarded to all full-time personnel of the Armed Forces wherever serving, provided they had served for 28 days at least between 3 September 1939 and 2 September 1945.

The General Service Medal (Army and Royal Air Force) 1918-1964

The GSM was awarded for service in various parts of the world, except in India and East, West, and Central Africa. This medal, which has now been through six issues, has a total of 18 clasps in recognition of various actions. These clasps comprise small metal bars into which the name of the relevant campaign or theatre of operations was moulded, the clasps then being attached to the medal's suspension bar. The 1918 GSM was never awarded without a clasp. Squadron Leader Barnard's GSM is fitted with the South East Asia 1945-46 clasp. This particular clasp was awarded to British personnel involved in that area after the Japanese surrender of 15 August 1945, for various activities including guarding Japanese prisoners of war, maintaining law and order, and recovery of Allied prisoners of war. The qualifications for members of the RAF may be summarised as one operational sortie over the areas mentioned for the Army (Java, Sumatra, French Indo-China), or one sortie in connection with the removal of prisoners of war and internees in south-east Asia between 3 September 1945 and 4 October 1945, whether the squadron was based within the area mentioned for the Army or not. This service included Java, Sumatra, Malaya, Siam, French Indo-China, and the Andaman Islands. The GSM with South East Asia clasp was awarded to RAF personnel as a named medal, the recipient's details recorded upon the rim of the medal.

Note: The GSM medal worn by Donald is neither engraved nor impressed with his details, and his name is not given on the register or medal roll index. This raises a number of queries, not least whether or not Donald's unauthorised flight in Dakota KN593 on 2 September 1945, which carried over into the following day, fell within the clasp's qualification period, the commencement date for which was 3 September 1945. No. 117 Squadron personnel are indisputably eligible for the award of this medal and clasp. As Squadron Leader Barnard was flying and had collected prisoners of war, albeit on an unauthorised flight, this alone would suggest that he was entitled to the medal, with the question of that sortie being unauthorised being a different matter. But was Donald's name not submitted for the register or medal roll index as a result of his court martial? The answer to this is not known, and no evidence exists to indicate that his dismissal from the RAF resulted in the withdrawal of entitlement to any of his medals.

Donald Barnard's medals.

ENDNOTES

Chapter 1

1. The seat of government of the Windward Islands until 1956 lay in Grenada. A fourth island, Dominica, formerly part of the Leeward Island group, was attached with effect from 1 January 1940.

2. It covers an area of 238 square miles, being 27 miles long and 14 miles across at its widest. Its population in 1942 was 73,770, but now is around 161,000.

3. Today, the 'Africans' form 82.5 per cent of the population of St Lucia, the Caribs only 2.4 per cent.

4. She was born on 20 October 1881 at 16 Richmond Place at Brighton in East Sussex.

5. Today Cranleigh provides an education for some 600 students from across the world.

6. *National Service* (HMSO, London, 1939), p. 38.

7. Alternatively Donald could have applied for a permanent commission.

8. The Reserve was the Reserve of Air Force Officers, commonly abbreviated to RAFO.

9. Denis Richards, *Royal Air Force 1939-1945, Volume I: The Fight at Odds* (HMSO, London, 1953), p. 14.

10. Also later enlisting in the RAF or RCAF were four other St Lucians, none of whom survived the war: Pilot Officer D. C. D. du Boulay, RCAF; Flight Sergeant H. E. M. Dulieu; Pilot Officer D. Shingleton-Smith; and Flying Officer H. T. S. Etienne. (Information from http://www.caribbeanaircrew-ww2.com/?cat=41).

11. By March 1939 there were thirty-four E&RFTS scattered the length and breadth of Britain.

12. Other, higher, grades of flying ability were 'Above average' and 'Exceptional'.

13. French (15103), whose DFC was gazetted on 3 June 1918, during the First World War, had served on 30 Squadron in Iraq in the early 1920s. By the early 1930s, still in Iraq, he was a flight lieutenant Personal Assistant to the Air Officer Commanding, Iraq Command – Air Vice-Marshal E. R. Ludlow-Hewitt CB, CMG, DSO, MC.

14. Quine's Military Cross was gazetted on 18 January 1918.

15. Sadly, Lewis was to be killed on operations within three months of the start of the Second World War. On 14 December 1939, in broad daylight, 99 Squadron's Wellingtons were attacked off the island of Wangerooge by Me109 fighters. Five Wellingtons and their entire crews, thirty airmen, were lost. A sixth Wellington crashed on return to base, with the loss of a further three crew.

16. John Terraine, *A Time For Courage* (Macmillan Publishing, New York, 1985), p. 78.

17. Greig's service number was 07114. He won the DFC (28 October 1921) for services in Mesopotamia. His AFC was gazetted on 4 June 1928.

18. Even the monthly editions of The Air Force List (see that for March 1939, for example) were already carrying HMSO adverts for the publication 'On Air Raid Precautions', a Home Office Circular that had been published as far back as 9 July 1935.

19. John Blackwell Sinclair Monypenny (29098) was killed with all his crew when their 9 Squadron Wellington, L7795, crashed off the German coast on an operation to Wismar on the night of 19/20 July 1940.

20. Curiously, this posting is not noted in Donald's RAF records.

21. The squadron badge, with the '9' in Roman numerals, IX, had been authorised in November 1936, and so it was thereafter referred to, internally at least, as IX Squadron.

22. Healy was commissioned pilot officer in August 1922.

23. Medical records indicated that operational aircrew were liable to develop signs of 'flying stress' if they did more than thirty.

24. *RAF Medical Services, Volume II: Commands* (HMSO, London, 1955), p. 64.

25. Wing Commander John A. MacBean and Major Arthur S. Hogben, *Bombs Gone* (Patrick Stephens Ltd, Wellingborough, 1990), pp. 65-6.

26. *The History of 9 Squadron Royal Air Force*, p. 48, compiled by Flying Officer T. Mason (1965).

27. The internal bore of the bomb was increased by an eighth of an inch, thus saving 2½ ounces of magnesium per bomb. The authors acknowledge *Bombs Gone*, MacBean and Hogben.

28. *RAF Medical Services, Volume I: Administration* (HMSO, London, 1954), pp. 199-200.

29. Flying Officer John Nigel Loring (86297) was a Member of the Royal College of Surgeons and a Licentiate of the Royal College of Physicians. He was Mentioned in Despatches on 11 June 1942.

30. Quoted in Sir Charles Webster and Noble Frankland, *The Strategic Air Offensive Against Germany 1939-1945, Vol. IV* (HMSO, London, 1961), p. 205 There is no reason to suppose, though, that the bombers' effectiveness up to that point was any better – or worse.

31. All six crew are buried in the local Communal Cemetery at Ostend. W. R. Chorley, *RAF Bomber Command Losses of the Second World War 1939-1940* (Midland Counties Publications, Earl Shilton, 1992).

32. For a fuller account of the adventures of the Parkes crew, see Oliver Clutton-Brock, *RAF Evaders*, (Grub Street, London, 2009), pp. 19-22.

33. Wing Commander R. G. C. Arnold, killed on operations on 9 June 1941, was one of those immensely brave pilots who remained at the controls of a doomed aircraft in order that his crew could bale out.

34. Official figures for non-operational losses were as follows: killed 8,090; wounded 4,203; died other causes 215; missing now safe 83; POW now safe 54. *The Strategic Air Offensive Against Germany 1939-1945, Volume IV* (HMSO, London, 1961), Appendix 41, p. 440.

35. Wing Commander Alexander Black Olney was another to survive the war, still a wing commander, apparently without ever receiving a flying award.

36. This was possibly the raid to Bremen on 21/22 October 1941.

37. Campling had won his DFC (gazetted 3 March 1942) for an attack on the German warships *Scharnhorst*, *Gneisenau*, and *Prinz Eugen* as they made their bold dash up the English Channel on 12 February 1942. He was awarded the DSO (27 July 1943) while serving on 460 (RAAF) Squadron as a wing commander.

38. 1310507 Harper is commemorated on Panel 85 of the Runnymede Memorial.

39. Harker and his crew are buried in the Hanover War Cemetery. On this Kassel raid, 142 Squadron lost five Wellingtons, five men in each, from which only five crew survived, as prisoners of war.

40. *The Bomber Command War Diaries*, p. 268.

41. Mentioned in Despatches on 2 June 1943, Simmons was killed in an aircraft accident on 17 March 1945, his name being commemorated on Column 283 of the Alamein Memorial, Egypt.

42. This Wellington survived its operational time only to be lost on 104 OTU (Nutts Corner) when it flew into high ground coming out of cloud over County Antrim, Northern Ireland, on 1 October 1943.

43. The authors would like to believe that the victory shout 'Pauke' is an abbreviation of the German phrase *mit Pauken und Trompeten*, literally 'with drums beating and trumpets sounding' or 'with full honours'.

44. *The London Gazette* No. 36975.

Chapter 2

1. In May 1942, the chief of the PAT line, Pat O'Leary, had asked for its name to be changed to PAO.

2. In his unpublished memoirs Albert Buckell, the wireless operator, says that he was the one who let out the front gunner, Ralph Forster, from the front turret.

3. Donald was not only extremely skilful with his aircraft handling but also immensely fortunate, for the story goes that the field in which he landed was the only flat piece of ground for miles around.

4. This poster was unusual in that it actually named the wanted RAF personnel. To be able to do this, of course, the Germans had to have somehow discovered the names. The posters were printed at a works on the rue du Maréchal Pétain, St Omer, a small town with a population of 16,000 at this time. The orders shown on the poster were authorised by Hauptmann und Kreiskommandant Gottwald [captain and area commander]. Significant numbers of these posters were printed and distributed to mayors' offices across the district, with orders to display them.

5. Donald called this place 'Fanqueberg' in his diary.

6. This isolated café 'Chez Nicolas' was between Fauquembergues and Coyecques.

7. This was Albert Cousin, who was also a member of a local Resistance group.

8. Within the last few years the Lifeboat Hotel has been demolished and a block of flats built in its place.

9. Ray Glensor had arrived in Renty on 18 September – see Chapter 6.

10. Issued in 1942 under the RAF stores reference 22c/739, this was the Buoyant Type Taylor Suit. Designed in a dull yellow material, it was fitted with full-length leg zips to assist with dressing. These suits were capable of accepting the electrically heated inner gloves and socks specifically designed to protect the exposed air gunners. The suit, heavily padded with extra pockets to accept buoyancy pads, also held a torch in a pocket on the right leg and a fluorescent sea-marker pack on the right leg. According to Ralph Forster (interview 24 August 2010) the suit was more brown than yellow.

Chapter 3

1. The only other survivor was 2nd Lieutenant Albert W. La Chasse (bombardier), who became a prisoner of war.

2. Roger A. Freeman, *The Mighty Eighth: Units, Men and Machines of the US 8th Air Force* (Military Book Society, London, 1973), p. 18.

3. See Chapter 5, page 126, for the next part of their evasion.

4. *The Way Back* (Cassell & Co. Ltd, London, 1957), p. 105. The actual relationship of the 'sisters' is not clear. Donald just called them 'two English women', though this does not preclude them, of course, from having been sisters.

5. 1st Viscount Trenchard GCB, OM, GCVO, DSO (1873-1956).

6. *The London Gazette*, 23 May 1946.

7. In an attempt to block the main railway line from Italy to France, RAF Bomber Command attacked the railway yards at Modane on the night of 10/11 November 1943, and at Cannes on 11/12 November 1943, but there were no raids from England on the northern Italian cities at this time.

8. His wife, Patricia, was also commended by the King for brave conduct: 'British resident in Monte Carlo. For special services during the enemy occupation of France.' (*The London Gazette*, 17 December 1946).

9. It is unlikely that any civilian at that time in the war had been flown over from England just to see their offspring.

10. Beatrice was born in New York on 2 August 1914, and died on 7 April 2001 in Los Angeles, California. Michael, also born in New York, on 1 September 1916, died on 4 January 2004. When up at Cambridge University in the mid-1930s, Michael became a member of the Communist Party and one of the so-called Cambridge Apostles. He worked for the KGB along with Guy Burgess, Donald Maclean, Kim Philby, and Anthony Blunt, who recruited him for the KGB.

11. For a more detailed account of these escapes see *RAF Evaders*, Chapter 5, pp. 100-103.

12. Donald's hosts were Dr Georges and Fanny Rodocanachi, with whom Ray Glensor had earlier stayed.

13. This was the Canal du Midi.

Chapter 4

1. In his official report Donald stated that they left Toulouse for Banyuls (near Port Vendres) on 6 December.

2. Philip D. Caine, *Aircraft Down!* (Brassey's, Washington, USA, 2000), p. 95. The authors, having spoken with Donald's relatives, and in the light of Donald's further account, believe Bob Smith's recollections to be somewhat exaggerated and, perhaps, fanciful. But then there are two sides to every coin …

3. Robert Gilliland was appointed OBE (Civil Division) on 2 June 1943.

4. Madrid to Seville is some 530 km and Gibraltar a further 200 more, a total of 730 km or 450 miles.

5. 'Humbert and Woof' cannot be found. Donald possibly meant Williams & Humbert, founded in 1877 by Alexander Williams, who later married Amy Humbert. Sherry, a fortified wine, is blended not 'brewed'.

6. The *Ville d'Oran*, 10,172 tons, built in 1936 in France, was originally capable of a speed of 22 knots. Since 1940 she had been laid up for lack of fuel, only beginning her British trooping career in January 1943, under the flag of Cunard White Star. See Appendix III for details of some of the other ships in the convoy.

Chapter 5

1. His name is given as Chelingworth by French historian René Lesage.

2. On 1 September 1942, Squadron Leader Lockhart DFC, as he had now become, evaded again when his 161 (Special Duties) Squadron Lysander aircraft hit a French ditch as he made a landing in the dark and had to be burnt. Returning to England and to operations, he was killed on 27 April 1944 (Friedrichshafen), as a wing commander DSO, DFC & Bar, in Lancaster JB676, 7 Squadron.

3. Alex Nitelet had also been hit by five bullets, one of which had hit his eye, one was in an arm, and two more were in his thigh.

4. The Abwehr was the German Army's counter-intelligence section. It was not at this time a part of the Gestapo.

5. For the full story of Merlin and Becker see Appendix VI, *RAF Evaders*.

6. Crosby was to be shot down and to evade again in January 1945.

7. Glensor Diary, p. 38. Unpublished, no date, courtesy of the estate of Raymond Edwin Glensor, via Patricia Glensor.

8. Helen Long (William Kimber, London, 1985), pp. 204-11.

9. In the Belgian Air Force after the war, he rose to the rank of Colonel Aviateur, and died on 6 January 1981.

10. This despicable character was liquidated by his countrymen soon after the liberation in 1944.

11. She was born on 5 November 1881, in rue de la Liberté, Cahors.

12. There is doubt as to whether she was awarded the George Medal and/or the OBE.

13. Glensor Diary, p. 2.

14. Ibid., p. 9.

15. Ibid., p. 12.

16. Ibid., p. 12. In his diary Ray mentions Donald's nervous state on several occasions. It seems quite probable, therefore, that Donald was suffering from operational fatigue, officially called 'flying stress'.

17. Ibid., p. 17. See Appendix II for the full French and English versions of the message.

18. Ibid., pp. 40-1.

19. Ibid., p. 41.

20. Adams was pilot of the only B-17F to be shot down on 8 November 1942 (Lille). He flew back to RAF Portreath, Cornwall, on 24 April 1943.

21. Glensor Diary, p. 44.

22. Ibid., p. 46.

23. *The Unknown Courier* (William Kimber, London, 1953), p. 39.

24. Text for the citation from Group Captain C. M. Hanson OBE, RNZAF (retired), *By Such Deeds* (Volplane Press, Christchurch, New Zealand, 2001), pp. 212-3.

25. This aircraft went missing on 2 April 1942 (Le Havre) with a 12 Squadron crew, all six of whom survived, five as prisoners of war and one as an evader.

26. Tillard and crew were killed on 26/27 March 1942 (Essen). Z1245, 305 (Polish) Squadron, was lost on 28 August 1942 (Kassel). One of the two survivors, Flight Lieutenant A. Kiewnarski, was one of the fifty officers murdered following the 'Great Escape' from Stalag Luft III (Sagan) on the night of 24/25 March 1944.

27. Flying Officer Stanley Bryan Critchison and crew were lost without trace on the night of 9/10 July 1942, shot down on a mine-laying trip in the North Sea. Z1287 was also lost, on 25/26 July 1942 (Duisburg).

28. Arrested on 9 October 1943 and cruelly tortured by the Gestapo, he died on 12 January 1944.

29. It is noted that there is also a village a few kilometres to the north of the same name, Rebergues.

30. Appendix C, Eric Doorly's report M.I.9/S/P.G. (-) 1129, in The National Archives file WO 208/5582.

31. This was sent on 26 March and simply said: 'QUITE WELL DON'T WORRY SIX LETTERS SENT ONE RECEIVED LOVE TO ALL'.

32. McBeath had been shot down on 21/22 December 1942 (Munich).

33. Wartime Memories of Warrant Officer Albert Edward Buckell, p. 2. Recorded by John Buckell. Bayenghem is adjacent to Lumbres (Pas-de-Calais), which had a

population then of around 2,550.

34. The authors are most grateful to Richard Oliver for sight of this letter.

Chapter 6

1. The National Archives file WO 208/3242.

2. This was usually at this time the Great Central Hotel at Marylebone Station, but Donald clearly states in his diary that both he and Ray 'went to the Charing Cross Hotel'.

3. *Sunday at Large* (William Kimber, London, 1977).

4. *Secret Sunday* (William Kimber, London, 1975), p. 52.

5. TNA file KV4/320. Unfortunately, details of the 'proof" are not given in this file.

6. The award was published in *The London Gazette* on 22 September 1942.

7. The DFC was gazetted on 6 June 1941, when he was flying Whitleys on 102 Squadron.

8. In 1943, 5,337 patients were admitted to Rauceby. Of the 607 aircrew admitted for psychiatric care, only 47 were later admitted to hospital.

9. Mel Rolfe, *Looking Into Hell* (Arms and Armour Press, London, 1995), p. 90. Chalk was not to survive the war, being killed in a second mid-air collision, on 28/29 January 1944 (Berlin), when his 77 Squadron Halifax HR841 hit a German night fighter.

10. Ibid., p. 96.

11. In December 1942, 142 Squadron had been posted to Blida, Algeria, in support of the Allied landings in North Africa the previous month (Operation Torch).

12. No. 20 MU was in No. 52 Wing of No. 41 (Maintenance) Group, Maintenance Command. The commanding officer of the group, Air Vice-Marshal George Laing CB, CBE, had been appointed to that post on 28 July 1939. Born in 1884, Sir George (he was knighted on 1 January 1945) had served during the First World War as an equipment officer and had served in that field ever since.

13. This venerable aircraft, built late in 1939, survived not only its time on 115 Squadron but also the war, being struck off charge on 26 April 1945.

14. Wing Commander Roper Guy Aymer Vallance (service number 11072).

15. BM315 also survived the war, being struck off charge on 15 January 1946.

16. Franks was probably one of very few serving RAF officers to have His Majesty's Royal Licence and authority to wear the Insignia of the Fourth Class (Military Division) of the Order of Al Rafidain, the decoration having been conferred upon him by His Majesty the King of Iraq in recognition of valuable services rendered by him in the capacity of a Member of the British Military Mission in Iraq. For his long service in Iraq – he had been there since late 1931 – he was awarded the AFC on 9 June 1938.

17. Sergeant Andrew E. Joyner, *Royal Air Force Cosford: The War Years* (produced by permission of the Station Commander, 1994), p. 5.

18. Ibid., p. 15.

19. Alex Henshaw, *Sigh for a Merlin: Testing the Spitfire* (John Murray (Publishers) Ltd, London, 1979), p. 123.

20. One curious fact about G. R. Beamish (1905-67), later Air Marshal Sir George, was that on attaining the rank of air commodore in 1942, he became the first RAF-trained officer to achieve air rank, all other air commodores before him having first served in some branch of either the Army or Royal Navy.

21. Elmas, known today as Cagliari-Elmas Airport International 'Mario Mameli', had been opened on 3 May 1937.

22. In 1842, General Sir Charles James Napier (1782-1853), on quelling the Muslim rulers in the Sind region is alleged to have sent to his superiors the one-word Latin message '*Peccavi*' – 'I have sinned.'

23. Donaldson was CO of 177 Wing, which comprised 31, 62, 117, and 194 Squadrons.

24. 'CC' for Combat Cargo.

25. From the Despatch of Air Chief Marshal Sir Keith Park GCB, KBE, MC, DFC, Allied Air Commander-in-Chief, South East Asia, to the Secretary of State for War. Submitted in August 1946, it was not published in *The London Gazette* until 19 April 1951.

26. A long ton is the British 2,240 lb, whereas the short ton is the American 2,000 lb.

27. McLean's AFC was gazetted on 1 January 1944, and his DFC on 14 November 1944.

28. Great Britain and Northern Ireland by comparison cover 94,000 square miles, while India proper in 1941 covered 1,581,000 square miles.

29. The highest mountain in Burma is Hkakabo Razi at 19,295 feet (5,881 metres).

30. From Leese's Despatch submitted to the Secretary of State for War on 4 February 1947. The despatch was not published in *The London Gazette* until 12 April 1951.

31. Ibid.

32. Sir Keith Park, op. cit. Park gives neither the date nor squadron number involved in the 'epidemic'.

33. From the Despatch submitted to the Admiralty on 2 May 1945 by Vice-Admiral Sir Arthur J. Power KCB, CVO, Commander-in-Chief, East Indies Station, which was published in *The London Gazette* on 26 April 1948.

34. McLean was awarded a DSO on 19 October 1945. In the same issue of *The London Gazette*, fellow Australian members of 117 Squadron, Squadron Leader J. W. Maloney (Aus.406252), Flight Lieutenant H. E. Orchard (Aus.407589), and Flying Officer D. G. Orchard (Aus.407452) were awarded the DFC. A fourth member of the squadron, Pilot Officer W. A. Smith, RAF (191677), also received the DFC.

35. Today, Shah Amanat International Airport.

36. It was estimated that during the first six months of 1945, 50,000 men, many requiring hospitalisation, were airlifted from frontline areas by Dakota support squadrons to base airfields.

37. Colin Cummings (compiler and editor), *The Price of Peace: A Catalogue of RAF Aircraft Losses between VE-Day and End of 1945* (Nimbus Publishing, Yelvertoft, no date), pp. 241-3.

38. The Pegu Yomas is a range of low jungle-covered hills between the Irrawaddy and Sittang rivers.

39. From http://en.wikipedia.org/wiki/Burma_Campaign.

40. From http://en.wikipedia.org/wiki/Jiffs.

41. Both 'Supplies Delivered' and 'Estimated Total' were measured in short tons.

42. No. 110 squadron, and No. 82, were flying in support of Operation Dracula, the seaborne invasion to capture Rangoon on 1/2 May 1945. Saunders was killed on 11 July 1945 when the aircraft in which he and two others were flying, Beechcraft Expeditor HB158, disappeared without trace. He was appointed OBE on 1 January 1946.

43. He is buried in the Kanchanaburi War Cemetery.

44. Park Despatch, op. cit. He would use the 'trans-Atlantic' term again in his Despatch.

45. RAPWI = Release Repatriation of Allied Prisoners of War and Internees. RAPWI Controls 'were responsible for the co-ordination of executive action in all matters of supplies for RAPWI, and the evacuation of personnel by aircraft and white [Royal Navy] and red [Merchant Navy] ensign ships.'

46. From the citation for his MC in *The London Gazette*, 5 April 1946.
47. Colin Cummings, *The Price of Peace*, pp. 425-6. For crew details see Appendix IV.
48. *RAF Medical Services, Volume 1: Administration* (HMSO, London, 1954), p. 584.
49. From Norman Davies's account at http://www.bbc.co.uk/ww2peopleswar/stories/16/ a7445216.shtml.
50. Letter of 27 April 2005 to Colin Pateman. Barons originally wrote: '... an Officer in the Dutch Air Force'.
51. *RAF Medical Services, Volume I*, pp. 596-7.
52. A list of all the casualties aboard the Dakota, both crew and personnel, is given in Appendix IV.
53. The Bar to his DFC, awarded for services over Burma, was announced in *The London Gazette* in June 1946, and noted, 'Since deceased, awarded with effect of the 7 September 1945.' As the DFC cannot be awarded posthumously, this explains the date of the award being the day prior to his death. The 37-year-old James Forbes Cuthbert is commemorated on Column 445 of the Singapore Memorial.
54. Itagaki, found guilty of war crimes, was hanged at Sugamo Prison, Tokyo, on 23 December 1948.
55. Published by HMSO, London, 1939, by Command of the Air Council, Air Ministry, 1 July 1939.
56. 'Cashiering is the more ignominious form of dismissal. Sentences of cashiering and dismissal do not take effect until promulgation.'

Chapter 7

1. Powell was born in Cardiff on 11 August 1907; he died on 8 March 1999.
2. When Powell flew H.P.42 *Helena* to South Africa in January 1933, it was the very first four-engined aircraft to go there.
3. Air Commodore 'Taffy' Powell, *Ferryman: From Ferry Command to Silver City* (Airlife Publishing Ltd, Shrewsbury, 1982), p. 123.
4. Ibid., p. 124.
5. Silver City was taken from the name given to Broken Hill 'because of a silver lode discovered in 1883'.
6. *Ferryman: From Ferry Command to Silver City*, p. 138.
7. DT-970 was a registration of the Netherlands East Indies Air Force not the RAF.
8. From the end of the war until January 1948 Stoney Cross was used as a staging post for transports to the Far East. During the war Blackbushe was known as RAF Hartford Bridge.
9. G-AHBT, an Avro 691 Lancastrian 3 (basically a 13-seat conversion of the Lancaster bomber), was first registered to the Ministry of Supply and Aircraft Production on 20 February 1946. It was sold to British Aviation Services on 17 August 1946. Operated by Silver City Airways and named *City of New York*, it was sold to Skyways Ltd on 6 June 1947, and was used as a tanker on the Berlin airlift. It was withdrawn from use in 1952.
10. Including G-AHRK (bought 1946), G-AIBF (1946), G-AIKY (1946), G-AJGH (1947), and G-AJNG (1948).
11. A. J. Jackson, *British Civil Aircraft 1919-1972: Volume 1* (Putnam, London, 1987), p. 30.
12. In *The Argus* Classified Section for Saturday, 4 March 1939, Intercontinental were advertising flights 'Twice weekly to England and the East.'
13. It is worth noting that in February 1946, Viscount Knollys, chairman of BOAC, said in a summary of his article 'Air Transport and The Public' in *Flight* magazine

that there 'were those who wanted to fly very fast right through from England to Australia. This class of traveller had been met by the 63-hour Lancastrian service between U.K. and Sydney.'

14. VH-ASV was sold on to Burma, where it was registered on 13 April 1948 as XY-ACD and flown by the Union of Burma Air Force. Its ultimate fate is unknown.

15. Jennifer Gail, *From Bullocks to Boeings* (Australian Government Publishing Service, Canberra, 1986). Cecil Arthur Butler was born on 8 June 1902 in Warwickshire, but emigrated with his family to New South Wales in about 1910. He died on 13 April 1980.

16. From: http://www.adastra.adastron.com/company/chron-40.htm.

17. By this time Adastra Airways had been incorporated within the British company Hunting Aerosurveys Ltd.

18. This aircraft was sold to Bush Pilots Airways in 1951. The Dragonfly was a British 1930s-designed twin-engined, touring biplane.

19. This aircraft, built in 1952, has had a long life, later becoming OY-DHJ. After it was damaged on 26 April 1987 at Marbæk, Frederikssund, Denmark, it was rebuilt with parts from OY-ATF.

20. No. 1 CAACU was at Hornchurch, No. 2 at Langham (Norfolk), No. 3 at Exeter, No. 4 at Llandow (combining with No. 3 at Exeter in 1954), and No. 5 at Llanbedr in Merionethshire, North Wales.

21. Donald records having flown Vampires Mk FB.5 VV482, VV687, VV689, WA240, WA282, WA286, WA357.

22. Quotes from http://www.raf.mod.uk/rafneatishead/aboutus/whywearehere.cfm.

23. Note that the record in the marriage index for Kensington 1953 June quarter shows Rosalina not Rosalind.

24. Letter courtesy of Richard Oliver. Donald's letters are seemingly rare to find.

Appendix I

1. Source: http://www.resistance62.com/message_fillerin_oct1942.htm.

2. *La relève* had been introduced by the Vichy regime to encourage the French to volunteer to work in Germany in order to secure the release of French prisoners of war.

Appendix II

1. Former US Coastguard cutter *Itasca*.

2. Former US Coastguard cutter *Chelan*.

3. Sometimes referred to as one of the Leith Class, HMS *Grimsby* was sunk by aircraft off Tobruk on 25 May 1941.

Appendix V

The medals of Squadron Leader Donald Barnard DFC: *Left to right:* (1) Distinguished Flying Cross; (2) 1939-1945 Star; (3) Air Crew Europe Star; (4) Burma Star; (5) Defence Medal; (6) War Medal 1939-1945; (7) General Service Medal 1918-1964 with South East Asia 1945-46 clasp.

BIBLIOGRAPHY

Buckell, John (recorded by), *Wartime Memories of Warrant Officer Albert Edward Buckell*

Caine, Philip D., *Aircraft Down!* (Brassey's, Washington, USA, 2000)

Chorley, W. R., *RAF Bomber Command Losses of the Second World War 1939-1940* (Midland Counties Publications, 1992)

Clutton-Brock, Oliver, *RAF Evaders* (Grub Street, London, 2009)

Colvin, Ian, *The Unknown Courier*, (William Kimber, London, 1953)

Cummings, Colin (compiler and editor), *The Price of Peace. A Catalogue of RAF Aircraft Losses between VE-Day and End of 1945* (Nimbus Publishing, Yelvertoft, no date)

Darling, Donald, *Secret Sunday* (William Kimber, London, 1975)

Darling, Donald, *Sunday at Large* (William Kimber, London, 1977)

Frankland, Noble and Sir Charles Webster, *The Strategic Air Offensive Against Germany 1939-1945* (HMSO, London, 1961

Freeman, Roger A., *The Mighty Eighth. Units, Men and Machines* (Military Book Society, London, 1973)

Gail, Jennifer, *From Bullocks to Boeings* (Australian Government Publishing Service, Canberra)

Glensor Diary, Unpublished, no date, courtesy of the estate of Raymond Edwin Glensor, via Patricia Glensor

Hanson OBE RNZAF, Group Captain C. M., *By Such Deeds* (Volplane Press, Christchurch, New Zealand, 2001)

Henshaw, Alex, *Sigh for a Merlin. Testing the Spitfire* (John Murray Ltd, London, 1979)

Hogben, Major Arthur S. and Wing Commander John A. MacBean *Bombs Gone* (Patrick Stephens Ltd, Wellingborough, 1990)

Jackson, A. J., *British Civil Aircraft 1919-1972: Volume 1* (Putnam, London, 1987)

Joyner, Sergeant Andrew E., *Royal Air Force Cosford. The War Years* (produced by permission of the Station Commander, 1994)

Mason, Flying Officer T. (compiled by), *The History of 9 Squadron Royal Air Force* (1965)

Powell, Air Commodore 'Taffy', *From Ferry Command to Silver City* (Airlife Publishing Ltd, Shrewsbury, 1982)

RAF Medical Services Volume II Commands, p.64 (HMSO, London, 1955)

Rexford-Welch, Squadron Leader S. C. (edited by), *R.A.F. Medical Services, Volume I, Administration* (HMSO, London, 1954)

Richards, Denis, *Royal Air Force 1939-1945, Volume I. The Fight at Odds* (HMSO, London, 1953)

Rolfe, Mel, *Looking Into Hell* (Arms and Armour Press, London, 1995)

Terraine, John, *A Time For Courage* (Macmillan Publishing, New York, 1985)

Unknown author, *The Way Back* (Cassell & Co Ltd, London, 1957)